LEFTOVER
IN CHINA

LEFTOVER
IN CHINA

THE WOMEN SHAPING
THE WORLD'S
NEXT SUPERPOWER

ROSEANN LAKE

W. W. NORTON & COMPANY

Independent Publishers Since 1923

New York | London

The names and other identifying characteristics of many people who appear in this book have been changed. Certain characters are composites.

For information about permission to reproduce selections from this book, write to
Permissions, W. W. Norton & Company, Inc., 500 Fifth Avenue, New York, NY 10110

For information about special discounts for bulk purchases, please contact
W. W. Norton Special Sales at specialsales@wwnorton.com or 800-233-4830

Manufacturing by LSC Communications Harrisonburg
Book design by Chris Welch
Production manager: Lauren Abbate

ISBN 978-0-393-25463-1

W. W. Norton & Company, Inc., 500 Fifth Avenue, New York, N. Y. 10110
www.wwnorton.com

W. W. Norton & Company Ltd., 15 Carlisle Street, London W1D 3BS

1 2 3 4 5 6 7 8 9 0

For my dear parents, Rosa and Ken—
it doesn't look like I'll ever become an ophthalmologist,
but I hope this makes you proud.

For Steven Lake—the little brother like no other.

Os quiero!

CONTENTS

PREFACE

Just after Chinese New Year, I returned to the office of the Beijing television station where I had been working to find that all of my usually chipper young female colleagues were in decidedly different spirits. Even Shan Shan, the megawatt producer, had toned it down several joules and was uncharacteristically mum for a Monday morning. "Did everyone have a nice holiday?" I asked. I got a few unenthusiastic nods, a few forced smiles, and was handed a half-eaten bag of sesame balls that had been circulating around the newsroom. Puzzled, I went to see one of the network supervisors, a woman who was about ten years older than most of the women on staff. "They are sad because they are not getting married," she said, as if this answer would make perfect sense to me. She then turned back to her computer, leaving me to wonder if China's answer to Mr. Darcy was coming to town, or if the Communist Party had just issued millions of free honeymoons to the Maldives.

Sitting down to lunch with Shan Shan later that day, I learned that Chinese New Year is famous for being the time of year when red envelopes are stuffed, dumplings are steamed, and singletons skewered. As the grand apotheosis of the Chinese lunar calendar and the longest yearly holiday that most Chinese workers are entitled to, it's heralded by the mass migration of over 300 million people traveling home to feast and set off fireworks with their families. Yet as extended clans unite to eat, drink, play, and be merry, tidings of betrothals commonly take center stage. Gathered around tables festooned with fish heads, singles over age twenty-five are often assailed with well-meaning but often completely misguided offers of blind dates. Women, especially, are targeted in this marriage offensive, as it is considered imperative that they tie the knot by a certain age, lest they risk becoming "*sheng nü*" or, literally translated, "leftover women."

In addition to finding it highly objectionable that my still young and presumably fertile colleagues (the oldest just a few days over twenty-seven) were being referred to as the stuff of doggie bags and garbage disposals, I struggled to understand how this was all happening in modern China, the world's largest economy,* which by no coincidence is also home to 650 million women—the largest female population in the world. In a country where, until fairly recently, women had few personal, social, economic, and even bipedal freedoms (see: foot binding), my colleagues were a stunning deviation. They were a fleet of educated, independent young women who were doing things that their mothers and grandmothers could never have dreamed of. In my eyes, they were the toast of the nation—a glittering testament to the increased edu-

---

* According to the IMF, China's economy is the world's second largest economy by nominal GDP and the world's largest economy by purchasing power parity.

cational and professional opportunities that Chinese women had accumulated over the past thirty-odd years, though their label clearly indicated otherwise.

While at the studio, I found I was spending most of my time surrounded by a dynamite team of young female writers, editors, directors, and producers like Shan Shan. Quite naturally, over the course of delayed flights to Inner Mongolia, sleeper trains to Shanghai, and delirious overtime hours in our Beijing office, we bonded. Gradually, I became privy to their more personal conversations—the juicy ones—regarding their family histories, their aspirations, and increasingly, their love lives. The more I learned about the quirks of their dates and the complexities of their courtships, the more I was confused, surprised by what appeared to be a glaring inconsistency.

At the time—2010—the reports in Western media with regards to Chinese women had a very sanguine glow. As articles in *Forbes, Newsweek,* and *Time* were indicating, Chinese women were at the top of their game. They represented the highest percentage of self-made female billionaires in the world, and with 63 percent of GMAT takers in China being female, they were attaining MBAs with a ferocity that was making the boys blush. According to National Bureau of Statistics reports, 71 percent of Chinese women between the ages of eighteen and sixty-four were employed, and they accounted for 44 percent of the country's workforce. The first one would soon be sent into space.

From what I could see, this was all true. Professionally, these women were so tenaciously pushing the limits of what was possible for their half of the sky, as far as I was concerned, they were all astronauts. Yet personally, and when it came to matters of the heart in particular, they appeared beholden to the playbook of another galaxy—a distant, anachronistic realm that seemed straight out of a Jane Austen novel. Much to my surprise, the recurring topic of our conversations quickly became marriage. They spoke of it as one might speak of an ingrown toenail—with urgency, a niggling element of pain, and the full knowledge that if it wasn't addressed in the imminent future, things would only get worse.

Sensing that something wasn't adding up, I began to do some digging beyond the scope of my newsroom comrades. Three years and several hundred interviews later, my curiosity has led me to understand the story of China's rise and development under a radically new lens. It's a story that begins with an impoverished Communist nation where marriage was universal, compulsory, and a woman's only means to livelihood. Fast-forward thirty-plus years to an urbanized, globalized, economic superpower where marriage is swiftly becoming more discretionary and an institution that increasing numbers of educated women are committing to only after developing themselves and their careers a bit more fully, if they're committing at all. Factor in the aftershocks of a nation still reeling from an onerous one-child policy that has saddled it with a walloping gender imbalance, and the plates in this wildly tectonic shift of social, economic, and demographic proportions begin to take shape.

Central to this shift is the idea that despite China's dazzling superlatives, there are strands of its culture that remain inextricably rooted in tradition, the most significant and inexorable of which is the societal pressure to wed. Although this pressure exists in varying degrees across many cultures and religions, it is particularly strong in China, where marriage retains the equivalent social force of a steamroller. This force makes it so that marrying off a child is the mission of just about every parent with offspring under the age of thirty. After thirty, the mission becomes a crusade.

In most cases, parents mean well. They genuinely believe that the best thing for their children is to assure that they are dutifully snuggled into wedlock as swiftly as possible, but there is a formidable cultural disconnect between progenitors—who were raised through poverty and revolution—and their progeny, who grew up through an economic boom and the birth of the individual in an otherwise fiercely collectivist society. This cultural disconnect is the essence of the infinitely textured and complex set of sparring values, obligations, traditions and tensions that define modern China, where like the perennial wind chime, changes in marriage policies and patterns have heralded the most significant shifts in China's sociopolitical climate. This has been true for the past five thousand years: a time during which—it's critical to note—marriage has been the cornerstone and pinnacle of a woman's life.

In the span of just over thirty years, all of that has changed. For women especially, marriage has become less of an imperative, largely because of the unprecedented educational and professional opportunities that accompanied China's reforms, beginning in 1979. Elements of this evolution will surely sound familiar in the Western world, where women were once meant to be seen (in the kitchen) and not heard (in the workplace), though there are a few salient factors that make the situation in China especially alarming. Of greatest significance are the more than 30 million female abortions and infanticides which occurred during the peak years of the one-child policy and have resulted in a surplus of poor, uneducated, rural males who are doomed to remain without a bride because there are simply not enough women in China to marry. On the other side of that potential demographic disaster are urban only daughters: women whose parents chose to allow a daughter into the world during a time when everyone else wanted a son. These are women who for lack of competing XY chromosomes in the family were given unprecedented opportunities and resources that may have previously been reserved for male offspring. They came into the world at a point when China was aggressively expanding its number of institutions of higher learning, and were pushed to study, succeed, achieve, and bring honor to their families as if they were sons. Yet contrary to what Mao and his modern-day disciples might have us believe, women have not been able to seamlessly slip in alongside the men and work as equal comrades.

The bedrock of a population of educated women that are entering the white-collar workforce in numbers that rival and surpass those of men, China's "leftover women" are the ultimate linchpin to the country's rise and development. They are broadcasting a cultural shift so massive that it defines not only contemporary China, but also the single greatest demographic movement of our era across the world.

For the magnitude of the transition to be fully absorbed, it must be contextualized in the grander scheme of development. Half of the world, the United States included, has gone through the thick of it. American women have been the dominant earners of college degrees in the United States since 1981, but it wasn't until 2014 that professional college-educated American women became just as likely to marry and have children as their lesser-educated counterparts. Previously, to be educated and to be ambitious often meant foregoing a life partner in favor of a career, but lines are blurring, timelines are changing, and new priorities are emerging. We are becoming a globalized world of classes, instead of cultures. A well-educated, professional woman in Beijing or Shanghai now has more in common with a well-educated, professional woman in New York or Los Angeles than she does with a female Chinese factory worker from a town just an hour's train ride away. One generation ago this would have been unheard-of.

Whether this is a cause for celebrating globalization or lamenting homogenization is still up for debate, though it's clear that when you strip away the idiosyncrasies of China's demographics, economics, and socio-political baggage, what remains is a country where women are starting to face the very same challenges that American women have been weathering for decades. Why are we not joining forces and voices? How much more could be learned and accomplished if these issues were considered on an international scale?

Across the world, an increasing number of women are standing up for their right to determine their own futures. Whether that means being able to decide where or what to study, whom, when, or if to marry, whether or not to have children, or how to best define and achieve that ever-elusive ideal of "having it all," the population of women taking bolder steps to map out more fulfilling lives is expanding. So must the conversation.

LEFTOVER
IN CHINA

1

ULTRASOUND CHECKS AND IMBALANCES

养女儿不如养条狗囤

It is more profitable to raise geese than daughters.

—CHINESE PROVERB

Only Daughters

On the morning of her seventeenth birthday, Christy Yang woke up, showered, and sat down to breakfast. She arrived at the kitchen table to find that her mother had prepared a bowl of her favorite noodles, although she recalls spotting two unsolicited ingredients swimming in the spicy red broth she so regularly delighted in: one sausage link (1) and a pair of hard-boiled eggs (00). After two mouthfuls, Christy realized something: these ingredients represented her mother's wish that her daughter would get a perfect score on the Chinese college entrance exam, which Christy would be taking later that morning.

As an only child and an only daughter born during the very onset of China's one-child policy, Christy explains that her parents cast all of their hopes and resources into securing her a bright future. "It's hard to say what things would have been like if I'd had a brother," she says. "Tradition seems to dictate that he may have gotten the lion's share of the family's care and focus, though I can't really imagine my parents operating that way." What she does insist on making very clear, however, is her feeling that despite all of the horrors it prompted—the millions of abortions and female infanticides in families where parents were determined to have a son—China's one-child policy had an unexpected outcome. It forced parents to value their daughters.

Christy, like the one-child policy, is now over thirty years old. Though over time, the policy's stipulations have become significantly more relaxed, it's critical to consider that the policy has essentially turned out three generations of only daughters.* What often gets overlooked as the very fine silver lining of an otherwise very gruesome cloud is that China's "surviving" (non-aborted) daughters—especially the urban-born ones like Christy—were pushed tenaciously by their parents to achieve. With little exception, they were given more resources, opportunities, and liberties than any generation of females before them, the results of which are starting to play out in unexpected ways.

While Christy never did get a perfect score on the college entrance exam (that's virtually impossible), she scored well enough to attend a top university in the southern megalopolis of Chongqing, where she graduated with a bachelor's degree in economics and a master's in English. After gaining experience working in the offices of a few marketing and communications outfits, she now runs her own public relations firm, servicing a series of upscale hotels, restaurants, bars, and private clubs

---

* Following an amendment to the one-child policy in 2013, married couples were allowed to have a second baby if one of the parents was an only child. Certain ethnic minority groups whose first child was a girl or disabled were also allowed to have a second child. As of January 1, 2016, all couples in China are now permitted to have two children, but more on that later.

around Beijing. She loves managing her own schedule, having autonomy over the projects she takes on, and her innate sociability makes her perfect for the job.

Although there is very little about Christy's work that her parents understand, they're proud of her. Her success affords her an enviably comfortable lifestyle; one which she very generously and regularly shares with them. They are able to boast of vacations to Europe, new appliances, and an extensive home renovation, all financed with help from their only daughter. She has provided them with luxuries they might otherwise have never experienced, and as far as daughters go, they emphatically agree that she would be completely without reproach if she would just—get married and get pregnant. Ideally this would all happen before her next menstrual cycle, but on the chance that's asking for too much, she was told in 2012 that a minimum of nine months before the end of the lunar calendar would also be acceptable. There's nothing quite like a grandchild born in the year of the dragon!

"I don't mean to stress you, but I simply cannot relax until you are married," Christy's mom recently said to her. "You're thirty-four already. How can you be sure you're still ovulating?"

Though Christy would love for her mom to get a hobby, or at least a rigged Magic 8-Ball that's perpetually set to YOU MAY RELY ON IT, she weathers the mild insults, the mania, and the occasional outbursts because she's all too familiar with the greater picture. Whether she buys into it or not, Christy knows that by Chinese marriage standards, she's a dinosaur. If she doesn't find a man soon—as her parents, grandparents, aunts, uncles, friends, neighbors, colleagues, boss, and one particularly loquacious Beijing taxi driver are all quick to remind her—she'll curdle up, mold over, and be 嫁不进去, or "unworthy of any man's home."

From a purely numerical perspective, it should be a cinch for

Christy to find a man to marry. By 2020, the Chinese Academy of Social Sciences estimates that there will be 30 million more men of legal marriage age (age twenty-two in China since 1980) than women. While this may sound like a heavenly bounty of potential mates to choose from, the reality is that geographically, educationally, socially, and economically, the majority of these surplus men live in a different universe from women like Christy.

Only Sons

In a quiet corner of Xiaoshan, a small city in Zhejiang province, is a village that appears to be entirely made up of churches. Clustered together, with crosses soaring from their rooftops— one taller than the next—they seem to be a surprising addition to an otherwise decidedly agnostic local landscape. Until, upon closer inspection, it becomes apparent that the buildings in question are not churches but three-story residential homes. Their soaring T-shaped protrusions are not crosses but gargantuan lightning rods.

Yearly precipitation records for Hangzhou, the capital city of Zhejiang province, show it is an area of China that receives a fair amount of rain, lightning, and thunder, but hardly enough to warrant such oversize rods. What gives?

Like many areas across China, Hangzhou suffers from a severe gender imbalance. As recently as 2010, the sex ratio at birth (SRB) was 113; or 113 males for every 100 females. For purposes of comparison, the world's natural gender ratio at birth hovers around 105 boys for every 100 girls. However, the onset of China's one-child policy in 1979, when combined with the widespread availability of ultrasound technology in the late 1980s and a deeply entrenched cultural preference for males, led to a rise in the abortion of female fetuses. As a result, China now has the most imbalanced sex ratio in the world.

Though sex-selective abortion is certainly not exclusive to China, of the 163 million females estimated to have been aborted in Asia between 1985 and 2005, roughly 32 million were Chinese. In addition to "missing" a female population equivalent to the entire citizenry of Poland, throwing things even further off kilter is the fact that the resulting shortage of females is not evenly spread out across the country. As reported by Mara Hvistendahl in *Unnatural Selection: Choosing Boys over Girls, and the Consequences of a World Full of Men*, there are places in China like Yichun, in Jiangxi province, where the ratio is 137 males for 100 females under age 4. That imbalance rises to 153 males for every 100 females of the same age group in Guanxi, and in Tianmen, Hubei, it escalates to a perilous 176 to 100, or the mathematical equivalent of 1 in every 3 men being unable to find a bride. What becomes evident when connecting these demographic dots is that with little exception, the vast majority of China's surplus men were born in the most rural and impoverished areas of the country. As only sons, they were required to stay behind and tend to their family farms, whereas any females born into their same villages were free to migrate in search of menial jobs, and often husbands who would provide them with better lives. Now grown bachelors in a land where women their age are already in short supply, they face fierce competition to attract a wife and are known as *guang gun*, or "bare branches." In Chinese, the term is most commonly used to refer to a man whose circumstances force him to be single (or who simply chooses to remain a bachelor), while also hinting at the strong likelihood that he will never produce "offshoots" of his own.

"Bare branches" face great difficulty in China, where to be

married is to be on track; it's the hallmark of a properly functioning member of society, and the official sponsor of adulthood. Failing to produce an heir is among the most egregious violations of *xiao*, or filial piety, a concept that the Chinese continue to approach with extreme reverence. Further complicating matters are still prevalent Confucian ideals of the male as chief provider, which require that men not only out-earn their wives, but that they own a home in which to welcome a future wife. China's fiercely hierarchical household registration system—known as the *hukou*—doesn't make things any easier. Under this system, rural-born residents have rural *hukou*, and urban-born residents have urban *hukou*, both of which are issued for life. As a result, rural male citizens, in addition to being poor, are forever linked to their rural status, making them the nadir of the Chinese marriage chain.

None of this was an issue in the days when Chinese work units known as *danwei* automatically provided their (male) employees with housing, but following the privatization of the Chinese real-estate market in 1998, property prices have soared, forging a formidable chasm between the country's haves and have-nots.

Which is where the lightning rods come in.

Average Zhou

To help their sons get married, the parents of rural surplus men often pour all of their life savings into property, reasoning that a deed will improve their sons' marriage prospects. This is true to the extent that in a recent study, Shang-Jin Wei, a professor of finance and economics at Columbia University; Xiaobo Zhang, a professor of economics at Peking University and a senior research fellow at the International Food Policy Research Institute in

Washington, DC; and Yu Liu of Tsinghua University found that the intensity of competition in the marriage market in China has considerable consequences for housing value and size. Specifically, they estimate that 30 to 48 percent of the real-estate appreciation in thirty-five major Chinese cities between 1998 and 2005 (or the equivalent of US $8 trillion), is directly correlated with China's sex-ratio imbalance and a man's need to acquire wealth (property) in order to attract a wife.

Wei, Zhang, and Liu arrived at this percentage after examining different regions of China with a significant variation in the gender imbalance for the marriage-age cohort, and discovering that across both rural and urban areas, there is a strong positive association between the local sex ratio and the ratio of home value to household income. In other words, the more skewed the average sex ratio, the more expensive the average home.

As a control, the researchers looked at rental prices and discovered that they did not appreciate at the same rate as housing prices, adding credence to the idea that the elevated home prices are less indicative of a demand for living space than they are of the need to hold a deed. They also found that the increased home value is a result of two main factors: people paying a higher price per square meter for their homes, and a trend of buying bigger homes.

Just how much bigger?

Zhang, courtesy of whom I came to know of the "church village" in Xiaoshan, also introduced me to the concept of homes with "phantom third stories." This type of construction refers to a two-story house with an unfurnished, unfinished third story built expressly to make the house appear more grandiose from the outside. The trend has taken off in neighborhoods where the competition for a wife is particularly fierce, and in some areas, it has become mainstream to the extent that matchmakers won't schedule an appointment with a man's family unless his house has the requisite phantom floor.

For an extra edge in the marriage market, parents who are especially keen to see their sons married have taken to adding height to their phantom third story abodes by bedizening their rooftops with lightning rods. Zhang explains that this has turned into something of a competition, with proprietors visibly striving to outdo their neighbors by upping the size of their rods to delirious proportions. While having the tallest house in town may warrant some unsolicited attention for a lonely bachelor trying to improve his odds in the marriage market, it's critical to understand why his family must go to these lengths, widths, and heights to have him married: the odds are completely against them otherwise.

More baby boys than girls have been born every year in China since even before demographers began to take notice. Prior to ultrasound machines, the one-child policy, and the ensuing female abortions that caused the gender imbalance, female infanticides were already happening across the country. Even in cases where female babies weren't killed upon birth, China's strong cultural preference for boys entitled male babies to a somewhat higher rate of survival. During times of hardship, for instance, male offspring were generally given a greater share of resources (in other words, food) to ensure their survival, resulting in a higher mortality rate for young females. A demographic study cited in Nicholas Kristof and Sheryl WuDunn's *Half the Sky* found that thirty-nine thousand baby girls die annually in China because parents don't give them the same medical attention they give to their sons—and this is just in their first year of life.

I mention this not to be grim, but to convey a more complete sense of the accrued surplus male population in China. In other words, when we see that a province has 120 males for every 100 females born during a certain year, it doesn't simply mean that twenty-five or thirty years later, when those males and females are looking to be married, that 1 in 5 of those males will be without a wife. In real terms, it means that 20 males out of every 100 from that year of birth, plus all the other males born before them who didn't find a wife in previous years, will all be in search of one.

"It's like going to the movies," says Christophe Guilmoto, a demographer at the Centre Population et Développement in Paris, who likens each seat in the movie theater to a woman available for marriage. "As a man seeking a wife, you go to the afternoon showing, but it's sold out," he explains. "You try again later that evening, queuing two hours in advance this time, but there are still no tickets because a new batch of theater-goers has arrived ahead of you, and they've already gotten in." Since there is only one theater in town playing this film, what is a man to do? He either keeps trying to get into future showings—thereby continuing to increase the demand for a wife—skips the movies altogether (remains a bachelor), or goes to see another film.

In the case of rural Chinese men with limited resources, that other film might be *Bride-Buying*, starring Vietnam, Cambodia, Laos, North Korea, and a few other neighboring Southeast Asian countries. It is well documented that China's gender imbalance and resulting marriage squeeze has manifested itself in increased instances of bride trafficking and other unsavory practices, but perhaps most alarmingly, there is little sign that balance will be restored any time soon. Between 2001 and 2010 alone, an average of 1.3 million more boys than girls were born in China each year, indicating that sex-selective abortions are still occurring and continuing to upset the laws of nature. In other words, what we're seeing play out today is just the beginning of a marriage squeeze that China's rural bachelors will face for generations.

Urban Oasis

As China's countryside saw the boom in baby boys that has led to its current gender imbalance and marriage squeeze, a very different story was unfolding in cities. Though birth records from Beijing and Shanghai indicate a gender imbalance strong enough to prove that sex-selective abortions had taken place, they represent a fraction of what was happening in more rural areas. In addition to a more balanced gender ratio, city life for only children—regardless of gender—was also very different. Urban only sons were raised as the proverbial "little emperors." Showered with all of the attention and resources that two parents and four grandparents living in a suddenly much more open economy could possibly offer, they reaped the best of everything. And as luck or the lack of competing XY chromosomes would have it, urban only daughters did too.

Born in an urban area, Christy already has one of the most desirable *hukou* available and doesn't need to marry into a better one. Educated and well employed, she also has enough capital to purchase her own home, in addition to one day inheriting the Beijing apartment that her parents currently occupy. As far as living conditions go, she is light-years ahead of China's bare branches, and yet her struggle to find a marriage partner is just as pronounced, but for radically different reasons.

"We didn't give it any thought—we just accepted the child we were given," explains Christy's mom. "My mother-in-law wasn't too keen at first, but I was happy to have her, and my husband stood by me." Christy can overhear our conversation and I see her nod. She later tells me that she's long sensed her paternal grandmother's preference for a grandson. "She has made us very proud," continues her mom. "But she works so hard—we've always encouraged her to—it is very dangerous for a woman in China not to have her own livelihood, but now she must make space in her life for a man."

Like so many women in her age group, Christy is among the first generations of females born under the one-child policy to have reached the age by which according to societal prescriptions, they should be wives and mothers and after which they become known as *sheng nü,* or "leftover women." The prefix "sheng" is the same as in *sheng cai,* or "leftover food"—hardly a palatable association. In more rural areas, this term may be applied as early as age twenty-five, whereas in larger cities, it kicks in closer to thirty, or what is generally considered the last stop before spinsterhood. In extremely progressive circles the lifeline may be pushed to the early thirties, but beyond that, it's commonly acknowledged that a Chinese woman has limited her dating pool to bulbous sexagenarian divorcés who suffer from severe halitosis and are the fathers of at least one irascible adolescent.

Brookings Institution demographer Wang Feng estimates that there are 7 million never-married women between the ages of twenty-five and thirty-four in urban China. They are concentrated in China's top-tier cities, with Beijing, Shenzhen, and Shanghai topping the charts, and like most things in China, they are a phenomenon of the last thirty years. Wang notes that in 1982, less than 5 percent of urban Chinese women in their late twenties were unmarried. That percentage doubled by 1995, tripled by 2008, and is advancing, full-steam ahead, toward 30 percent. For a country where just over thirty years ago, marriage was obligatory and universal, that's a considerable change of course.

"Women in China are still seen primarily as biological beings," says Wang, who as a demographer and sociologist, has studied marriage in China for over twenty years. He adds that since age twenty-seven or twenty-eight is still considered the ideal for child-bearing in China, thirty has become the threshold after which a woman becomes "leftover" based on the simple logic that she is out of her child-bearing hot zone. "It's a very dangerous characterization," he says, "because it unnecessarily squeezes women over 30 out of marriage. At that age, their fertility window is still fairly large."

But as far as the general Chinese public goes, thirty is the magic number. "男人三十一枝花," or "Men at thirty are still in bloom," begins a delightful Chinese idiom, which reflects the commonly accepted notion that a man entering his third decade is still well within his prime. The second half of the idiom, "女人三十豆腐渣," is slightly less poetic. It likens women over thirty to tofu pulp—the insoluble parts of the soybean that cling to the tofu press or cheesecloth, after the rest of the soy milk has cooperatively passed through and coagulated into a big, smooth block.

Though "leftovers" in China are viewed with a sundry mix of disdain, awe, and sympathy, it is generally agreed that they are the products of their time. They are a living testament to the increased educational and professional opportunities afforded to Chinese women over the last three decades, which have made marriage less of an immediate necessity or priority for them. Though not all of these women are only daughters, the majority are characterized as being well-educated, career-oriented women whose life experiences and relative financial independence have made them more discerning in what they seek in a mate. Refusing to marry because they've reached a certain age, or because everyone around them is telling them that they must, their attitude toward marriage is often considered irreverent, though as it turns out—not entirely without precedent.

Renegade Reelers

At the turn of the nineteenth century, in a little pocket of the Canton River Delta, lived a group of female renegades. Master runaway brides before the dawn of sneakers, they were known to escape from home on the morning of their marriages or bolt from their bridal sedan chairs and hide from their grooms in empty graves until everyone had given up looking for them. Of those who did accept marriage vows, many took fierce precautions to avoid one of their side effects: pregnancy. On the night of their nuptials, these renegade ladies were known to stay awake and vigilant, barricading themselves from their betrothed with as much furniture as they could muster. Using a technique called "body-wrapping," some would mummify their genitals using a whopping undergarment equipped with several layers of fabric. Sewn into the garment like human dumplings, they remained stitched inside for as long as three consecutive days, taking pills to suppress nature's calls.

While the methods of these renegade women varied, their mission was the same: to keep marriage and motherhood at bay. This, in the China of the 1890s, was supremely saucy. As discussed in Janice E. Stockard's fascinating *Daughters of the Canton Delta*, an unmarried woman during these times—in addition to being a social anomaly—was a source of great distress. Her spirit was believed to cause crop failure, infertility, and a host of other misfortunes. It was said that grass would not grow on the site where an unmarried woman had died, so moribund maids were taken out to pass away in deserted areas where the damages incurred by their spouselessness could be minimized. Then of course there was the predicament of an unmarried woman's soul, which, lonely and restless, might come back to haunt the living and the wed.

Central to the bravado of these unmarried women was the fact that they were all reelers; silk reelers. During the peak years of their marriage-resistant activities (between 1890 and 1930), the Canton River Delta area of China where they lived was responsible for one-ninth of the entire world's silk production. Stockard reveals that by 1930, the region had more than 300 filatures, and nearly 4,000 tons of silk were produced there annually, creating an unprecedented economic opportunity for young women. Hired to complete the highly challenging job of pulling silk threads from their cocoons, silk reelers were paid handsomely for their skilled work, which required excellent eyesight and extreme dexterity, and was critical to the silk-making process. They earned up to $1 per day, or nearly double the salary of field-laboring men.

As a result of hard work and high silk-sales, silk-reeling women spun themselves a cocoon of financial independence. And when their families decided it was time for them to marry, few of them got hitched without a fight. Those who didn't run away from marriage bought their way out of it, writes Stockard. They contracted what were politely known as "compensation marriages," or a marriage in which a reeler woman paid her betrothed's family about $300—the rough equivalent of one year of her salary. This fee was for the groom's family to use toward the purchase of a *muijai*, or little maid. Essentially an outsourced wife, the *muijai* would bear children, care for in-laws, manage the desires of the man of the family, and do all of the other wifely things that renegade reelers would rather not do themselves. Despite not being present, this exchange allowed reelers to earn an official marital status. This came with the perk of a dignified burial place within the man's family plot, where their souls could rest peacefully in the afterlife.

More enterprising reelers saved themselves the compensation fees by marrying dead men. Known as "spirit marriages," these were arrangements between a woman and the family of a prematurely deceased bachelor who feared he would be lonely in the afterlife. They were all the rage in southeastern China of the 1900s, and dead men a shockingly hot commodity. As recounted by one of Stockard's sources, "It was not easy to find an unmarried dead man to marry! When the family of a deceased son decided to arrange his marriage, the news spread quickly." According to Stockard's accounts, upon hearing that one was available for marriage, women would often fight viciously among themselves to marry him.

Though this singular economic opportunity for Chinese women ended when the Great Depression bottomed out in '32, prompting a sharp decline in the demand for silk, the marriage-resisting renegade ladies of the Canton River Delta appeared to be onto something.

Much like the silk reelers who preceded her, Christy's financial independence allows her to keep marriage at bay and, if she chooses, to skip it altogether. Alhough fortunate in that she doesn't have to run away, buy off her in-laws, or marry a dead man, there are some departments in which Christy's spinning sisters of yore were arguably better off. For instance, despite being pressured into marriage, the women of the Canton River Delta were praised for their economic fortitude. Parents who compensated or contracted ghost marriages were proud to have a silk-reeling daughter who continued to work, as it meant a great financial contribution to the family. In *Daughters of the Canton Delta*, Stockard suggests that in an otherwise very patriarchal China, "This was the only place where the birth of a girl was an occasion for joy."

Likewise, the nineteenth-century spinsters of New England

were described as "highly moral and fully womanly creatures." It was commonly acknowledged that their spinsterhood was "the outcome of intricate choices," and they were even praised for "having the courage to remain single because the right man never came." Spinsters were, in fact, a social phenomenon. "Why Is Single Life Becoming More General?" ran the headline from a March 1868 article in *The Nation*. The article references Frances B. Cogan, who in her book, *All-American Girl: The Ideal of Real Womanhood in Mid-Nineteenth Century America*, describes how an increase in spinsterhood goes hand in hand with the "process of civilization." She writes, "Men and women can less easily find any one whom they are willing to take as a partner for life; their requirements are more exacting; their standards of excellence higher; they are less able to find one person who can satisfy their own ideal and less able to satisfy anybody else's ideal."

While it's fair to say that in its five thousand years of dynasty-studded, paper-, compass-, and gunpowder-inventing history, China has been a great enabler of the "process of civilization," it has been remiss in the particular aspect of civilization that Cogan is referring to. How might one otherwise explain that single Chinese silk-reeling women of the 1890s Canton River Delta were celebrated for their work and financial fortitude, while modern-day career women like Christy—no matter how impressive their educational and professional accomplishments—are still antagonized and devalued if they haven't married by a certain age?

Before beginning to answer the various components of that rather loaded question, it's essential to keep in mind that leftovers are a dramatic deviation from what until thirty years ago was the overwhelming norm in China: married women. As wives and mothers, Chinese women were destined to be the building blocks of families, which in turn, were the building blocks of the nation.

Pursuant to a post–Qing Dynasty pearl of wisdom that continues to drive the governance of the Communist Party: the home is a miniature model of the state. A harmonious home is the foundation of a harmonious nation, and for this, women are key. A home comprised of a single woman—and especially a self-reliant one— is different, destabilizing, and by some accounts, dangerous.

Ideally, as embodied by the often cited adage, 男主外, 女主内, "a man's place is on the outside; a woman's place is on the inside," a Chinese woman will raise happy, healthy children while tending to the home so that her husband will be unfettered to work, socialize, and focus on more important, external matters of strengthening the nation. Though this definition has modernized over time, a woman's propensity for the inner realm traditionally made her a prized wife, and is still often the criteria by which many Chinese men refine their search for a partner.

"Two years ago, I organized a New Year's Eve party at a high-end club—the replica of a French château," explains Christy. "I invited this man I had been seeing, and he came." She recounts how he danced, drank, and appeared very merry, but mysteriously stopped calling her after the event. When she finally asked him why, he explained that when he saw her in a cherry red silk dress, surrounded by so many people and so vigorously fluttering around to make sure that everything was running smoothly, he felt she was *"bu anchuan,"* or "unsafe."

"That party was a major career milestone for me," says Christy, fully aware that from a personal perspective, it was less of a success. "Of course, there could have been other things, but it was probably poor judgment to let him see me in that kind of environment so early in the relationship. He's not an exception—many Chinese men would react this way." She readily cites another instance: a PhD candidate her mom was especially anxious for her to meet because he had studied in the United States and was likely to be more accepting of Christy's "modern" tendencies. Freshly divorced with a one-year old child, he told Christy—on their first date—that his relationship with his previous wife (also Chinese) did not work out because she (also a PhD candidate) was neglecting her duties to the home.

Christy knows that her profession, and the fact that she is very much a citizen of the *wai* (outer) instead of the culturally prescribed *nei* (inner), can work against her in the dating world. She keeps this in mind, but isn't willing to stifle her career just to improve her chances at marriage. Ideally, she would like to find a partner who supports her professional pursuits, or at least isn't deterred by them. Mathematically, this should be possible, as more than 60 percent of urban Chinese women work. The demands of China's economy make it so that living on the inside isn't an option for many wives, who contribute to the financial stability of their families, and in many cases even out-earn their husbands. True to the culturally dictated "outer/inner" dichotomy, it is likely that in addition to the time they put in at work, Chinese wives must also shoulder the brunt of the housework. However, it seems that from a professional standpoint they may have a few advantages over their unmarried compeers.

"Female Astronauts: Single Women Need Not Apply," ran a headline in the Chinese state-run newspaper, the *Global Times*, during the period leading up to the much-buzzed-about decision of who would be China's first female astronaut. The article went on to explain how according to some aerospace experts, "single women will be deemed unfit for the job," further specifying that female astronauts should be "psychologically and physically as strong as their male counterparts."

In what many foreign media outlets had a field day reporting, the article also mentions that, according to Pang Zhihao of the Beijing-based China Academy of Space Technology, astronauts cannot have bad mouth odor, scars, or foot diseases. "A bad mouth odor may annoy other astronauts (who, being male, are presumably odorless?), and scars may bleed in outer space," he told Xinhua, China's national news agency.

The article continues, "Aspiring female astronauts should also be married with children," as the space flight might have an impact on their fertility. "There's no evidence that shows space life impacts women physiologically, but after all this is the first time for China [to send a woman into space]. We must do it more carefully," said Xu Xianrong, a professor with the General Hospital of the People's Liberation Army Air Force, on Chinese National Radio.

It should be recognized that nine years after sending its first man into space (2003), China sent a woman there. While this generally bodes well, to imply that an unmarried woman is unfit for space travel because she is "psychologically and physically inferior" to her married counterparts is also a giant leap backward for Chinese womankind.

"A woman's ability to manage her family is a reflection on how she can manage her employees," confides Christy's friend Xu Li, who is the manager of the global expansion department at a major telecommunications firm. She wants to get divorced, but fears it will jeopardize her job. "I supervise 140 people and am the breadwinner in my family, so I can't take that kind of risk." Instead, Xu lives three hundred miles from her husband, who is not employed full-time but takes care of their daughter in another city. Alone in Beijing, Xu purchased an apartment and took on a lover to keep her company. Her boss doesn't know about the lover, but she's less worried about him somehow finding out. "From a professional standpoint, I'm better off as an adulteress than as a divorcée," she says.

At least for now, being single in Christy's field works to her advantage because it keeps her evenings open for all of the events she must attend to keep growing her network. "Marriage is something I definitely aspire to," she says. "I'm proactive about finding a partner, but not to the extent that it gets in the way of other ambitions."

If only her family would agree.

As she sets out for a Sunday-morning Champagne brunch with friends, Christy's grandfather has returned from Beijing's Temple of Heaven Park. Week after week, he congregates with fleets of other septuagenarians all in search of spouses for their grandchildren. They gather on a large tree-studded square lined with Xeroxed tomes featuring collections of marriage résumés that include the name, age, height, occupation, salary, astrological sign, and sometimes even the blood type of singles approaching their expiration dates. Other ads are more personalized, composed by their elderly authors in wobbly ink and brush on a piece of cardboard. The one Christy's grandfather has made for her is of this kind, and describes her as "fair-skinned, fair-tempered, and youthful."

"Have a look at these," he says, showing Christy a small stack of résumés he's brought home with him. She indulges him sweetly, but privately concedes that she's horrified to be peddled in the park.

"At your age, you can't afford to be fussy," he reminds her sternly. Bracing for another barrage, Christy takes the papers from her grandfather, and then just shy of his earshot asks with a playful smile, "I wonder if I'll meet any dead bachelors?"

2

"GOLDEN TURTLES"

结婚就是给自由穿了一件大衣活动不便但很温暖

Marriage is like putting a winter coat on your freedom. It
makes it harder to move around, but keeps you warm.

—CHINESE PROVERB

Zhang Mei is from a small town outside of Harbin, the capital city of the icy Heilongjiang province located in Northeastern China, not two hours from the border with Siberia.
It's famous for an annual ice festival that draws in millions of
tourists, as well as a legendary Siberian tiger park, where visitors
can choose to become live spectators of the park's renowned tiger-
feeding sessions. Selecting from a savory menu that includes
ducks, chickens, goats, and cows, visitors may purchase a treat
for the ever-hungry felines, and then watch as it is thoroughly
and rapaciously devoured.

Though proud of her glacial origins and chock-full of innova-
tive tricks for combatting subzero temperatures, Zhang Mei left
Harbin at the age of twenty-three after completing her master's
degree in history. It was time to put all she had studied to use and
see what sort of job offers she could rustle up in the big city. Get-

ting her parents on board with her move to Beijing was no easy task. At her age, they thought it was nearing a good time for her to return to her small hometown, accept a steady, rubber-stamp job at the bank where her father had been working for over three decades, and start thinking about settling down. After all, her older sister, Chen—Zhang Mei's parents were allowed to have a second child because their first was a daughter—had gotten married at age twenty-one. Chen hadn't gone to college because she was much more interested in running her own clothing stall—a dream she had since achieved, to relative success. Zhang Mei struggled to see herself doing the same. She bargained with her parents for three years of "freedom" in the capital—just time enough for her to gain some solid professional experience—and then promised to be back in Harbin well before the twilight of her twenties.

It is important to keep in mind that over the past twenty years, China has seen 300 million people migrate from rural to urban areas in search of better education, jobs, and lifestyles. In addition to being the reason for China's prodigious economic boom, this activity represents what Jamil Anderlini of the *Financial Times* has referred to as the largest yearly mammalian migration on Earth, with bats—at 90 million—following at a distant second.

Of China's migrants, women have represented the majority, as rural men were more likely to stay behind and inherit the family farm or business. This is worth underscoring because leftovers are often clumped into the category of "well-educated urban women with ambition and promising careers," but that's only one facet of a much larger story still developing in the wings. More than a label, being a leftover woman means living outside conventional norms—it's a mind-set that exists independently of degrees, salaries, nationalities, and even the rural/urban divide.

Chinese Lessons

I met Zhang Mei shortly after moving to Beijing because she was my Chinese teacher. She was twenty-five at the time. Upon arriving at the language school for my first class, I was told by the headmistress that I would be given a short lesson by three different teachers and that I could choose the one I liked best. After the sample lessons were over, Zhang Mei emerged as the clear favorite. I spoke zero Chinese and she nearly no English, so we weren't able to communicate much, but I remember being charmed by her expressive nature and the large furry pompoms on her kitten heels.

One evening before class, another foreign student at the school came bursting into the lobby, eyes blown up like a pufferfish. She had just split with her boyfriend of several years, and had been crying all the way to the study center. As I fumbled for some words of consolation, Zhang Mei strolled over, smiled, gave the girl a playful slap on the shoulder and said, *"Mei shi."* I had heard this expression before and knew it was like the Chinese equivalent of "Hakuna matata." It's the same thing Zhang Mei had said to me after a scooter accident left me with a hideous gash down the front of my left leg and mortified by the prospect of going to a local Chinese hospital for stitches. Though I mustered the courage to seek medical attention before things got ugly, the student in the lobby didn't look so convinced. *"Ni xian zai hui hen zi you,"* Zhang Mei said to the still grieving woman: "You'll have a lot more freedom now." By this point, the student's pupils appeared to be on the verge of herniating, and she was clearly not comforted by the prospect of becoming Lady Liberty.

When Zhang Mei and I got into our little classroom and shut the door behind us, I expressed sympathy for the student in the lobby, only to receive a slap on the shoulder myself. "*Ai-yah*," she said (in this context, Chinese for "Don't be ridiculous"), before teaching me the phrase that would later become my north for mapping romantic relationships in China: "Love is for teenagers, but when it comes to marriage, one must be practical." As soon as we worked out the kinks of the translation and I was sure I understood her intended meaning, I was miffed. Wet wipes and cargo shorts are both marvelously practical, but on what planet should their kind be a basis for marriage?

I asked her to elaborate—more than anything to see if there was any nuance I might have missed. To my surprise, she defended her statement with the tenacity of the tigers in her hometown. "There is a time for romance, and a time to be responsible," she said. And almost by definition, she insisted, those lines could not cross.

By age twenty-six, Zhang Mei's parents were starting to get jittery about getting her home and wed. According to their calculations, after three years of life in the capital, their daughter had long overstayed her term away, and needed to start thinking about her future. Most of her classmates were already married, and the neighbors were starting to talk. Slowly, her mother began to plant the marriage bug in her ear. Whenever she would call to make the usual round of inquiries (What did you have for dinner? How is the weather in Beijing? Have you gotten a raise? Are you eating less chocolate?), she started to slip in small updates about all of the engaged or pregnant girls in town. "When are you going to bring someone home to us?" her mom would then coo. "Work is too busy these days for such things," was Zhang Mei's stock answer.

"If young women didn't have to leave their hometowns in search of better education and job opportunities, there would be no leftover women in China," Zhang Mei explained to me with great conviction and a hint of distress, one day during our class. "This only happens to us because we leave home. At home, everything is simple. If you don't meet someone on your own, your parents, relatives, or acquaintances present you with a few options, and you just end up marrying one of them. But in a big city like Beijing where you're all on your own? The playbook is completely different."

Now twenty-eight, Zhang Mei lives in a small single dormitory-style room about a one-and-a-half-hour commute west from her work. She shares a bathroom with eight other women and is on call six, often seven, days a week as a private language tutor, depending on how charitable her boss is feeling. While she delights in the "freedom" she has bought herself by migrating to a larger city, she realizes that it has also made her somewhat of an anomaly.

Zhang Mei's biggest challenge is that when she returns home to visit her family, she is reminded that everyone she went to high school with who didn't pursue higher education is already married and with a child. "I see my former classmates—the girls— and they are like spinning tops. Their lives are spent in perpetual service to their husbands, their mothers-in-law, and their child. I don't want that life."

Listening to her speak, I am reminded of how China has grown to become the world's largest economy. For all of its flaws, it is a country that has had the foresight to actively include women in its objectives for economic expansion. Young Chinese "Factory Girls" are the reason the plan worked so well, as they flocked to assemble the Nike sneakers and iPods that put China on the worldwide manufacturing map. Known as "golden turtles," they used their earnings to support their parents, to help pay for the weddings of their brothers or the educations of their younger sisters (in cases of families with more than one child), and to have a small taste of disposable income before returning home and dutifully getting married. Today, while they continue to be a powerful economic motor, they're increasingly trading smokestacks for syllabi and migrating for college—an experience after which it's much harder to fit back into a traditional box.

Further complicating matters is that many of China's young migrant women find pink-collar jobs in environments with few eligible men. "The only men I ever really interact with are married ones," says Zhang Mei, referring to the middle-aged base of Korean and Japanese male professionals who represent the bulk of her students. All of her colleagues are young women, many of them in a situation similar to her own. She often socializes with them on weekends, most often for hotpot and a movie, or a bit of karaoke. They begin their evening early, have dinner at around five thirty or six p.m., and are home by eleven at the latest, in order to be able to catch the last rounds of public transportation back to their respective living quarters.

Because none of this is very conducive to meeting eligible mates, one of Zhang Mei's colleagues decided to take a leap and try online dating. She took a selfie, her bangs partially covering her eyes and her lips pursed in a playful pout. She held up two fingers next to her face in the classic Asian-girl V sign, and uploaded the picture with the following text: "I'm on this site because I spend most of my day around married men." A few days later, she got a message back from a young gentleman wearing black-rimmed frames (which appeared to have no lenses), spiky hair, and a similarly playful pouty face. "I'm on this site because I spend most of my day around married women," he wrote. She was intrigued. They began to chat online, and she soon discovered that he was a photographer specializing in children's snapshots. His days were filled with bouncing babies and beaming mamas. This revelation produced a communal swoon among the girls in the office. The pair went on a few dates, but nothing materialized. Soon, each went back to days filled with married members of the opposite sex.

Zhang Mei tried online dating too, but was much more mum about the results. "I messaged a few men, but nobody interesting wrote back," she said, and that was the end of that.

Over the course of my lessons with Zhang Mei, I took endless pleasure in the quiddities of the Chinese language. That an avocado is referred to as *e li*, or "alligator pear," is just one example of the magically visual nature of the language. (A more comic example is *pi yan*, which translates as "the eye of the butt," or how the Chinese say "anus.") Likewise, expressions such as *qi lü zhao ma* were also the source of colorful gateways to conversations with locals. This particular expression means "ride the donkey while looking for a horse," and I found it exponentially more entertaining upon discovering that it is used in reference to both jobs and boyfriends. *Mou gu* and *mu gou* are examples of words I've struggled to get straight. The former means "mushroom" the latter means "(female) dog," which I've tried to order on multiple occasions. Fortunately, the consumption of dog is illegal in most parts of China—despite being a winter delicacy in regions like Guangdong—and since only a handful of Beijing restaurants carry it, my request for fungi was almost always eventually understood.

Then there were those three little words—*wo ai ni*, that were impossible to mistake or confuse. Their English equivalent, "I love you," is probably the third phrase Chinese students learn in English class after "hello" and "nice to meet you." In China, I've seen it written liberally on everything from notebooks to bedsheets, wall stickers to breakfast treats. My dentist once even gave me a promotional keychain that said "I love you" on it after I had a cleaning. It was touching, though a toothbrush would have been preferable.

While "I love you" seemed ubiquitous in China, never having been privy to a Chinese world of close romantic attachment, I had more or less assumed that *wo ai ni* was used more seriously, much like its English equivalent. "No," explained Zhang Mei. "For us, 'I love you' is beautiful in its brevity, universality, and vagueness in another language, but *wo ai ni* is still very unchartered territory."

Curious to know more, I fired off an email to thirty of my closest Chinese friends. About twenty-five of them got back to me. While I'm fully aware that this is hardly a representative or scientific sample, I found the results to be more illuminating than expected. For starters, few of my contacts born in the '70s or before admitted to ever saying *"wo ai ni."* One told me a story about an afternoon she spent watching a film with her husband, whom she married at age thirty-eight. The film was based on a story written by John Keats, and was full of effusive expressions of emotion. After the film was over, her husband said he didn't think the man really loved the woman in the film, because he just said a lot of things, but there was very little he actually did to make the woman happy. "Love is not a matter of words," she wrote in response to my email. "If you love someone, you care for him/her and do everything possible to make him/her happy." How could I argue with that?

My friends born in the '80s were of a slightly different school of thought. They seemed more tortured about how and when to say those three little words, and most admitted to having done so either to disastrous or comical effects. Zhang Mei reported that she loved her cat more than she had ever loved any man since her middle school crush. A married friend of hers dismissed the words *"wo ai ni"* as "the silly talk that leads to marriage, but stops right after the wedding." Of those who had yet to say *"wo ai ni,"* or hadn't said it in a long time, many ladies, especially, expressed wanting to one day feel the desire to say it. Christy described it as "something very private and difficult to say," adding with a series of smileys and assorted winking emoji that the kind of "soul mate" she was looking for (a corpse groom) wouldn't be able to speak anyway.

Over drinks one evening, my dear friend Guang—a dashing Australian-born Chinese with a penchant for velvet blazers and classic literature—lamented in an uncharacteristically layman's fashion: "Love is like a double cheeseburger. When you have it in your hands, there is nothing better in the world. But if you have it every day and for too long, it will destroy you." To be fair, when I asked Guang this question, his ticker was on the mend. "Broads and burgers," he said, gazing wistfully into his wineglass, "can only lead to heartbreak and bypass surgery." He then paused for dramatic effect, knowing well that I was enjoying the spectacle.

Other Chinese gentlemen who responded to my inquiry were more tight-lipped, and quickly resorted to Taoism. They played down the emotional significance of *wo ai ni*, instead insisting that China is still a place where feelings are conveyed indirectly, or more through actions than words. (Those must be the men who always take out the garbage, I reasoned, but when I ran this logic by a recently married Chinese friend, she responded with a hiss.)

As for the '90s cohort, these young devils were the most radical of the generations. For them, *wo ai ni* is neither positively nor negatively charged, but something that just comes up—in text messages, in a dark corner of science class, or while smushed in closely on the subway ride home.

Despite the relatively small age gaps, I was surprised by how each generation seemed to have its own distinct relationship with the words "*wo ai ni*." In fact, the only common thread that emerged across generations turned out to be parents. Of my two dozen friends, none had ever heard their parents say "*wo ai ni*" to each other, or to their children. This discovery caught me off guard, and I wondered if I should take it as evidence of Zhang Mei's utilitarian description of marriage.

For as much as she seemed disinterested in romance, Zhang Mei—like just about everyone I've met in China—responded with great reverence to a rather romantic concept known as 缘分, or *yuan fen.** Loosely defined, it's the affinity or binding force that links two people together in a relationship—be it fraternal or romantic. On a daily basis, *yuan fen* can be defined as coincidence. For example, if you're scheduled to meet a friend for dinner one evening but happen to bump into him earlier in the day at a coffee shop, you could say that your *yuan fen* is very strong. Two passengers who sit next to each other on a train and end up having a meaningful exchange are also said to have *yuan fen,* as it is assumed that the serendipity of their meeting and hitting it off at that precise moment in time is something special, given the otherwise small odds of that happening in such a large universe. By the same logic, lovers are said to have *yuan fen.* It's the fate that brings them to meet, but it can also be the feeling that they've known one another a very long time (perhaps because they've met in a previous life).

To Zhang Mei, *yuan fen* was something to be heeded. *"Kan kan yuan fen, ba"* or "Let's see what *yuan fen* brings," is a phrase she often spoke, most frequently in reference to her search for a husband. I could sense she really believed that *yuan fen* "had her back," or would somehow come through and provide for her, although this conviction seemed to waver around the Chinese New Year holiday.

---

*   For those well versed in philosophical concepts, *yuan fen* is sometimes likened to Swiss psychologist Carl Jung's concept of synchronicity.

Home Sweet Home

"My parents have been living in the same housing unit for over thirty years," explained Zhang Mei to me one day, just a few weeks before the holiday. "Virtually none of our neighbors have changed over time—they're all my father's colleagues from his work unit at the bank. Twenty years ago, we all moved into a new building because the old one was razed, but none of the inhabitants changed; they've known me my entire life."

I thought it was sweet that Zhang Mei had grown up with what seemed to be a big extended family around her, but she quickly corrected my rosy assumption.

"When I go home to spend Chinese New Year with my family," says Zhang Mei, "I have two options. I can either fly to Harbin, or take the train. I can afford to fly and would much prefer to, but I always take the train instead, because it's the only way of arriving in Harbin late at night. This is more complicated for my sister because it means she has to drive in the dark and on icy roads to pick me up at the train station, but arriving late gives me the great convenience of avoiding my neighbors. We live in the last apartment building in a row of six. In order to get to my front door, I need to pass the homes of five other neighbors on foot. If I do that during the day, at least one person from each building is bound to pop out and start asking me personal questions. I just can't face that, so I tell my family that I'm scared to fly alone, and they accept that I take the train, instead."

Indeed, as was confirmed to me by Christy, for young Chinese men and women, Chinese New Year is the most stressful time of year for singles. "Some mothers literally start to whistle and steam," she explains. "I play along because I know it means a lot to my mother, but sometimes I can't help but feel like a generation of chickens has given birth to a generation of ducks," she says, referencing the bouts of maternally induced seasonal man pressure she and her unmarried friends experience around the holidays. "Our mothers want the best for us, but what they think is best is totally different from what we want!"

Yet while Beijing girls like Christy get their blind dates spread out over the course of the entire year—a young government official here, a male ballet dancer there, and a few academics in between—Zhang Mei's case is different. Her mother has her in close proximity for only a few days each year, time that she fully expects to make the best of. As a result, she begins plotting her marriage offensive in the early fall.

"My mother gets really crazy around the holidays, but honestly, I really don't think she's that stressed out about my lack of husband," explains Zhang Mei. "It's just that the neighbors give her social pressure, so out of desperation, she has to pass that pressure along to me."

"How can you be so sure?" I ask her. The answer dazzles me.

China has a curiously nationalized heating system. In most households, heating is not controlled by individual residents, but by the government. In Beijing, for instance, the "public" heat comes on starting November 15, and lasts until March. While there are some apartments with "private" heat, which means their occupants can turn the heat on and off as they please, residents of apartments with "public" heat (the grand majority) have access to heat only during the time period that corresponds to their city. In Harbin, because it's so cold, the public heat kicks on sooner—October 15. Since all of this heat is powered by burning coal, however, the beginning of each cold season is often accompanied by a great deal of pollution.

"My mother didn't say a peep about marriage for the entire

month of November," explained Zhang Mei. "The pollution was so thick, she wasn't going outside to see her friends. Without them all flocking together to mingle and meddle, I seriously think she forgot all about my situation. I don't need to check the Harbin weather report to know that the AQI (air quality index) levels have normalized. I can feel it in the tips of my ears—they're starting to throb. The skies have cleared, and she'll soon be out socializing. After getting wind of the latest engagements and births, she'll be back on my tail."

As we're walking down the street after the end of class, Zhang Mei's phone rings. She and her mother speak every Wednesday evening after Zhang Mei's last class, so the call was expected, though its content suspiciously strayed from the usual banter. I could overhear their conversation, which Zhang Mei rather graciously allowed me to reproduce here, as she said, "for the good of Chinese female kind."

ZHANG MEI'S MOM (ZMM): *Lao er* [a term of endearment], you're on your way home now?

ZHANG MEI (ZM): Yes.

ZMM: Have you had dinner yet?

ZM: I'll just pick up some noodles on the way home.

ZMM: *Ai-yah*, isn't it lonely eating on your own?

ZM: Meh, it's fine, it's late anyway.

ZMM: But if you had a boyfriend, you'd have someone to eat dinner with.

ZM: Ma, what are you getting at?

ZMM: Nothing, I would just feel better if you had someone to look after you.

ZM: [silence]

ZMM: What will you do this weekend?

ZM: Relax, do a bit of shopping, reading, see a few movies online.

ZMM: *Ai-yah,* why don't you go out for a walk? See, if you had a boyfriend, there would be someone to accompany you on walks—it would be good for your health and you wouldn't have to spend your own money!

ZM: Ma, what are you trying to say?

ZMM: Why are you off work anyway? If you don't work, how will you earn money?

ZM: Ma, do you want me to work seven days a week? If I do that, how will I even have time to spend the money I earn?

ZMM: Well, if you don't have a boyfriend, you have nothing interesting to do during your free time, so you might as well work to save money!

Sensing a conflict, Zhang Mei changes the subject.

ZM: Are Dad's allergies getting any better?

ZMM: They're better, no need to worry about him. We're more concerned about you. We'd like you to bring a boyfriend back for Chinese New Year.

ZM: Ma, Chinese New Year is in two months. Where am I supposed to find someone so quickly?

ZMM: We don't care where you find him, just bring someone home!

ZM: Ma, you realize that if I bring home a random person and we get married, our relationship is unlikely to last very long?

ZMM: Not necessarily.

ZM: OK, but there's definitely a greater chance of divorce if I marry a stranger. You'd rather increase my chances of getting a divorce?

ZMM: At least you will have been married!

After this doozy of a conversation, I ask Zhang Mei what her game plan is for finding a life partner in the next sixty days. "I have no idea," she says. I offer up a few foreign male friends who might be willing to travel home with her and play the part, if it means they get a few free days to explore Harbin and its tiger park. "Nah," she says. "I know a girl who did that. Her dad saw right through it. He said the guy was far too handsome to ever be attracted to his daughter. What if my dad does the same?"

I took the evening to brainstorm about anything I might be able to do to help. Zhang Mei shot down most of my suggestions, until I brought up the idea of a rent-a-boyfriend. I had heard there were Chinese men who rented themselves out to single women at a daily rate over the holidays—it sounded risky and like far more trouble than it might be worth, but much to my surprise, Zhang Mei was willing to give it a shot.

At our next class, we logged onto Taobao.com. The crown jewel of Jack Ma's Alibaba (NYSE's largest IPO, to date), Taobao is an online marketplace selling everything from fake hymens to porcelain claw-foot bathtubs and imported organic quinoa. It has the kind of traffic and selection that makes Amazon look like a lemonade stand, and as I soon discover, no shortage of young Chinese men who are willing to rent themselves out for a bit of extra cash over China's biggest holiday.

As I typed in the Chinese character for "rent" (租) in the search bar—this was my lesson, after all, and Zhang Mei had no intention of letting me slack off—the predictive text followed up with 女友, 男友, 车, 情人, 女友服务, 婚礼服装, in that exact order. Neither of us could believe it. The site's top rental hits were for: girlfriends, boyfriends, cars, lovers, girlfriend services (which further investigation revealed was for women to cuddle and watch movies with from time to time), and wedding clothes.

We promptly homed in on the rental boyfriend section and found ourselves with a motley list of search results. The first specimen was from Beijing. His hair was bleached a blazing shade of pineapple, and in most of his pictures he wore variants of an oversized tee, saggy jeans, purple high-tops, and thick black frames which didn't appear to have lenses in them, either. He seemed friendly, but didn't quite exhibit the qualities Zhang Mei thought her parents would be impressed by—even if it was all just for show.

The second man in the search results was from Guizhou. He was shirtless in his photos, flashing a tanned, rippled torso and a pair of stonewashed jeans. In another picture, he sat behind an oversized wooden desk wearing a suit made of iridescent gray fabric, clutching what appeared to be a large marble globe. He claimed to have a master's degree and to speak four languages.

The third man we came across had several reviews from women he had already accompanied home. One referred to him as "very lovely and discreet." Another said "trustworthy and reliable," and a third said, "large face, but otherwise handsome."

We looked into his rates. He was charging 700 RMB ($100) per day during non-peak seasons, and 1,000 RMB ($145) during Chinese New Year. Those rates increased to 1,000 RMB and 1,500 RMB ($220), respectively, if he was required to travel to more remote provinces, like Tibet, Xinjiang, or Inner Mongolia. Unlike some of the men advertising their services, his offering was pricier, but all-inclusive. He didn't request additional fees for smoking cigarettes (usually billed at 10 RMB or $1.50 per cigarette), giving kisses (5 RMB or 75 cents per kiss on the forehead), holding hands (20 RMB or US $3, flat rate), and drinking rice wine (10 RMB per shot).

"What do you think?" I asked Zhang Mei.

"It can't hurt to call," she said.

3

DOORS AND WINDOWS

One man is best suited to four women, as a teapot is best
suited to four cups.

—XINRAN, *THE GOOD WOMEN OF CHINA*

Although many Chinese parents name their daughters after things found in nature (like Fragrant Mountain and Flowering Lotus), Ivy earned her English name from the first married, moneyed man she ever slept with. "He was mesmerized by the length of my legs," she said, "and since I think the name suits me, I've kept it."

Indeed, Ivy's legs are veritable trellises upon which any plant would be challenged to climb, though it's doubtful they would have brought her such spectacular returns if it hadn't been for her masterful mind and her determination to end life on a far more stratospheric notch of the social ladder than the one she started on.

"Chinese men want a wife who is four things," she explained with an authoritative puff of a cigarette.

1. Beautiful
2. Doting and wifely
3. Hardworking
4. Willing to turn a blind eye when they cheat.

"Basically, they want a fairy tale," she said. "It's no wonder they must look elsewhere to have all of their desires fulfilled."

One good look at Ivy reveals that she is beautiful, though probably not considered "wifely," or "doting" by Chinese standards. She smokes with a vigor unlike any I've ever seen before. Just after exhaling smoke, she re-inhales it with the force I imagine a dragon might have in its nostrils. She rarely smiles, though she listens carefully and with a quiet intensity. She speaks with candor and confidence about her choice to complete someone else's fairy tale in exchange for her own version of a happy ending.

Originally from a middle-class family in the second-tier city of Chengdu, Ivy relied on her striking good looks, determination, and her talent for the arts to gain admission into one of China's most legendary drama schools—a hotbed of extremely gifted but also devastatingly attractive actresses and emerging movie stars. Despite being talented, Ivy could sense that she would never outshine her more politically and socially connected peers, so after a careful appraisal of her most marketable talents, she estimated that her legs presented the greatest opportunity for advancement. Shortly after this realization, she met a man at a business school networking event that a friend had invited her to. Upon seeing him arrive in an Aston Martin, she used her spindles to catch his eye, and soon after had found her new calling as a mistress.

For context, it's worth recalling that extramarital activity has been a driving force of China's history for dynasties. The country's most powerful leader—Wu Zetian—served as a Forbidden

City concubine during the Tang dynasty. By ruthlessly pitting the reigning emperor against his son and pinning the murder of her one-week-old daughter on a rival consort, she eventually became empress and supreme ruler of China. By 700 CE, she had amassed a huge fortune and to this day is still ranked as the wealthiest woman of all time. In its five thousand years of history, she is also the only woman to have officially ruled China as emperor.

Though current methods for seeking wealth and power through affairs and marriage are presumably more subdued, the practice is still flourishing in China, where the transition to a market economy has presented fortune-seekers with a glittering new world of possibilities. Making this transition all the more fascinating is the fact that China went from being a country with essentially no "old money" to having its own full-blown Gilded Age. Thirty years ago—barring exceptional government connections—there were very small differences between classes. Urban professionals all lived in the same cement block housing provided by their *danwei* (work unit), ate in their largely uniform work unit cafeterias, and married within a similar socioeconomic bracket—often as arranged by a work superior. Life was routine and heavily regimented; couples couldn't even divorce without the approval of their employer, and requests to do so were rarely granted.

Marriage was so deeply ingrained and enforced as a prerequisite for adulthood that even the process for giving wedding gifts was standardized. In the 1980s, it was customary for a groom's family to provide their new daughter-in-law with "three rounds and a sound": a bicycle, a watch, and a sewing machine, plus a radio or an alarm clock. By the 1990s, these three objects were upgraded to include a TV, a fridge, and a washing machine, but since China's economic boom, the sky has become the limit.* Between 2000 and 2015 alone, China's middle class grew from 5 million to 225 million households, and 50 million more are expected to join their ranks by 2020. In parallel, following the establishment of China's private real estate market in 1998—prior to this time, all property belonged to the government—housing prices have skyrocketed, producing *Freakonomics*-worthy repercussions on the market for status symbols like apartments and cars.

Alongside this lust for material goods obtained through marriage is the timeless adage that, prior to the Cultural Revolution, had guided the work of Chinese matchmakers for centuries: *"men dang hu dui,"* or "matching doors and matching windows." Essentially, this idea implies that marriage partners should be from similar households and socioeconomic backgrounds, ideally with the man's family being slightly better off so as to justify his position as the head of the family and its chief "provider." Although this model is still generally considered ideal, the emergence of a suddenly very wealthy Chinese class, when combined with the continued existence of a very poor class and a quickly growing middle class with exposure to an exponentially larger catalogue of things to covet, has provoked a sharp change in the rules of the game. Unlike in India or other caste-heavy systems, in China a woman of any background can now take the express elevator to a better life by hitching herself to a wealthy man, and for those enterprising enough to shop around until they find the man

---

*   Before De Beers appeared in China in 1993, there was no tradition involving the exchange of diamond engagement rings; gold and jade were used instead. Since then, China has become the second largest diamond market in the world after the United States, which suggests that more than a few Chinese women have required their fiancés to "put a ring on it."

with the most desirable set of doors and windows, great profits lie in store.

Changing Tides

"As the water rises, so does the boat," says Dr. X. I had originally been connected with him as a source for a story I was writing about marriage in China, because as a former government official and executive vice chairman of a somewhat mysterious NGO promoting cultural exchange between China and the rest of the world, he had facilitated the work of two American marriage counselors in China. On our first meeting, he welcomed me in his Beijing office with a very fine pot of tea. After a few pleasantries and a bit of Chinese fortune-telling—which according to Dr. X's interpretation revealed that we had been close friends in a previous life—our conversation surprisingly veered toward the topic of mistresses.

In retrospect, this makes perfect sense. For a Chinese man of Dr. X's standing—well off, well connected, well educated, and well into his fifties—a mistress (or two, or three) is practically a requirement. But when I first met him—still only in my salad days of understanding the dynamics of extramarital relations in China—his ideas and observations seemed extraordinary, if not completely farfetched. "If a man in China doesn't have a mistress, it's because his economic situation doesn't allow for it," he announced, as casually and assuredly as if he were reporting the latest figures for China's GDP. "And if a very successful man doesn't have a mistress, his wife will be puzzled as to why he doesn't."

Dr. X delivered his words with such ease and conviction that it was actually very easy to hear him out, despite my moral objections to what he was saying. When I asked him why he thought mistresses were so popular—especially among men of his stature—he taught me a new word: *jingshen* (精神). According to Dr. X, this word, which translates roughly as "vitality," represents the mix of spirit, energy, and invigoration that fuels men in an endless quest for the revitalizing company of women roughly half their age.

It would be simple to demonize Dr. X. He does, after all, represent the ruling class of Chinese men who philander from one plum government posting to another. From what I'm able to infer, his life is a revolving door of meetings (professional and recreational) in hotel lobbies, from the St. Regis, to the Ritz, to the Kunlun. Yet to his credit, he plays the part of a Lothario with far more zest than his contemporaries. He has style—something that seems to escape the majority of the high-ranking officials of the Communist Party. Though there is barely a gray hair among them (Chinese men don't spend millions on facial creams and toners like their Japanese and Korean counterparts, but they certainly do not skimp when it comes to hair dye), most elite party members appear to dress in a similarly stultifying uniform. Dr. X is different. He is practically a dandy. In the dead of winter, I spotted him in a blue-and-white checkered blazer, playfully accented with a magenta-and-chartreuse silk paisley pocket square. He wears cologne, has a sense of humor, and delights in traveling abroad. After a trip to Barcelona, he explains that he fell so in love with *jamón ibérico* (Spanish ham) that he brought back an entire pig's leg, as well as the *jamonera* required to slice it on. He spoke of this cured meat with more zeal than any Spaniard I've ever met, including my Iberian relatives who treat their consumption of *jamón* as a religious experience.

"I can have almost anything I want in this world," he explains, just after telling me that two more Spanish hams will be arriving in the mail. "Except a wife." He delivers these lines with a hint of regret and more than a dash of frustration. Only after getting a bit deeper into our conversation does it become apparent as to why.

Dr. X was married in his twenties, but only for a year. Now in his fifties, it appears that he has a strong desire to remarry, but the only problem, according to him, is that the types of women he would like to wed are not interested in marriage. "They have so many suitors, they'd rather remain free agents and benefit from the attention and assets of several men at once. They can get much more out of their relationships this way."

I had a feeling Dr. X was not referring to jewelry, handbags, cars, or any of the other "gifts" commonly given to mistresses in exchange for their company. I was just about to request that he elaborate when Dr. X preempted my question and opened my eyes to a new level of mistressing. "These women already have all the accessories they need. They also already have their own cars and apartments," he said. "Material possessions aren't what they require—they're after connections and capital." In other words, they become mistresses in order to network.

Dr. X then takes out his phone and flips through photos of several women. He rattles off a list of things they've acquired from different men. One got just under US $1 million in investment to put toward her own cosmetics line. Another obtained US $2 million to start her own advertising agency. Yet another, now based in Paris, used the money she'd accumulated from her paramours to launch her own fashion line. "And when they don't need capital, they go after connections," he explained. "I estimate that 80 percent of Chinese women with their own businesses are somebody's mistress."

Dr. X's revelations were turning my preconceptions about gender dynamics in China on their head. In his version, women (mistresses, in this case) were coming out on top. They were exquisite profiteers, using men to their great advantage. While it was a mind-rattling discovery, I couldn't help but wonder if it was symptomatic of gender inequalities in China even greater than I had considered. The women Dr. X was describing sounded resourceful, sharp, and extremely competent. From the pictures he had shown me, they were also significantly more beautiful than the men to whom they attached themselves. Why did they bother?

What if these women needed this sort of male "sponsorship" because the gender cards in Chinese society are so stacked that it was one of the only ways to get ahead? It seemed like a radical theory, but I wasn't immediately willing to dismiss it. Despite all the fuss that has been made over the "women hold up half the sky" epithet that was proclaimed by Mao, I'd long suspected that the feminine half of the Chinese heavens was still somehow the less sunny of the two. I was well aware that many business deals in China are made over dinners accompanied with excessive amounts of *baijiu* (a famously strong rice wine) and followed up at karaoke places where "hostesses" serve as prostitutes. For these reasons, women aren't usually involved, unless they're part of the entertainment.

A Chinese media personality and businesswoman who is also among China's strongest voices on feminism told me by phone that she must regularly pay some of her male employees to go drinking with her prospective clients after she has dinner with them because she knows that the best wheel-greasing opportunities happen in after-hours scenarios she can't partake in. This sentiment was echoed to me by China scholar Gwendoline Debéthune, whose doctoral research examines the Chinese provinces where a woman can't obtain micro-credit to start her own business, unless a man (presumably, her husband) signs off on it. Piecing these anecdotes together, I was starting to wonder if "making it" in the professional world could be especially challenging for a woman without the male connections that seemed necessary to get a business going. Was it challenging enough to warrant becoming a mistress?

Dr. X then told me about a Shanghai matchmaking event he'd recently taken part in. I already had a vague idea of how these events operated. Chinese men with cash to burn hand over several thousand RMB in order to be set up on dates with cherry-picked women who conform to an exacting list of requirements that the men may stipulate. These usually include some variant of very well proportioned body measurements and exceedingly fair skin. After attending with high hopes, Dr. X explained that the woman he was most interested in told him that she was currently seeing five other men. "I have no intentions of marrying any of them in the near future," she told him squarely, in what must have been a sizable blow to his *jingshen*.

While I was struggling to process this information, to Dr. X, it was the most natural thing in the world. According to him, being a mistress was just a logical progression in a woman's personal and professional trajectory. In fact, he argued, smart, savvy, hardworking women (in other words, the ones who I assumed were the least likely to become mistresses) were actually among the best paramours, because their educations and life experience made them even more enterprising.

But I wasn't about to take his word for it.

The Mistress Slayer

Wei Wujun is China's answer to Sherlock Holmes, but instead of a deerstalker, pipe, and magnifying glass, he's known for smoking tarry Zhongnanhais (classic Chinese cigarettes) and his knack for imperceptibly tacking GPS tracking devices onto the underbellies of cars owned by cheating husbands. Commonly referred to as the *er nai sha shou* or "mistress slayer," the sixty-year-old detective has made such a name for himself hunting down doxies that he recently had to announce his retirement on Shanghai TV, just so his phone would stop ringing.

"Most private detectives in China are in the mistress business," he tells me. "This was my livelihood for twenty-one years. I made so much money, I ended up driving nicer cars than some of my clients."

Wujun describes one of his more memorable cases—a Taiwanese businessman living in Guangdong who had eight mistresses. "This was in 1995," he explains. "For the Taiwanese, having a mistress on the mainland was commonplace. The cost of living in China was so low, you could have a mistress for 3,000 RMB (US $430) a month."

Why any man who already had a wife and two daughters would want to add eight more women to his life was bewildering to me, but according to Wujun, this was nothing out of the ordinary. In fact, the gentleman in question (let's call him Wild Oats) had an arrangement with his wife, who not only approved of his extramarital activities but often played mahjong—a Chinese tile game requiring an even number of players—with her husband's lovers.

Things took an ugly turn when Wild Oats decided to get his younger brother—also a partner in the family business—a mistress of his own. Although the brother's wife didn't oppose her husband's infidelity, she had failed to give birth to a son and feared that her husband (whom we'll call Little Oats) might try to have one with his lady companion.

And so she called Detective Wujun.

"Cavorting is costly, but procreating is exorbitant," says Wujun, explaining that Little Oats's wife didn't so much fear another child but a drain on the family finances. As it turns out, it's a common scheme among mistresses to try to have a son for their men—and possibly abort if they become pregnant with a girl—because the act of providing a male heir means they'll be entitled to financial support for a longer period of time, even once they're too old to live off their looks alone.

There are significant "social compensation fees" for having a child out of wedlock in China, where the progeny of unmarried parents are so frowned upon that they're not even entitled to a *hukou*, or residence permit. Without a *hukou*, a child can't attend school, access basic social services, or even apply for an identity card. These limitations fuel a black market for fake *hukou*, which is usually how the children of men and their mistresses become legitimized—unless Wujun is able to intervene beforehand. Over the course of his career, he admits to having participated in at least one high-speed chase to a maternity ward, in a bid to blow the cover of a man and his mistress on the way to give birth.

Mistresses who don't secure a financial link through childbirth often open businesses, explains Wujun. "They open beauty salons, luxury boutiques—all territory they're very familiar with," he says. However, if they haven't invested well or if they don't have a good head for business, as they age and lose market value, many retire with much less than they're accustomed to. "They end up lonely and living day to day," he says, just before adding, "I think the happiest ones are those who eventually get married."

Costly Cavorting

If marriage was a part of Ivy's master plan, she was certainly in no rush to complete it.

Though she is only twenty-seven, one gets the impression that she has lived well beyond her years. The first time I met her in person, she had a Cartier watch encircling her wrist, a Dior bag dangling from her forearm, Chanel earrings illuminating her ears, a cashmere Burberry coat cinched at her waist, and LV patent pumps with small golden bows adorning her feet. She was a veritable pageant of luxury branding, and yet somehow—shockingly—she made it all work.

"In the eyes of many Chinese men, a beautiful girl can only be beautiful so long as she's useless and completely lost and destroyed without a man supporting her," she said as we sat down to Hong Kong–style sweets at a small café near her apartment. We were surrounded by royal-purple velvet furniture, endless mirrors, and swirling tentacular chandeliers—a decorative theme that I sensed has somehow become the coat of arms of China's nouveau riche. "And a smart girl can only be smart so long as she isn't too beautiful to be taken seriously or to be perceived as too much of a threat," she added.

As for a smart, beautiful woman? That, Ivy proudly proclaimed, is a mistress.

Shortly before meeting Ivy, I came across a report in Chinese media of a busted "mistress ring" run by a Shanghai Finance University student surnamed Ding. He had allegedly recruited female students from fourteen leading mainland universities, including Peking University, Tsinghua University, and Renmin University, and was charging a premium (between 400,000 RMB and 600,000 RMB or US $60,000–$90,000 a year) for their services. As part of the deal, he even promised prospective sponsors copies of the female students' academic achievement certificates and English proficiency tests. This news struck me as surprising—all along I'd been under the impression that Chinese men shied away from intelligent women. It turns out they do—when it comes to finding a wife. But where mistresses are concerned, as Dr. X hinted, it seems brains and beauty pack an extra-special punch.

There's a historical explanation for this preference. In China as recently as the early 1900s, the brothel, courtesan house, or otherwise designated location where a man might procure what in modern terms would be defined as a "mistress," was a place of extreme social importance. Here, a client's masculinity was either validated or denigrated by the women he frequented, as courtesans were the arbiters of a man's sophistication, class, and refinement. There were even guidebooks instructing male callers on how to behave when in the company of a courtesan. If a man failed to comport himself appropriately, he risked shame, ridicule, and ran the danger of being perceived as a "country bumpkin" by other customers.

This was equally true for prostitutes, who, although of lesser standing than courtesans, were still among the most elite women in society and the social equals of aristocrats, scholars, government officials, and the like. More than carnal pleasure, they provided the pleasure of their company through music, poetry, singing, and dancing, as conveyed by the Chinese character for prostitute, 妓, which means "female performer."

During the Tang dynasty (618–907), even a special governmental institution called the *jiaofang* (教坊) was founded, where prostitutes trained in music, dancing, literature, calligraphy, chess, and literary drinking games. Considered a conservatory or high-end finishing school of sorts, it existed at a time when women were otherwise completely deprived of education, which made courtesans and prostitutes a scintillating and welcome escape from innocent and homely wives. Their worldliness and prestige made them privy to situations and conversations that "virtuous" women would never have access to, and their talents and charms made them the darlings of respected men and poets. As noted by Ginger Huang in *The World of Chinese*, of the 49,000 poems in *The Complete Poetry of the Tang*, 4,000 are related to prostitutes and 136 are written by prostitutes themselves.

Even in modern China, politics and extramarital activity remain intertwined. Known in some circles as China's unofficial "Queen of Mistresses," Li Wei was born into an impoverished family in war-torn Vietnam and has since become a billionaire thanks to her clever and strategic conquests. Much like Wendi Deng—the former wife of Rupert Murdoch who is largely seen as a hero in her native China—Wei used powerful men as stepping-stones to even more powerful men. Yet whereas Deng is admired for having skillfully manipulated herself out of poverty (and out of China) by seducing a married American man—to whom she was briefly married before wedding Murdoch—Wei's story has an extra pinch of drama. In addition to amassing an enviable fortune through her escapades, Wei also put several of her paramours behind bars.

As reported in a searing cover story by *Caijing Magazine*—one of China's most respected publications—Wei started small. In the late '80s, as a modest tobacco trader keen to build a network of business connections, Wei first became the mistress of the man who would help her—and her sisters—obtain the residency papers and fake IDs they needed to facilitate business travel between Hong Kong and the mainland. She then upgraded by marrying a local government official working in China's tobacco bureau, and through him she met her next victim: Li Jiating, the governor of Yunnan, a Chinese province that produces a prodigious volume of tobacco. He was jailed in 2001 for taking millions of dollars in bribes, and although Li Wei was also arrested for exploiting her husband's contacts to bring in backhanders, she was eventually released. Following their divorce, she became mistress to the crown jewel of her collection: Du Shicheng, then the Communist Party secretary of Qingdao, a coastal city in the northeast that is something like China's answer to Atlantic City, minus the casinos.* Through Shicheng, Wei gained access to huge plots of land at bargain-basement prices in Qingdao, which at the time was gearing up to host the water sports events at the 2008 Olympics. Wei won numerous contracts to develop prime seafront locations, including a luxury marina, an upscale shopping mall, and an opulent mansion, the latter of which she used to host legendary parties for party members. As reported in the *Daily Mail,* "Fine wines flowed. Obscene sums of money changed hands. Multi-million-pound deals were agreed. Flirtations were initiated and future lovers seduced. And in every encounter, Li Wei reigned supreme."

Unfortunately for Shicheng, he made the mistake of introducing his mistress to Chen Tonghai, then chairman of Sinopec; the Chinese oil and gas goliath. Sensing the opportunity to diversify her portfolio, Wei became his lover and pumped him for gas-station rights and Sinopec shares worth millions of pounds.

Perhaps most intriguing in Wei's never-ending game of "man monopoly" is the fact that while virtually all of her pawns served time for corruption charges, despite a few slaps on the wrist and brief stints behind bars, she remains free. She has testified in court against many of her former lovers and, by extension, has toppled a portentous list of powerful men. Du, the party secretary

---

* Gambling is illegal under Chinese law, which begins to explain why casinos around the world—including in the special administrative zones of Hong Kong and Macau—are often filled with zealous Chinese gamblers.

of Qingdao, died in jail. Chen, the former chairman of Sinopec, is still in jail, as are other men to whom Wei has been connected, including the former deputy of the supreme court, the former deputy governor of the China Development Bank, and the former vice mayor of Beijing, as far as can be known. It is impossible to say for sure, but Wei may have been spared much jail time for her own misdemeanors because, like a catfish, she sucked details (and money) out of greedy, high-level men and made the work of the Chinese graft-busting police infinitely easier by keeping all the information in a journal.

A police official associated with one of the corruption cases told the *Daily Mail,* "It showed that behind every successful woman, there are many bad men."

Though a superlative example, Wei is not an exception. A survey of Chinese corruption cases conducted in 2000 and reported in John Osburg's book *Engendering Wealth: China's New Rich and the Rise of an Elite Masculinity,* found that 93 out of 100 cases involved mistresses and often the sticky fingers of these convicted men were revealed through testimonies from their extramarital female companions. "In this world, only the kiss of a woman will send you to your doom," noted Li Zhen, a former party secretary and tax bureau chief from Hebei province. While he was in hiding, his mistress, whom he referred to as a "little lamb turned poisonous snake," leaked his whereabouts to the police, a revelation that led to his execution for graft in 2003.

Thinking back to Empress Wu Zetian, the actions of China's modern mistresses are not so different from those of their concubine sisters of yore, who used their feminine charms and privileged proximity to men in power as a means of gaining access to sensitive business information and networks they would not otherwise have had. While this doesn't say much for equality between the sexes, it underscores the curious persistence of a system that has been in place for centuries. It also highlights the importance of its female protagonists, who, consciously or not, may have redressed prevalent gender inequalities in their society by obtaining sizable sums of wealth and power, while simultaneously reinforcing these inequalities at the expense of other women—namely, the wives.

Still, for better or for worse—and until a corruption scandal do it part—mistress culture is so embedded in Chinese culture at large that March 3 is known in some circles as "Mistress Day." The date was coyly chosen because in Chinese, one of the two most common ways to say mistress is *xiao san* or "little three." March 3 (3/3), therefore, was considered the most opportune day for a group of third wheels called the Association for the Care of Little Threes, to publish an open letter on its now defunct (presumably censored) website, Xeixe.com, establishing March 3 as a day of respect and awareness for the third wheels of the world.*

Though the site was full of tutorials and friendly forums where "little threes" discussed the gifts they received, the going rate for monthly allowances, and shared tips for taking revenge on dishonest men, some of the most interesting entries attempted a more metaphysical approach to mistressing.

According to SuXiaoman.com, another now defunct site that I was redirected to from Xeixe.com, there is a very critical differ-

---

* Mistress Fun Fact: Today, Valentine's Day in China is celebrated by couples with roses, chocolates, and candlelit dinners, much like it is in the West, but until the 1990s, Valentine's Day, translated into Chinese as "Lovers Day," was largely understood otherwise. Since the word "lover" at the time was still almost exclusively associated with extramarital affairs, many Chinese believed that Valentine's was actually a special holiday to celebrate mistresses. "Mistress Day" (March 3) didn't come along until two decades later.

ence between a *xiao san* and an *er nai*, the other common term used to reference a mistress, which literally translates as "second breast." *Er nai*, it's generally acknowledged, are the more self-interested breed of mistress. The primary objective of their relationships is generally understood to be money, whereas for *xiao san*, feelings trump finances.

As explained on the site:

- A *xiao san* treats the affair as a real emotional relationship, whereas an *er nai* is just looking to make money
- A *xiao san* is with a man because she wants to be, an *er nai* is with a man because it's her occupation
- A *xiao san* needs to hear the words *"wo ai ni"* (I love you), whereas an *er nai* needs to hear the words *"wo yang ni"* (I'll pay for you)

It concludes: In today's modern society, wives are the ones who manage money, *er nai* are the ones who require money, and *xiao san* are the ones who just want love.

I ran these definitions by Dr. X, who I am not surprised to discover is friends with Wei, whom he affectionately and cheerfully refers to as Wei Jie, or "sister Jie." (She must have spared him in her chain of conquests in favor of a bigger fish.) Dr. X didn't dispute the definitions, and decided to build on them. "Chinese culture dictates that for a woman to marry, she must find a man with superior education, societal status, and earnings. Today, given everything Chinese women have achieved, the number of these men in proportion to single women just doesn't work out, and so in order to get what they want, some women have to become mistresses instead."

Although it was hard for me to imagine that Ivy became a

mistress as the result of an unfavorable numbers game, I decided to ask her anyway. "It wasn't a difficult decision," she said. "I'm not the type of woman men want to marry, but it turns out I'm exactly the type they want to have an affair with. Rather than change my nature, I chose to use it to my advantage."

As she spoke, I couldn't help but think about how much she has in common with Christy, Zhang Mei, and other so-called leftover women I'd gotten to know. She was resourceful, ambitious, and—while it may not seem obvious—fiercely independent. "Being with several men gives me the freedom and the resources to avoid becoming the property of one," she admits, in a rare moment of emotion. This idea reminds me of an earlier conversation I'd had with Christy after she had finished a particularly taxing week of work. "I don't work this hard because I want to," she said. "I do it because I need to know that I can support myself." In China, little girls grow up hearing the phrase "It's better to marry well than to study well," Zhang Mei once explained to me during a lesson. "But that's a very foolish thing to think and a very dangerous way to live."

4

MARRIAGE AND MORTARBOARDS

女子无才便是德

Women of high intellect die young.

—CHINESE PROVERB

hen June Ma goes out on a date with a Chinese man, she hikes up the virgin factor. Instead of wearing an open cardigan and a necklace, she stows away her cleavage and is demure in a modest sweater and scarf. Throughout the course of the date, she is careful to let the man do most of the talking, to appear interested in everything he says, and to react with sufficient wonder to ensure that he is—at all times—very comfortably marinating in his own ego.

This proves somewhat challenging for the twenty-seven-year-old Beijinger, who is by no accounts a shrinking virginal violet. She graduated at the top of her high school class and was admitted to Yale, where she earned her BA and began her JD, then worked briefly at a Manhattan law firm before returning to Beijing to be closer to her parents. Animated, affable, and razor sharp, she is also endlessly inquisitive, a habit she developed in the United States—which for the information-deprived Chinese student, was an all-you-can-ask buffet.

"Pay attention to your laugh!" warns her mother as June is getting herself ready for a date one evening in Beijing. While it isn't necessary to cover her teeth, her mother is constantly reminding her to tame her expressions of amusement to a titter when in the company of a Chinese gentleman. Equally invested in his daughter's marital future, June's father—a respected scholar—more radically suggests that she mute her laugh altogether, and instead encourages her to "smile like the *Mona Lisa*." Anything more exuberant might convince a prospective suitor that she is assertive, worldly, charismatic—in short, not a good wife.

June is a prime example of the obstacles Chinese women with advanced degrees encounter when seeking a marriage partner, especially once they've had exposure to foreign men while living or studying abroad. Back in China, June feels as if she's living a double life. She finds that most of the local men she is set up with aren't interested in casual dating; they are looking for wives—blushing, tender, baby-making wives. June plays along out of respect for the family members and friends who set her up, but in her free time, she dates Western men and other "return turtles" (Chinese who have studied abroad but are now back in China) whom she meets when out on the town. Like them, her education, exposure to a foreign dating culture, and higher emotional expectations all make her an anomaly in modern China, where traditional courtship mores of propriety and practicality still dominate. Though determined to avoid finding a husband of the "shake-and-bake" variety—that is, the kind who, shortly after shaking his hand, you are married to and baking his children—as she has discovered, these types of arrangements abound in China.

"We like our wives to be yogurts," said the thirty-five-year old Chinese investment banker sitting across from me. "Plain yogurts—so that we can flavor them as we'd like." On paper, this man—a friend of a friend who had kindly offered to provide his perspective on leftover women, is a solid match for June. Like her, he's ambitious, well educated, works in a prestigious field, and speaks excellent English. When I sat down to talk with him at his office in the Central Business District of Beijing, I thought I might even play matchmaker and offer to introduce him to one of my accomplished female friends. As it turned out, however, he is surrounded by high-achieving single women at work. While he enjoys their company, he's not at all interested in marrying his educational or professional equal. Besides, he's already engaged.

"My fiancée is a plain yogurt," he explained to me, just two days before his wedding. "She's low maintenance and doesn't really have her own ideas. I like her because she's easy to manage." And then, leaving me to question whether he was engaged to a human or a dairy cow, he left the office to board the high-speed train that would take him back to his hometown for his bachelor party.

While I wasn't enraptured by his logic, after working in television journalism in Beijing and forming a tight-knit group of friends over five years, I was familiar with his viewpoint. A general distaste for wives of the flavored variety is dominant enough in China to warrant the now commonly acknowledged idea that the more educated a Chinese woman becomes, the more difficult it is for her to find a life partner. This axiom is true to the extent that Chinese female PhDs are commonly referred to as a "third sex," because very few men are willing to marry them—not even fellow academics. According to my now betrothed informant, the educations and salaries of more educated women put them on a par with elite males, who have a tendency, if not a cultural obligation, to shy away in favor of more tractable wives.

This wasn't an issue in the days when boys were considered more worthy of higher education and girls were barely schooled past early adolescence, but over the last sixty years in China, that coin has been flipped.

In 1949, roughly 75 percent of Chinese women over the age of fifteen were illiterate. By 1980, that percentage had dropped to 10 percent, and at present, it is one of the lowest in the world. The push for literacy first began during the Cultural Revolution, as Mao wanted as many people reading his Little Red Book as possible. It has also helped that since 1998, China has tripled the portion of its GDP dedicated to education. More than 60 percent of high school graduates now attend university, as compared to 20 percent just thirty years ago. In the last decade, the number of institutions of higher education in China has more than doubled, and the number of students enrolled in degree courses has sextupled. Leading the charge have largely been Chinese women like June, whose higher-education enrollment rates greatly exceed those of males, and who, since 2011, according to United Nations statistics, have come to represent the majority of bachelor degree earners in China. The downside to this rapid female educational advancement is that for well-educated Chinese women, a dangerous paradox emerges.

"Whatever you do, don't get physical!" yells June's mother as her daughter heads out the door for her date.

Far from a histrionic, modern-day Mrs. Bennet, June's mom is more of a practically minded dating coach. Well aware that her daughter's education makes her highly appealing to prospective employers, yet highly intimidating to prospective mates, she's trying to help render her more wifely in the eyes of suitors who might be shaken by her confidence and accomplishments. "After you reject a man physically, you need to lavish him with praise," she instructs her daughter.

June nods knowingly. "Modern China is like a giant episode of *Sex and the City*," she says. "Except that instead of bawdy Samantha, we have our practical and traditional Charlotte-like mothers." She goes on to explain that traditional Chinese men want to marry virgins, and that most of the marriage-minded blind dates she goes on are completely devoid of romance. "They're like business meetings," she says. "It's not uncommon to talk about marriage on the first date, though physically, it's imperative for things to move much slower. There's lots of nodding, and absolutely no touching."

That her mother is suddenly so proactive about her dating life has come as a surprise to June, whose parents had strongly discouraged her from socializing with the opposite sex until her last year of college (as do many Chinese parents). I know this sounds wildly paradoxical, especially since most parents expect their daughters to get married as soon as they graduate from college, but welcome to the gnarly crosshairs of young adulthood in modern China. As an only daughter, June is all her family has. Her parents are aware of how fierce the job market in China is, and they want to give her every opportunity to succeed and bring honor to their family. At the same time, they also know that if she generates too much success or too much honor, she runs the strong risk of alienating a potential father for their future grandchild; hence the hurry to get her hitched.

Despite being treated like a burning building surrounded by the urgent flames of fading looks, waning fertility, and plummeting value on the marriage market, June doesn't regret the energy she has put into her education. She just completed an MBA in

Beijing and is considering doing a PhD in the United States. Her desire to learn is what makes her so sharp, charismatic, and endlessly resourceful. As we speak about her different degrees, she makes it clear that as a young girl, she didn't realize how her educational pursuits would affect her romantic prospects. "The bottom line is: we all need advanced degrees to remain competitive in the workforce with men," she says. "But the new reality is that those same advanced degrees may later bite some of us in the back when it comes time to get married."

For a country still in the throes of development, China's numbers of excelling females are commendable, but not entirely surprising. It's worth noting that between 1975 and 2006, the percentage of American women with at least a four-year college degree nearly doubled—from 18.6 percent to 34.2 percent, but the male percentage only increased one point—from 26.8 percent to 27.9 percent. Today, American women are responsible for over 60 percent of all four-year college degrees earned, over 60 percent of all master's degrees, and over 50 percent of all PhDs—and they are not the exception. In 67 of 120 nations, including places as diverse as Iran, Venezuela, the Philippines, Kyrgyzstan, Israel, Brazil, Belarus, Armenia, Jamaica, Panama, Cuba, Italy, Hungary, and Germany, women have gone through a similarly rapid expansion on the educational front, and now earn more college degrees than men.

According to demographers Albert Esteve, Joan García-Roman, and Iñaki Permanyer of the Centre d'Estudis Demogràfics in Barcelona, an increase in female educational attainment has a very direct influence on marriage patterns across the world. In their study, "The End of Hypergamy," the demographers hypothesize that as countries progress toward more gender-balanced educational distributions, the prevalence of hypergamy tends to diminish. In other words, the age-old idea that a woman must "marry up" to a man with a higher educational level than her own will erode as more and more women attain higher levels of education.

To test their theory, they accumulated marriage and educational data for fifty-six countries spanning the period from 1968 to 2009. Based on this data, they were able to show a steadily decreasing level of educational hypergamy across the world. From 1970 to 1975, for instance, it was more common for women to marry "up" (female hypergamy) than to marry "down" (female hypogamy), but by the year 2000, trends had changed drastically. In twenty-six of the fifty-one countries for which they had data, a majority of women were married to men with lower education than themselves. These included countries as diverse as the United States, France, Jordan, Mongolia, Slovenia, and South Africa.

The demographers conclude that although women's levels of education have already caught up with and exceeded men's, highly educated women have not been left high and dry in the marriage market. On the contrary, their research shows that as women's educational levels increase, there's an almost simultaneous decrease in the trend of men wanting to marry plain yogurts.

While these conclusions bode favorably for the marriage prospects of well-educated women around the world, the demographers are aware that there are a few flagrant exceptions to their findings, even after factoring in different economic and educational development timelines. And as luck (or a heavily paternalistic society) would have it, China is one of them.

In what may sound like a social engineering project gone awry, as Chinese women pile on the mortarboards, their marriage prospects dwindle. That hardly seems fair, but more important, how and why is it true? Do Chinese men have a natural aversion to well-educated wives? Or does the fact that well-educated marriage-seeking women are generally older (because they've spent time focused on their studies and careers) work against them more heavily in the mate market?

The answers to all of my questions came in the form of Yue Qian, a now assistant professor of sociology at the University of British Colombia, who at the time I met her, was still a PhD candidate at Ohio State University. On one of Qian's trips home to China, I meet her at a small café tucked away on the campus of Renmin University (literally "The People's University"), one of three establishments—the others being Tsinghua and Peking University—attended by China's best and brightest students. Qian is fresh-faced, with long black hair and bangs that sweep across her forehead in a soft demilune. Something about her smile and her pep reminds me of Sailor Moon, though her voice and composure give her all the trappings of a budding scholar.

As we sit down, she pulls out her doctoral research and treats me to the smorgasbord of log-linear models she used to carefully determine the greatest inhibitor of a Chinese woman's marriage prospects.

"Generally speaking, Chinese women under the age of twenty-nine get married at much higher rates than Chinese men of the same group," she explains. This pattern holds true across all levels of educational attainment, except for college-educated women in China, who have a tougher time finding husbands, as their education is perceived as being "linked to strong career aspirations and appears to clash with the role of good wife and mother." And while the disadvantage that college-educated Chinese women have in finding a mate is pronounced under age twenty-nine, once they hit thirty, Qian says, it soars.

After thirty, however, it not only becomes more complicated for college-educated women to find partners, but for *all* Chinese women, regardless of their level of education. In other words, it's as if a Chinese woman is driven off the showroom floor on her thirtieth birthday; she instantly loses her retail value. Add a few graduate degrees, and she's essentially on clearance.

This is not so for Chinese men, who, as they approach thirty, enter much greener pastures. Men between thirty and forty-nine with a vocational degree or above begin to see an increase in their likelihood of marriage, something that is especially true for college-educated males, who, as they age, all seem to morph into George Clooney and become four times more likely to get married than their female graduate counterparts. This is not true for under-thirty, less-educated males, who are one and a half times less likely to get married than their female counterparts. Basically, Qian's findings suggest that highly educated men have much better marriage prospects if they delay their marriages until their thirties. For highly educated women, the exact opposite is true: a hitch in time saves *nein*.

Although marriage is one of Qian's prime academic interests, much to her mother's dismay, it's not a domain she plans to personally familiarize herself with, anytime soon. Qian's mother lives back in Wuhan; a Chinese city with a population of about 4 million.

She describes her mother as "very social," and even admits that she's quite the reputed matchmaker. In fact, Qian's mother once set up the daughter of a family friend with a man who embodied the elements most sought after in a Chinese male marriage candidate—tall, handsome, well-educated, and from a prominent local family. But before meeting this star young bachelor, it seems the young woman was skeptical of the arrangement and asked

Qian's mother, "If he's so wonderful, why don't you introduce him to your own daughter?" Hearing this greatly upset Qian's mother. It was a reminder of just how helpless she feels in the face of her daughter's marriage arrangement.

"She's learned to acknowledge that I am different," explains Qian. By "different," the young scholar is referring to the fact that she lives on the other side of the world, and is therefore not very geographically compatible with anyone in her hometown, but also that her parameters for a life partner—when she begins to seriously consider that aspect of her life—will also likely be "different."

By the time she finishes her PhD, Qian will have spent eight years living and studying in the United States. She'll also be thirty-one years old, which, according to the research from her own master's thesis, indicates that she'll be in the red zone when it comes to finding a mate in China. Finding a mate in her hometown of Wuhan—where her parents hope to spend their golden years near their only daughter—will be even more challenging. Though it is a large city, it is significantly more traditional than places like Beijing and Shanghai. Its inhabitants tend to marry earlier, leaving Qian with few desirable options.

When I ask Qian about the prospect of marrying an American, she responds with mixed feelings. "I'm not familiar enough with the nuances of American culture," she says. "I think there may be too many inherent differences for that to work out."

But as our conversation evolves, one last aspect in which Qian is decidedly "different" from the majority of her female compatriots emerges. She cites research from developing economies that shows how in places like China and India, women are far more likely to become engineers or study IT. This isn't always because they enjoy math or computer science more than women in other parts of the world, but because they know these fields are more lucrative and provide more secure job opportunities.

"Their motivation for studying is external," says Qian, explaining that external factors (likely pressure from parents) guide their choice of profession. This is in contrast to women like Qian, whose educational pursuits are internal (individually decided), and in many cases, even directly oppose what their parents would have wanted them to study.

On the surface, this all may sound paradoxical. How can Chinese parents, on one hand, push their daughters to do well in school and drive them into fields where they are more likely to find jobs and earn good salaries, while on the other discourage them from doing too well in school or too well at work, at the risk of alienating future mates?

Zhiwei Xu of the Institute of Computing Technology at the Chinese Academy of Sciences (often described as China's answer to MIT) is all too familiar with this paradox. As a senior professor and doctoral thesis adviser, he is responsible for nurturing the minds of China's top computer scientists, a duty that also happens to include managing their marriage prospects. "After a student has been accepted into our doctoral program, I make the effort to meet his or her parents," he said. "On more than one occasion, parents with a daughter in the program have expressed concern that she might not find a mate. They worry that she'll be too old for marriage upon completing her post-doc, or simply too educated or intimidating to be desirable as a wife," he added. Xu, whose own daughter, Xiaomeng, is a happily married assistant professor at the University of Idaho, reassures all jittery parents with great aplomb.

"He's a bit of a matchmaker," says Xiao Li Juan, one of his happily hitched post-doc students, who, at thirty-four, has recently had a baby but is already back to work at Intel. Though Professor Xu was not responsible for helping to initiate her romance with her former classmate turned husband, she admits that he's always been very vigilant of the love lives of his students.

Xiao Li Juan remembers how the professor would always try to organize group lunches or dinners, so that students from different years could mingle with one another. Once he got to know his students better, he'd ask them about their personal lives, often calling on other students to introduce friends or brainstorm for potential candidates they might get on well with. "It's an important part of their lives," he explained over a prodigious spread of dim sum.

As I learned more about how Xiao Li Juan met her husband, I realized that unlike Christy, June, or Zhang Mei, she's completely unfamiliar with what it's like to be a *sheng nü*, because she met her partner in school and married him right after graduation. "The odds were relatively stacked in my favor—my grad program had about six males for every female, so it was actually the men who were more nervous to find partners," she said. She admits feeling fortunate to have met her husband while still in school, because she can sense that the professional world is a completely different ball game. Though the majority of her peers are still male, most are already married, and the stresses of the daily grind hardly seem conducive to the same kind of courtship opportunities.

This conversation brings me back to my exchange with Qian—the bright young scholar whose discipline (sociology) happens to be filled with women. I think about how it's a field she entered against the wishes of her parents, whereas Xiao Li Juan chose to study computer science because at the time she was applying to university, it happened to be one of the hottest fields to enter. Things worked out—she seems to enjoy her work, and is certainly very good at it. As Qian's research suggests, Xiao Li Juan's post-doc also didn't pose a problem when it came time for her to get married—something she did before age thirty. But still, I couldn't help but wonder—what happens to Chinese women who don't have as many dating options on campus?

Tantrum Tactics

Rather than fret over a limited man supply, June prefers to be proactive. In fact, her ability to switch between "Chinese girl" and "overseas returnee Chinese girl with an Ivy League degree" is remarkable, and she insists, absolutely necessary if she wants to date in China, where in addition to playing down her education, she would be well served to improve her skills in the ancient art of *sajiao*, or the strategically executed temper tantrum.

According to the March 2012 issue of *Psychologies* magazine (Chinese edition), *sajiao* is an indispensable element in the dating arsenal of every Chinese woman. "A woman who knows how to *sajiao* knows how to make a man happy," reads the article. Though this may seem unlikely, given that *sajiao* is essentially a series of pouts, mewls, and foot-stomping, it is apparently the time-honored way of allowing a Chinese male to feel loved, needed, chivalrous, and just all-around manly.

An article about *sajiao* in the Beijing-based English magazine *The World of Chinese* provides further insight: "For the competent career woman in particular, *sajiao* is an indispensable tool for appearing neither too independent nor too self-sufficient for her boyfriend. *Sajiao* allows a woman to appear soft and feminine rather than hard and powerful; traits that challenge traditional notions of womanhood. By playing up to the male ego, she accomplishes the near-impossible: making her man feel like a man."

Although the idea of *sajiao* might sound unconscionable

to most American women, a gander through women's magazines published in the United States during the 1950s and '60s
is extremely sobering. "Warning! . . . Be careful not to seem
smarter than your man," instructs a 1940s advice book. "It's one
thing to be almost as smart, but to be or seem smarter—that is
taboo." According to Beth Bailey, author of *From Front Porch to
Back Seat: Courtship in Twentieth-Century America,* while most
advice books of the time cautioned against deliberately "playing
dumb," they did make it very clear that any hints of intellectual
superiority might "injure the masculine ego." To create a happy
balance, relationship experts instead encouraged intellectual
women to seek out very intelligent men, but then to play down
their smarts. "He'll know it's only an act. But you'll soon become
the little woman to be pooh-poohed, patronized and wed," reassured one article.

As reported by Bailey, in the 1920s American women made
such a sport of dating that groups of university girls were known
for classifying prospective suitors into categories which included:
"A" for a "smooth character," "B" for an "OK gentleman," "C" for
"pass in a crowd," "D" for a semigoon, and "E" for a "spook." There
are also myriad accounts from women of this time who would
refuse a date with a man just because he couldn't afford to take
her to the right soda shop. (The Model T was still quite new at the
time, and the drive to and from the soda shop was a big part of the
date.) How then, just twenty years later, did women end up with
the short end of the relationship bargaining stick, cooing and
watering down their intelligence in an attempt to keep a man?

Beginning in the 1930s, Bailey explains that as a result of
WWII, the United States (and Europe, for that matter) saw a significant drop in the availability of marriageable men. By 1943,
16,354,000 men, or almost every physically fit male between the

ages of eighteen and twenty-six, had been sent off to war. For the first time in history, reports Bailey, the United States had more women than men. In 1945, a *New York Times Magazine* article explained that as a result of war losses, 750,000 American women would be unable to marry (and psychologists argued that this would make them neurotic, frustrated, and mentally deranged). *Good Housekeeping* followed suit with a photo of a bride and a groom on the steps of a church, and a doozy of a caption: "She got a man, but 6 to 8 million women won't. We're short 1 million bachelors!" Readers were reminded that one girl in every seven would have to live alone, and were warned, "Unless you watch your step, this may be you."

Bailey explains how books of the *Win Your Man and Keep Him* variety filled the shelves, and cites a 1943 *Good Housekeeping* article that even offered up a new typology. Appropriately titled "Somebody's After Your Man," it recounts how merciless huntresses and hijackers who might steal a man at a moment's notice were broken down into four categories: the Vamp, the Pal, Big Sad Eyes, and the notorious Button-Twister, who weasels her way into a man's heart by coyly tugging at the buttons on his shirt.

As men were at the top of the list of war scarcities, Bailey writes that a cheeky correspondent for *Esquire* even suggested making polygamy legal, in order to solve the problem of what may be referred to as "American leftover women." But instead of being high on visions of polyamorous feasts, explains Bailey, the soldiers returning from war to a large surplus of women were spooked. While away, they had seen images of "Rosie the Riveter" and other women very competently filling the "masculine" jobs they once had. Still shaken from the Great Depression, they returned home more uncertain than ever of their abilities to fulfill the role of male provider.

This is where women swept in with a loaded shot of "beau-tox" to make men feel better about things. "How Feminine Are You to Men?" ran a 1946 survey in the *Women's Home Companion*, which attempted to stifle any hidden urges women might have to let their nails go unpainted or discuss business and world affairs with gentlemen. By and large, women played along, argues Bailey, because the alternative—being without a man—was far less desirable. This gave men the upper hand in courtship, allowing them to virtually mandate the submissiveness of women by rejecting the unfeminine ones.

But let's backtrack for a moment. China has not recently been to war. As previously discussed, there are actually 30 million more men than women of marriage age, as a result of the one-child policy and ensuing female abortions and infanticides. Why, then, are women still "playing along"?

Mandering

Professor Hu Deng teaches emotional psychology at Renmin University. Ratings show that he is one of the most popular professors on campus, largely because his classes offer wisdom in a subject area most twentysomethings are really eager to master: romantic relationships. In his lecture hall overflowing with students who can't officially get on his roster, he is known to fire up slides featuring Robert Sternberg's Triangle Theory of Love, which argues that love is composed of three qualities: passion, intimacy, and commitment. No relationship ever has all three of these qualities in equal levels, argues Sternberg, a point Professor Hu drives home by explaining to his students that traditionally, the majority of relationships in China are heavy on the "c" (commitment), but lacking in "a+b" (passion and intimacy). He mentions how during the Cultural Revolution, members of the

People's Liberation Army were matched politically, an arrangement that made them very committed to each other out of a sense of duty, but not necessarily out of desire or emotion. He then cites the hit blockbuster *The Hangover* as an example of relationships that are heavy on passion, but sparse on intimacy and commitment. That one can elope to Vegas and divorce the morning after is something a few of his students are mesmerized to discover.

Compared to most professors at Renmin University, Professor Hu is quite progressive. He speaks uninhibitedly about the mercenary marriages of revolutionary China, and warns his students that the marriage partners their parents and grandparents pick out for them are rarely going to make them happy. He presents his students with alternative marriage models—telling them of a Chinese couple that had two children out of wedlock, and after eleven years, finally got married. Something about marriage ruined their relationship, and it was only after their divorce that they were able to live happily again as a couple, explains the professor. For him to offer up this example in a country where having a child out of wedlock is illegal in almost every province, and where unwed mothers must pay "social compensation fees" that are sometimes six to eight times their yearly salary, seems very open-minded. But when it comes to *sajiao*, the professor is of a different mind.

We meet at his office, a Spartan room on the northern side of campus. His student assistant offers me a glass of scalding water from the hissing industrial-sized hot-water dispenser in the hallway—a staple at every Chinese university. "If a Chinese woman today doesn't know how to *sajiao*, it's very unlikely that she'll find a boyfriend," says the professor. I look him intently in the eyes, half expecting to call his bluff, but I soon realize that he's dead serious.

He explains that because China is highly populated and competitive, it's increasingly difficult for Chinese men to improve their lot in life. This was easier to live with prior to 1949, when a man's station at birth largely determined the rest of his life, but since Communism has begun to breed with elements of Capitalism, there has been greater pressure on men to excel. The problem is, the new opportunities have not been as great as the new pressures, which leaves many men floundering and feeling inadequate. If a woman can step in and artfully make a man feel esteemed, needed, and admired, she satisfies the feelings of achievement that a man can't get from his work or from society. According to Dr. Hu, *sajiao*, then, becomes a "fix" for the flaws, injustices, and inequalities in the Chinese social system, and arguably even a means of ensuring social stability.

I explain Hu's reasoning to June, who, though keen to do her part in contributing to the stability of her nation, remains incapable of mastering the art of the strategically executed temper tantrum. "I spent time over the weekend with some of my old friends from high school, and they all told me I don't have a boyfriend because I don't know how to *sajiao*," she tells me.

Although I had seen many stunning *sajiao* performances on the streets of Beijing—a Chinese woman whining to her boyfriend is as common as a stoplight—I had never realized that it was all done on purpose, and more important, I struggled to imagine June engaged in the same theatrics. After watching an online tutorial for how to *sajiao* your way to dinner at your favorite restaurant (yes, these types of tutorials exist), June tested out her best performance on me, and I felt obliged to be honest with her—she looked like a circus bear suffering from digestive ailments. After a few more stumbles, it became clear that she was not put on this Earth to feign subservience. *Sajiao* wasn't going to get her anywhere, but a seduction master class with one of Beijing's most beguiling sirens? That sounded far more promising.

Seduction, 101

I decided to introduce June and Ivy over dinner at an upscale Sichuan restaurant near Ivy's apartment. (It's always easiest to meet close to Ivy's home, as she is careful about where she is seen.) As June and I arrived, I spotted Ivy at a corner table with a jet stream of smoke above her head. Shortly after we sat down, a waiter came over and very politely—almost obsequiously—asked Ivy to put out her cigarette. She dismissed him coldly by saying that it was late, she knows the owner, there was nobody else in the restaurant, and we weren't bothering a soul. She waved him away, and then seconds later summoned him back to bring her an ashtray. (She had previously been stubbing out her cigarettes in a bowl of fragrant rice.) He looked terrified—so startled into obedience, even the tips of his bow tie appeared to stand at attention.

She then turned sweetly to June and me, and we began our conversation. We learned that Ivy is the daughter of a Chinese civil servant and a dancer from Inner Mongolia, which explains her untraditional beauty. Her eyes are larger than those of most Chinese women, and her face more almond-shaped. Her hair is collected in loose tendrils under her ears, a bit like Marilyn Monroe's, only it's so black, it's practically violet. I realize that there is an air of glamour about her, but also of mystery. She seems to have the ability to trigger innocence on command, morphing seamlessly from demanding patroness to charming conversationalist. If she were a cat, she'd most certainly be a Siamese.

We also learned that she loves to gamble. This year alone, she'd lost over US $50,000 playing poker, but that hasn't kept her away from the tables. I suspect some of the gambling might be related to her day job, as increased government crackdowns on bribes and corruption are prompting several companies in China to move their wheel-greasing efforts abroad, to Las Vegas, in particular. She's been there at least twice in the last ten months, "but my favorite thing to do is play mahjong," she says—imagine grannies engaged in a jovial battle of tiles and wits—in an about-face to innocence.

It was fascinating to watch June and Ivy interact. Though our meeting had been set up primarily for June to benefit from Ivy's prowess with men, the evening took a surprising turn. As June listened—simultaneously riveted and smitten by Ivy's alluring presence and all of the freedom and seductive power she seemed to command—I sensed that Ivy was being generous with her knowledge because she genuinely seemed charmed by June too.

Until meeting Ivy, June had been struggling in the man department. She had agreed to go on a few dates upon her mother's insistence, but was having trouble finding a polite way to taper off contact with one particular man she had met in person after her mother had chatted him up on a dating site, posing as her daughter. He was a lieutenant in the military, mid-thirties, well placed in his career, but a bit square and prone to sharp mood swings. She met him for a few dates, each time a bit less enthusiastically. "I felt like I had to keep meeting him just to come up with an excuse to stop seeing him that my mother would accept," June explained.

"I can't say he's unattractive—she'll just say that won't matter in ten years," said June. "I also can't say there's no chemistry or that I'm not attracted to him; she'll just say I'm being shallow. In her eyes, all problems fade away with time."

It took four more dates for June to come up with a more concrete excuse that her mother might actually accept: the man she was seeing was a passive-aggressive sociopath!

"You know when someone is trying really hard to be nice, but deep down you can tell they're angry?" she says. "Well, since I didn't really like this guy, I started showing up a little late to our dates. He tried not to show his annoyance, but it came out in really odd ways. He'd start asking me about my career, the demands of my job, and if I had any plans to scale back. I told him no. Then he asked if we could text more to establish a closer relationship. I also told him that would be difficult because I was very busy. Then his eye just started twitching. He somewhat aggressively reprimanded me for my long work hours, telling me that they would render me less tender and womanly, but then very politely asked me to a movie."

After explaining this to her mother, June discovered that she still wasn't off the hook. "He's trying to make a good impression," her mother said. "It's normal that he's struggling to hide his true feelings!"

June's main problem—according to Ivy—is that she is not a *hua ping*, or "flower vase," as most men in China like their women to be. Despite being very beautiful, she is lively and self-assured in a way that men don't always appreciate. Continuing her very thorough analysis, Ivy infers that as an exceptional student from a very young age, June is also probably most comfortable learning new skills by studying or researching them, which—when it comes to men especially—is not the most winning strategy. As is true for many men and women in China, she has grown up with few examples of what dating should be like because after so many years of parentally orchestrated relationship brokering, the mores and manners of modern dating are still being established.

In a sign that class was ending, Ivy shared the bawdy details of her latest tryst with a heinously wealthy real-estate mogul. She paused for a few moments before explaining that although she has been generously compensated for her services, her line of work is also very exhausting. "I will retire soon," she said, to our astonishment.

"I'll start looking for a husband in the spring," she added. By "retire," she actually meant that she planned to get married.

Ivy then explained that she has made wise investments for her future knowing that her market value as "the other woman" will tank the older she gets. In fact, she has never been fully dependent on mistress activities for her livelihood, and right around the time she became a mistress, she was already working in film and television distribution in China—a job she continues to hold. Regularly attending star-studded film premieres and brokering deals for industry fat cats, she began moving in a social circle very distinct from the one she was born into. As her commissions started to roll in—supplemented by her first few escapades with moneyed and often married men—she was able to operate with greater confidence. In an industry where appearances are everything, she was suddenly able to dress her part, expertly accessorizing with designer handbags and, eventually, a glittering white Porsche Carrera. Now that she's achieved a significantly better life—for herself, and for her parents, with whom she has been very generous—it was time to think about the bigger picture.

"Do you worry about fidelity with your future husband?" asked June, the ever-inquisitive student.

"He will cheat," said Ivy. "Men of status always do. The trick is finding one who will be savvy enough to keep it a secret from you. In my experience, a bad man fools you once; a good man fools you forever."

Given all I had learned about Chinese marriages by that point, I couldn't decide if Ivy's logic was extremely tragic, or extremely wise. For her, infidelity was so much a part of marriage that after years of being an adulteress, she was fully prepared to turn a blind eye to her future husband's ineluctable philandering. Perhaps this was her self-imposed penance for years of transgressions—an attempt to make amends with karma? Either way, June wasn't sold on it.

"I just don't think I could ever accept that," she said firmly.

"When it comes to marriage, we all have conditions, standards, requirements, and responsibilities," replied Ivy, in her characteristically unflappable manner. "You just need to know very clearly which ones you value most, and prioritize accordingly."

"But what happens if you become interested in a person who doesn't meet any of those conditions or requirements?" asked June.

"Well, then that's love," said Ivy, with a complicit twinkle in her left eye.

Before June could get in another question, Ivy picked up her handbag, clicked open the doors to her white Porsche, and sped off into the night.

Long after the lights of Ivy's car had disappeared, June and I remained chatting outside the café. I could see she was furiously processing all of the new information she had learned. Because she didn't have a car of her own, I offered her a ride on my hot-orange electric scooter, which is essentially a Chinese manufacturer's take on a Vespa. Though lovely to look at, it has about as much power as a midrange hedge clipper when it's not fully charged (as was the case that night), so we don't exactly get off to a roaring start. As we finally picked up speed and braced ourselves against the wind—it was early March, and the northerlies from Siberia were still blowing in full force—we burst into uncontrollable laughter. "The mistress speeds home in a luxury sports car, and the two galoots with graduate degrees teeter home on an e-bike in the middle of a tempest," said June, still laughing in decibels that far exceed anything her mother would approve of. "So much for Yale!"

5

CHICKENS AND DUCKS

It is a misfortune to be unhappily married, but it comes near to being a disgrace not to be married at all.

—LEON H. VINCENT, *A SUCCESSFUL BACHELOR*, 1898

On June 21, at 7:47 p.m., user Snow Flower types:

"I think you're the missing half I've been looking for this whole time. I want to learn from you and be inspired by your courage; work with you, help you, and allow for the melting of our hearts together. I want to be your left hand and your right shoulder. You have moved me deeply from within. My dream is to have a happy life and family with you."

She continues, after waiting shortly, but receiving no response:

"Even though we are very far from one another, I put my faith in the wisdom of our elders. I have come to know and be charmed by you through my parents' descriptions. Our future together pulls on their heartstrings, and I think we should honor them by being together. We're both from the same region of China, so our personalities and customs will be similar, allowing us to happily fulfill our duties together. I don't know what your feelings are about all of this, but I eagerly await your answer.

Three hours, five minutes, and twenty-seven seconds later, user PhoenixPhoenix responds:

"I think this is taking things a little too far, as we have never even met each other in person. I understand your parents' feelings and I sympathize that time has a different meaning for women, but I hope you can realize that the love that must lead up to marriage is something that must develop naturally."

Snow Flower is Christy's ID on QQ, an instant-messaging platform that serves as China's equivalent to AOL Messenger. PhoenixPhoenix is the QQ id of a man living in the US whom she has never met, but whose contact information was given to her by her mother. Christy began chatting with him at her mother's behest, after a very elaborate series of afternoons in which the respective families of each singleton examined their compatibility—everything from their educational levels to their star signs to their blood types—and determined they were a heavenly match.

At first, their chats didn't yield much, as might be expected from two strangers on opposite sides of the world who were forced to chat online by their families. Sensing little chemistry or compatibility between the two, Christy tapered off the conversation, which is when her mother, in a cunning last attempt to have her daughter married to this well-to-do man with a green card, snuck into Christy's QQ account and sent the treacly messages reproduced above.

Three weeks later, Christy discovered what happened and became irate. She immediately messaged PhoenixPhoenix to apologize, but when trying to get a hold of her mother to let her know that she was wise to her online hijinks, Christy discovered that she was visiting PhoenixPhoenix's parents and delivering a box of candied fruits on her daughter's behalf.

"It's like a generation of chickens has given birth to a generation of ducks," explains Christy. "We're on completely different pages," she says. "They're the cog in the system that simply won't budge."

It's critical to understand that, like Christy's mother, parents with children who are now of marriage age were young adults during the Cultural Revolution, a time during which romance was reviled as a bourgeois sentiment and a selfish, dishonorable reason to marry. As was expected of them, many invested their lives in the revolution and were swept up in propaganda and proletarian love, only to become "unthinking and unfeeling body parts of the nation-building machine." They repressed their emotional and spiritual needs for national progress and wealth; a process that significantly distorted their values. Older now, they are disenchanted with idealistic notions of society and no longer believe in slogans or politics. Instead, they've thrust all of their hopes into money, property, status, and other perceived sources of stability because they've experienced life without any of these things. Striving for a materially comfortable life, they project their desires onto their children, often irrespective of their children's emotional needs.

For instance, Christy and her cohort, unlike their mothers, generally have enough education and financial independence that money, or the security it provides, is no longer their primary motivation for marriage. More self-reliant and assertive of their individuality than their mothers were ever allowed to be, they have a different set of priorities for seeking a partner, and are less willing to get married out of a sense of social duty or for material needs. Instead of a provider-cum-housemate with whom they happen to have a child, they want to marry someone they love. A concept that, for one of the oldest civilizations of the world—it appears—is actually quite new.

Love Meets Marriage

As noted by Stephanie Coontz, an academic whose work is on the history of marriage, "Until the late eighteenth century, most societies around the world saw marriage as far too vital an economic and political institution to be left entirely to the free choice of the two individuals involved, especially if they were going to base their decision on something as unreasoning and as transitory as love." In other words, romantic marriage is a relatively new concept of the last three centuries. From Renaissance Venice to colonial Mexico, marriage was, above all, a contract: an agreement about as romantic as a car lease. It was a communally decided system of social organization in which wealth, resources, status, rank, and class could be reproduced across generations.

According to Coontz, the two seismic social changes that instigated the evolution of marriage norms were the spread of wage labor, which made young people less dependent on their parents, and the freedoms of the market economy, which resulted in social relationships being based on reason and justice, instead of force. The combination of these two factors allowed the institution of marriage to transition from being a fundamental unit of work, politics, and social obligation to a refuge from work, politics, and social obligation. As a result, the ideal of a marriage based on love—unexplainable, unintentional, romantic love—gained wider acceptance. Less of a contract, marriage eventually came to be seen in most Western countries as a private arrangement between two individuals who themselves desired and chose to spend their lives together.

This was not, however, the case in China, an especially late bloomer on the love front. Arranged marriage was legal and widely practiced in China until 1950, and Confucian ideals nixed any stomach flutters and sonnets between spouses by instead emphasizing relationships between men. As per Confucian philosophy, the two strongest family relationships were between father and son, elder brother and younger brother. Any man who deviated from the norm and appeared openly affectionate with his wife was seen as someone of weak character.

Confucian ideals were so effective in cracking down on sentiments between a husband and his wife that until the 1920s, notes Coontz, there wasn't even a Chinese word to describe romantic love between spouses. Seeing the need to develop a word for this idea, a group of intellectuals coined the term *en nai*, or 恩爱. Literally translated, it means "gratitude love," and refers to the affections that a man exhibits toward his wife in gratitude for the sacrifices she makes for him. At this point in time, the Chinese word for the romantic notion of love, 爱情, was still only being used to describe an illicit, socially disapproved relationship.

More than romance, *en nai* was about respect between spouses and represented the traditional gender roles that each was tasked with upholding. A woman was expected to treat her husband with great reverence. Her husband, in turn, was to be a reliable provider for her and their children. Any "gratitude love" that grew between them was acknowledged in society as a pleasant by-product of their union, much like whey is a pleasant by-product of cheese. It sweetened the deal, but was certainly not the point. Furthermore, polygamy was still legal and liberally practiced, so a man could easily exhibit "gratitude love" with more than one wife.

Then, in 1950 (right around the time Christy's mother was born), something radical happened. The newly empowered Communist Party passed a law that abolished the practice of arranged marriage. It specified that marriage was to be based on the "free-dom of choice" between one man and one woman. The law was hailed as an effort to protect the interests and rights of women, and above all, to limit the self-interested intervention of parents.

Women, who had previously been the pawns by which families secured their own socio-economic and political advantage through strategic betrothal, were now legally free to choose their own life partners. And if things didn't work out, they could file for divorce. In the event of widowhood, they were freed from servitude to their in-laws and could remarry. And whatever the course their mar-riage took, women would retain rights to the property owned prior to the marriage, plus half of anything jointly acquired.

As described in Elisabeth Croll's *The Politics of Marriage in Contemporary China*, a nationwide campaign to familiarize peo-ple with the details of the new law was launched and became the ideal "marriage model" that all citizens were encouraged to fol-low. By 1953, there was a family-by-family, street-by-street guer-rilla campaign aimed at educating people about "free-choice" marriage, praising young citizens who held the "correct view-point in choosing life's companions."

This "correct viewpoint," as defined by the government, was outlined as follows:

> The relationship between husband and wife is first of all comradeship and the feelings between them are revolution-ary. By revolutionary it is meant that politically he should take her as a new comrade-in-arms . . . he should take her as a class sister and they should labor together.

Unless the word "labor" was code for something sexy, it's safe to assume that the "correct viewpoint" for a relationship between

a man and his wife was more ideological than physical or emotional. The government dismissed romantic love as "bourgeois
sentiment." As warned by a 1964 article in the *People's Daily*,
young people who become man and wife "on the impulse of the
moment and on the basis of good looks and love at first sight, dis-
regarding compatibility based on identical political ideas and
mutual understanding," were doomed to "quarrel and suffer
greatly." By contrast, those who were not attractive in their looks
but shared "revolutionary feelings" would experience a love that
is "forever green."

Young couples who pursued revolutionary love and dared to
"fight against the old thinking" were reassured that, should they
be met with parental resistance, the government would support
them, writes Croll. Political associations like the Central Com-
mittee of the Movement for the Thorough Implementation of the
Marriage Law (I wish I were making that name up) were set up
to champion the "free-will" marriages of young couples, and even
to defend them against the couple's parents in cases of discord.
Educational materials continued to be published, and instances
of young couples triumphing in their pursuit of free-choice marriage were widely publicized in an effort to encourage others to
do the same.

In essence, free-choice marriage represented an upheaval of
Confucian order, in which parents reigned supreme. Under this
new system, parents had to relinquish their power to strategically handpick their extended relatives and control how their
family would be represented in future generations. Instead, children were expected to court or date, a process that, as Croll notes,
was bound to trigger scandal, a maelstrom of wagging tongues,
and invitations to impropriety. Naturally, in an attempt to avert
such mayhem and preserve their gains from a child's marriage,

parents berated their freedom-seeking children and bribed local officials tasked with sustaining the new free-choice marriage law.

It also didn't help that young Chinese had no clue how to find a spouse, because there were no pre-established societal cues on how to date. The mandates of Confucianism had been so heavily ingrained in society that most young people feared the potential gossip, loss of dignity, and the disrespect they would bring on their families. Those who had free-choice marriages were disheartened by the lack of sympathy or support for their choice, argues Croll. And as for the government officials who were tasked with defending the free-marriage rights of Chinese youth? Their eyes were easily averted with a bit of cash from the elders.

Although customs are changing, Chinese parents of the same generation as Christy's mom still feel entitled to have a heavy hand in the personal lives of their children because it's what they endured from their elders. China's lack of a social safety net also makes children the nest eggs of their parents; they are expected to provide for and take care of them in old age. This means that ensuring a child marries by a certain age—and that he or she marries well—has become the guarantee of a comfortable retirement. Whether or not a couple is a good match from a social perspective still often matters more than how compatible they are as life partners, as long as they are married in a big, fanfare-filled wedding that gives face and peace of mind to the respective families of each. Keeping up appearances is still of paramount importance, and sex and sexuality are rarely discussed.

Skeletons in the Closet

In addition to being a mediocre brand of Japanese dairy sold widely in China, Suki is the name of Beijing's most sought-after bikini waxer. She has become such a household name among the community of foreign females in Beijing that she often comes up in conversations at cocktail parties. When two women discover that the same hands are tending their topiary, something magical happens, whereby like sugar wax to the pubis, they instantly bond. Part of this has to do with the shared intimacy of knowing that the same woman is plucking their privates, but also, I suspect, because of Suki's intriguing story.

Before becoming the door-to-door wunderkind of bikini waxing, Suki worked in the spa of one of Beijing's most upscale boutique hotels. (Beyoncé and Victoria Beckham stayed there when they were in town.) She had a solid following of regulars, but the working conditions at the hotel, despite its plush appearance, were deplorable. After one of her clients suggested she go solo and offer in-home beauty services at a fraction of the spa price, Suki handed in her notice at the spa and valiantly launched her own little waxing start-up.

Fastidious in her work, Suki removes wax as if conducting an orchestra. With little more than a medium-sized champagne-colored knockoff Longchamp tote containing all of her supplies, she shuttles between the homes of her clients, leaving everyone she touches marvelously glabrous. The quality and convenience of her services have led her to rack up a small fortune—much more cash than her husband, a barber, is able to bring home. According to Suki, he is very supportive of her job, and even helps pack up her supply bag on his days off. The only complaint she has is the very transient nature of her clients—mostly female expats who are in Beijing for a limited period of time. Though she is always getting new clients through enthusiastic word-of-mouth referrals, with her daughter approaching middle school and the rising cost of her educational expenses, Suki began asking around for suggestions on how to build a steadier client base. She was surprised to learn that many of her female clients had the same advice: expand waxing services to include men.

Despite the rather progressive nature of her profession, Suki still teeters on the line toward conservatism. She's from a small village in Shanxi province, and most of her life in Beijing is completely unfathomable to her family. "I tell my parents that I do facials," she says, which she also does, although the lion's share of her business comes from Brazilian waxes. Without getting too deep into the depilatory routines of Chinese women, I think it's safe to say that Brazilians are far from the norm. I've been in gym locker rooms where women have been aiming blow dryers at their nether regions, and many men, I've had confirmed, do the same. But gay Chinese men—well, they might just be a gold mine for Suki, if she were up for the challenge.

"Oh," she says, perplexed, when I mention this to her. "But where to find them? I've never met one."

This surprises me, though it shouldn't. The hotel where Suki was formerly employed occupies what may very well be among the gayest 500 square meters in Beijing. Its bar is the setting for a weekly gay happy hour that's like *The Wizard of Oz* meets Madonna. In warmer months when the terrace is open, the often impeccably coiffed men who gather there emit such a strong mix of cologne onto the surrounding sidewalk, I've come to call it Beijing's Duty-Free.

"Maybe my husband could help me with this?" Suki asks cautiously, still unsure of the viability of this idea, though certainly interested in the monetary prospect of it.

Suki is not the only person in China who doesn't understand homosexuality. Yet despite common misconceptions that may stem from a dubious record with regard to human rights and personal freedoms, China is not—at least on the surface— especially hostile to gay people. Beijing, in particular (which, of course, is not representative of greater China) is home to several gay bars.

Depending on the political climate of the times, a large-scale event (like the Mr. Gay Pride Pageant in Shanghai) might be shuttered by the government, but on the day-to-day club scene, the gay community appears to face minimal policing from the powers that be.

The home front, however, is a different story entirely. Though the World Health Organization removed homosexuality from its index of mental disorders in 1990, homosexuality was officially classified as a disease in China until 2001. Depictions of homosexuality on television have long been banned in China, but starting in July 2017, the China Netcasting Services Association (CNSA) prohibited the portrayal of "abnormal sexual lifestyles" in Internet video content—a category that, in the eyes of the censors, includes homosexuality.* Needless to say, homosexuality is still not very well understood, especially by parents who are all very keen to have their children married, but not to the extent that they'd tolerate their child marrying a member of the same sex, if that were even possible. The curious thing about the parental opposition to gay marriage, however, is that it is as much moral or ethical as it is a matter of losing face; it's seen as something that mars a family's reputation and jeopardizes its ability to function as part of the social order.

To get Suki's new business revving, I introduce her to my friend Leo, a gay Chinese man who has been with his partner for three years. "My mother knows I'm gay," he tells us, "and she kind of accepts it, but she still keeps hounding me to marry a woman. When I reminded her that I like men, she said, 'I don't care what you like, just give me a grandchild!'" She went so far as to suggest that Leo get married and have a baby with his part-

---

* In a telling example of how quickly the censorship tides change in China, they seem to have looked the other way when just a year earlier, Beijing Kunlun Tech Company—a Chinese gaming company—bought a majority stake in Grindr, perhaps the world's most iconic dating and social networking app for gay men.

ner's older sister (a leftover woman), as if that would lead to the creation of one, big, happy family.

The content of this conversation is rocking Suki's world. "There are gay men married to straight women?" she asks me later, in private. "Sixteen million of them," I tell her. She looks at me wide-eyed, realizing that her market potential is much larger than she had ever imagined.

Zhang Beichuan is the sexologist at Qingdao University who calculated the 16 million statistic based on his twenty-plus years of demographic research centered on China's gay community. He's not a gay activist nor gay himself, but explains that this area of research interested him because there was so little information available, and very few people working in it. He tells me that in the 1990s, an estimated 40 percent of the gay men he interviewed reported having suicidal thoughts. Over time, that percentage dropped to 20 percent, but Beichuan's work has shown a consistent rise in the depression rates of another group: China's *tong qi* or "comrade wives"—straight women married to gay men.

Despite their rather friendly moniker, most *tong qi* women don't often live happy lives as wives. Very few are aware of their husband's sexuality before marriage, something that, when it is eventually discovered, comes as a hard blow. By Zhang's estimates, 90 percent of *tong qi* are depressed, 70 percent report having experienced long-term emotional abuse, 40 percent experience suicidal thoughts, and 20 percent have experienced repeated physical violence from their husbands. His numbers are based on a sample of 150 *tong qi* wives who had been married an average of four years, with an average age of thirty-one. He also tells me that eighty of the women in his study discovered their husbands were gay as the result of intervention from a private detective. Roughly three women knew of their husband's homosexuality before their marriage, but didn't see it as an issue. "I thought I could 'fix' it," said one of his sources, who, Beichuan points out, was an accomplished college graduate.

Because the stigma surrounding homosexuality in China is still so strong (except for the nightclub scene, as mentioned earlier), many comrade wives don't know what to do when they discover they're married to a gay man. Christy, for one, was in complete shock.

I'd known Christy well over two years before she told me about her previous marriage. Over this time period, we'd become good friends, and she'd even been the inspiration for Chaoji Shengnu, a playful cartoon series that I created, almost as a precursor to this book.* Most of our meetings were high-octane ones. We'd sometimes catch up quickly at events or locations where she was in charge of the PR—fashion shows, nightclub anniversary parties, and boutique and gallery openings. Often, these events were attended by gay men—models, designers, art patrons, and owners of over-the-top entertainment establishments. She often joked that she knew more gay men than straight ones, but she had never mentioned that she'd once been married to one.

Christy met her former husband at a very young age, and according to her, it was love at first sight. "He was so sweet and handsome, I married him within three months of meeting him." Their relationship had been chaste prior to marriage, but following a few complications with small cysts on her ovaries, Christy's husband decided that the couple should stop being intimate until she was feeling better. Her doctor never told her to stop having intercourse, but as she was very young and somewhat startled by her condition, she decided to err on the side of caution. As Christy's sabbatical from sex approached the two-year mark, however,

---

* The full *Chaoji Shengnu* cartoon series was published in *The World of Chinese* magazine.

she became suspicious. Each time she attempted an advance on her husband, she would be dismissed, and he'd bring up the cysts on her ovaries, which had long ceased to be a matter of concern. "I started to think there was another woman," she recalls. "So I started checking his phone."

No leads.

"I always thought of him as someone very simple," explains Christy, "happy to just hang out with the guys." It wasn't until he left a chat program on his laptop open one day that she discovered his penchant for teenagers.

"My first reaction was total disbelief," she said, "but then I started connecting all the dots from our years together and things started to make sense. There was absolutely nobody I could tell though—my parents would be outraged, and he was begging me not to out him. I decided to treat it like an affair, telling him we could still *guo rizi*, or 'spend our days together.' He agreed most penitently, telling me he would give up his 'dirty habit.'"

Christy wanted to believe her husband, but she didn't trust him, so she kept an eye on his computer. There was no activity for two months, but then his lascivious chats with young men picked up again. Feeling distraught and helpless, she took refuge in the anonymity of the Internet, where she tracked down a support hotline for women in her situation.

Xiao Xiong's was the comforting voice on the other line that helped Christy cope with everything she was experiencing. Christy believed that she had "made" her husband gay because she was unattractive and inattentive to his needs. Xiao Xiong's counseling allowed her to understand that women don't make men gay. She listened, advised, and gently gave Christy the courage to peaceably end a marriage that was depleting her sense of self-worth, her confidence, and her happiness.

It's only a few minutes into my conversation with Xiao Xiong before I realize that she's also married to a gay man. The conditions of their marriage, however, are radically different from Christy's. Xiao Xiong is a lesbian, and she and her gay husband have what is commonly referred to in China as a *xing hun* or a "cooperative marriage." Though Xiao Xiong vehemently opposes marriages in which gay men are dishonest about their sexuality and wed straight women, she happens to be one of China's greatest facilitators of marriages between openly gay men and lesbian women looking to tie the knot with a member of the opposite sex in order to keep up appearances. In 2007, Xiao Xiong created the first QQ group for gay men and women in the market for a fake spouse. "Like any marriage," she explains, "both parties must really get to know one another and be very clear as to what their objectives are. But if men and women are honest with one another and have common goals and values, these arrangements can actually end up being a good way of mitigating the marriage pressure they face."

To date, over three hundred "cooperative marriages" have taken place between couples who met on the site, and Xiao Xiong is so familiar with the spouse-selection process, she practically has it down to a formula. The five most important questions a couple needs to discuss before deciding to get married are:

1. Will we live together? (she says not many couples do)
2. Will we have a child? (she says most Northerners don't want to have any children, but Southerners are more likely to want one)
3. Will we pool our finances? (usually couples living together may want to share finances)
4. Will we get a real marriage certificate? (many couples— especially those who opt to be childless—prefer to get a fake

marriage certificate, so they are not legally bound to each other. These fake certificates, often prepared by special agencies, cost around 200 RMB, (US $30), or twenty-five times the price of a real one)

5. Will we get a divorce? (some couples marry only temporarily to appease their parents, and then divorce after a year or two; other people have a big wedding for their parents to enjoy, then come out of the closet a few years later, once they feel they've done enough for their family and are entitled to do something for themselves)

Xiao Xiong reports that, overwhelmingly, couples decide to enter cooperative marriages due to pressure from their families. "Some parents even know their kids are gay, but they still want them to go through the hoops," she explains.

In Xiao Xiong's case, her parents have no idea that she is a lesbian. Marrying a gay man was simply the least confrontational way to address her obligation to get married. Her parents spent 200,000 RMB on the reception, and still don't know that the woman helping Xiao Xiong into her wedding dress was her partner.

She maintains a friendly relationship with her husband, but not a close one. "We each have our own lives," says Xiao Xiong, who lives with her partner. "We basically just see each other for meals over the holidays with our families," she says. "We don't communicate much otherwise, but my husband is great. When my mom got sick last year, he came with me to take care of her for a few days. I've done the same for his parents in the past."

As I listen to the terms and conditions of Xiao Xiong's marriage, I begin to realize that it's starting to sound like the most distilled version of what many Chinese marriages are—units of social organization whereby holidays are celebrated and elderly parents are taken care of. Our conversation reminds me of one I had with a friend of Christy's, who, because of her job, lives in a different city from her husband and has a long-term lover with whom she spends most of her free time. She's thought about getting a divorce but can't be bothered because, as she said to Christy, "then where would I spend the holidays?"

Still, I can't help but ask Xiao Xiong if it's difficult to keep "putting on a show" after more than five years of marriage. She responds with total nonchalance—"It's like being with a friend. If you're comfortable around the person, it's not difficult."

Xiao Xiong is lucky in that her parents aren't too pushy when it comes to her having a baby. "I have a friend whose mother is on a mission to have a grandchild," she says. "So my friend plays the 'we're trying' card. She even cries about it in front of her mother, complaining that fertility treatments are invasive and expensive.

"Obviously, this excuse wouldn't work for everyone," continues Xiao Xiong. Some women say their work conditions aren't favorable to having a child at the moment, others blame the air pollution for their struggles with conception. "We help each other brainstorm for the most believable ideas."

Throughout our conversation, Xiao Xiong is careful to reiterate that marrying a gay man is certainly not the ideal, but if two parties can come to an understanding, it's probably the most convenient solution to a "problem" that doesn't seem like it will go away anytime soon.

Dr. He Xiaopei is a friend of Xiao Xiong's, as well as the founder of Pink Space, an organization that promotes sexual rights, based in Beijing. When I catch up with her, she's just finished editing a documentary called *Our Marriages: When Lesbians Marry Gay Men*, which chronicles the cooperative marriages of four lesbians. The film includes footage of a cooperative wedding where there were six hundred guests in attendance. "Many of the bride's friends knew of her sexuality, but her parents and most of her family members are still completely in the dark," explained Dr. Xiaopei.

She then tells me about another wedding featured in the film, where the gay groom's mother is aware of her son's preference for men, but the bride prefers to keep her homosexuality a secret. Upon meeting her future daughter-in-law, the groom's mother apparently tries to persuade the couple "to have a normal life," but senses that her plea is falling on deaf ears. She cries and cries, until one morning, it occurs to her to go to a temple and have the *ba zi* of her son and his soon-to-be lesbian wife consulted. *Ba zi*, or "eight characters" are a complex system of numbers and symbols upon which the Chinese base a range of decisions, including marriage compatibility between potential partners. After the *ba zi* master describes the match as "tip-top" and the wife as "a real find," all of the groom's mother's apprehensions go out the window. On the wedding day, according to Dr. Xiaopei, the mother was among one of the merriest guests at the ceremony.

As part of her work with Pink Space, Dr. Xiaopei has also counseled many "comrade wives" like Christy, and as our conversation about them evolves, I can't help but ask her: are there also comrade husbands?

"We don't have the numbers, but I believe that men have greater pressure to produce an heir, and can divorce with less consequence," she says. "Not as many lesbians want to have a child, so gay men must find straight women. They also just think it's easier and less time consuming to lie and maintain a secret life on the side."

Would legalizing gay marriage in China make the situation better? Dr. Xiaopei really doesn't think so. As one of the women in her documentary said, "Even if gay marriage were legal, I'd still marry a gay man because cultures don't change overnight, and homosexuality will remain taboo for a long time."

Dr. Xiaopei elaborates: the biggest obstacle to gay marriage in China isn't legal, it's social. In the grand scheme of taboos, having a homosexual child trumps having an unmarried child in China. She explains that "homosexual," or 同性恋, which translates as "love for the same sex," still sounds wrong to most Chinese ears. This is true to the extent that the word cannot even appear in Chinese official media, be it in newspapers or magazines or on the radio. "Even if gay marriage were legalized, many Chinese would still think gays are 'sick,'" adds Dr. Xiaopei. And of course, she is very careful to point out, there's the larger underlying problem that affects everyone in China, gay or straight: the compulsory nature of marriage.

"If gays could marry, parents might just say, 'Well, then why don't you get married?' And of course there are also gay people out there who don't necessarily want to wed," she says.

"Marital pressures here are so strong, we even get inquiries from straight people looking for fake marriage partners. The pressure to get married in China—for both gay and straight members of society—simply does not allow one to live as a single and complete person."

I mention my conversation with Dr. Xiaopei to Christy, and she's not at all surprised. "Many of my friends have brought it up as a solution to their marriage woes," she says. "To be honest, it has even crossed my mind—marrying a gay man again—a friend, perhaps, but this time, with the full knowledge that he's gay, and a very thoroughly discussed marriage agreement. But then I think, what for? I too have the right to a more complete happiness."

6

FREEDOM AND SUBMISSION

嫁出去的女儿 泼出去的水

Marrying off a daughter is like pouring water
out of a jug.

—CHINESE PROVERB

Chinese New Year was just around the corner, and Zhang Mei was still without a plus-one. The rent-a-boyfriend she was considering ended up being booked for the holidays, something that Zhang Mei took as a sign from the heavens that she should just buck it alone. *"Suan le"* ("forget it"), she said decisively as she made arrangements to book train tickets that would get her into the icy city of Harbin after dusk.

When she arrived home for the holiday, she couldn't possibly have imagined what was waiting for her. One of her mother's friends—whom I'll just refer to as "the matchmaker"—had arranged for Zhang Mei to go on a blind date with a man from Hong Kong. The matchmaker proposed that they meet the following afternoon at a local teahouse; an invitation that Zhang Mei's mother gleefully accepted on her daughter's behalf.

As is customary on blind dates in China, five people—Zhang

Mei, her mother, the matchmaker, the young gentleman from Hong Kong, and his mother—gathered around a table, and awkwardness ensued. Most of the conversation transpired between the mothers and the matchmaker, while Zhang Mei and her potential suitor were sidelined on their own date. They sat in silence.

Zhang Mei could sense that her prospective mother-in-law had a steely exterior and was very protective of her son. She had been divorced for twenty years—something quite uncommon for her time—and had spent most of her adult years running the cosmetics empire she had founded as a young woman. Made up like a Peking Opera star, she eyed Zhang Mei suspiciously as the matchmaker very matter-of-factly summarized the supreme marriageability of the shy, borderline shell-shocked young man at the table: he owned a car, a large home, and held valuable stock in his mother's company. Zhang Mei glanced quietly at the man as this recitation was happening. They eventually exchanged a few polite words about their respective taste in movies, and by the end of the evening—when they were finally left alone—she even grew to like him, a tiny bit. "He's a very good listener," she reported. "I could tell he was sensitive and paying attention to what I was saying. He wouldn't cut me off, like some other men have." Just as I started to get hopeful that their first meeting might lead to a second, she added, "That's probably because he's been completely dominated by his tiger mother. She's terrifying."

The next morning, after having gotten word from the Hong Kong gentleman's mother that her son had enjoyed meeting Zhang Mei, the matchmaker rang Zhang Mei's mother to share the news and instruct her on next steps: Zhang Mei was to report to the local animal market at eleven a.m., where the matchmaker would be waiting for her.

Zhang Mei, who loves to sleep in, could not understand why she needed to trek across town in the cold to meet a bumptious old matchmaker at an animal market, but her mother did not give her time to dissent. After being hustled out the door, Zhang Mei arrived at the market to find the beaming matchmaker holding a small green creature in her left hand.

"There is something about your energy that is blocking your chances at marriage," she said, waving her free hand around Zhang Mei's head as if playing the castanets. "If we free up that energy—by allowing you to symbolically free this small animal—your chances will improve," she explained, again with far more gesticulation than necessary to make herself understood.

Before Zhang Mei could protest, she had been handed a turtle and was being led to a nearby lake. The lake was nearly iced over and she couldn't help but imagine that the turtle would die of hypothermia—thereby freezing her into singlehood for all eternity. The matchmaker was so persistent, however, that Zhang Mei had no choice but to play along. As they reached the edge of the water, she began to coax the turtle out of her hands, but he would not budge. Was he dead already? Zhang Mei tapped his shell. Somewhat panicked, she lowered him onto the lake's surface as gingerly and humanely as possible. Once there, she gave him a small nudge on the rear. He moved a few inches, then stopped near a small rock. As Zhang Mei left him to roam free—an action that she was vehemently reassured would be reciprocated as positive energy for her husband search—she saw a man in the distance. Walking away with the now very satisfied matchmaker, she couldn't help but notice that as they got farther, the man worked his way closer to her four-legged friend. They turned off the lake path before Zhang Mei could actually see what the man was up to, but she walked away with a strong sensation that he might be in the business of reselling the turtles purchased by naïve single women and their well-meaning, but entirely misguided, matchmakers.

That, or he was craving turtle soup.

Fate in Eight Digits

Back in Beijing, June's Chinese New Year holiday wasn't going any more smoothly. "I haven't slept for days and my ears won't stop ringing," wailed her mother, looking haggard and exasperated.

It wasn't until she spoke to her older cousin Wei Wei that June learned the reason behind her mother's sudden and mysterious case of tinnitus. In an attempt to assuage some of the holiday marriage pressures she knew June would be experiencing, Wei Wei thought it might be wise to have her *ba zi* checked out. As mentioned earlier, most often, *ba zi* are consulted to assess strategic partnerships and business transactions, though I've heard of them being used to determine everything from the most provident day to hold a wedding to the most auspicious day to take someone off of life support. A cross between astrology, fortunetelling, oracle bones, and a bit of good old-fashioned hocus-pocus, they are taken very seriously in some circles, allowing so-called *ba zi* experts the opportunity to charge significant sums for their services. Conveniently (or perhaps dangerously), a person does not need to be present for his or her own *ba zi* reading, which means that anyone with the knowledge of an individual's exact date and time of birth can commission such an assessment.

Wei Wei reasoned that if she had June's *ba zi* examined and the expert was able to confirm that marriage was indeed in her near future, June's mother would relax and allow June to enjoy the holidays as she deserved to. Wei Wei did not, however, consider what might happen if the *ba zi* report revealed otherwise.

"Your *ba zi* indicate that you'll get married at age thirty-four," Wei Wei explained to June. "I thought this was very good news, but your mother didn't." Apparently, June's mother was horrified that she'd have to wait another seven years before her daughter's wedding. "What will I do until then? I simply cannot relax until she's married," she told Wei Wei. June's mom then retired to her room complaining of tinnitus, insisting that nothing but news of her daughter's engagement would restore her aural health.

As an aside, in relaying these stories of histrionic mothers, I don't mean to give the impression that they are all crazed connubial conspirators. In fact, having met almost all of them, I can say with utmost sincerity that they are delightful women whose interests extend far beyond the ring fingers of their only daughters. Christy's mom is an avid community volunteer, having gone as far as Sri Lanka to assist in social welfare projects. June's mom is extraordinarily well read, in addition to being a very talented musician who is regularly called upon to give professional piano performances. Zhang Mei's mother is the leader of her local ladies' dance troupe, a stellar cook, and a wickedly sharp mahjong player. My understanding is that each of these women have their moments of acute marriage hysteria—moments that, according to my sources, have a tendency to center on Chinese New Year. For the most part, however, they are engaged, active members of their communities who genuinely mean well, but occasionally feel compelled to approach their daughters' search for a life partner with the same zeal as their extracurricular activities—often to disastrous outcomes.

In an attempt to gain some more insight into the eight little digits that threw June's mom into a tailspin, I thought it might be wise to speak with a *ba zi* expert. I wanted to get a better sense of what exactly these numbers could convey about a woman's marriage prospects and I was also curious to know how they were calculated. The few Chinese *ba zi* experts I reached out to were cagey with their information, but I eventually came across one in Kuala Lumpur who was very generous with her time and knowledge.

A self-proclaimed "wrecking ball of hopes and dreams," Bernice Low's family originally hails from China's Fujian province and she has a long history of dealing with unmarried women. More progressive and pragmatic than most *ba zi* experts, she will just as readily advise on a "friends-with-benefits" situation as she will a more marriage-minded one. In the very forgiving "*ba zi* for dummies" session she gave me, Bernice was quick to make clear that *ba zi* represent a person's destiny, but that destiny is only one-third of the equation. The other two equally balanced parts are *feng shui*, or the things that can be done to modify or tweak destiny, and *man*—the actions and choices we make that control our own destiny. *Ba zi*, in other words, are a bit like the blueprints of our lives. Whether we choose to follow them or not is another story entirely.

A *ba zi* chart, she explained, is made up of eight characters ("*ba*" meaning "eight" and "*zi*" meaning "characters") that are derived from a person's year, month, day, and hour of birth. By cross-referencing these characters with a special calendar known as the 10,000 Year Calendar or Chinese Almanac, the *ba zi* chart is assembled. According to Bernice, most Chinese households have one because it's the only calendar from which the ever-fluctuating date of Chinese New Year can be determined.

To make *ba zi* reading easier, a multitude of websites and app developers have created *ba zi* calculators to do all of the grunt work. So for example, if we take Christy's digits and plug them into a *ba zi* calculator, we're given the following chart:

Ba zi chart 八字				
Hour 时	**Day** 日	**Month** 月	**Year** 年	天干 Heavenly Stems
正财 DW — 癸 Gui Yin Water	戊 Wu Yang Earth	正印 DR — 丁 Ding Yin Fire	七杀 7K — 甲 Jia Yang Wood	
丑 Chou (Ox) Yin Earth	辰 Chen (Dragon) Yang Earth	卯 Mao (Rabbit) Yin Wood	豬 Zhu (Pig) Yang Water	地支 Earthly Branches
辛 己 癸 / Xin Ji Gui / 伤 劫 财 / HO RW DW	癸 戊 己 / Gui Wu Yi / 财 比 官 / DW F DO	己 / Yi / 官 / DO	癸 / Gui / 财 / DW	藏干 Hidden Stems

By looking at the Earthly Branches, we can see that the hour of her birth corresponds with the earth element and that the year of her birth corresponds with the pig. The interpretation of this chart can only be made by a *ba zi* expert, because in order to read a chart, one needs to have a substantial understanding of how different elements and signs interact, the permutations of which are endless. Yet for general purposes, Bernice explains that when tasked with assessing a person's marriage prospects, the first thing she does is locate a client's "spouse palace."

To me, a "spouse palace" sounded like a resplendent white building housing an elaborately upholstered throne upon which the doppelgänger of a person's future spouse can be found sitting as pretty as an emperor. As fanciful as that sounds, Bernice told me that I'm not too far off—she can sometimes detect certain physical attributes (height, chest size, hair color) of a person's future spouse based on the chart—but other than that, the spouse palace is simply the ideal place on a person's *ba zi* chart for his or her "spouse star" to inhabit. The spouse star, I then learn, can be located in different places on the chart, depending on the sex of the person being evaluated. Regardless of sex though, if there is a spouse star in a person's spouse palace, this bodes well for his or her marriage prospects. If there is no spouse star (which can happen), the person in question—according to Bernice—will be a good candidate for marrying someone he or she meets through a blind date or other "arranged" situation—ideally to a mate who doesn't have a spouse star either.

"It sounds straightforward, but the possibilities are endless," she says. "A man can have his mother in his spouse palace—when that happens, I tell a woman to think hard before saying yes, because it means she will be living with her mother-in-law forever."

Throughout our conversation, Bernice stresses that what she advises based on a person's *ba zi* chart is only "insight into what can be done to make the best of a situation." She explains that some people's marriage charts indicate low marriage luck, which doesn't necessarily spell doom; it just means that they'll have to work harder to make a marriage happen (and last). That may involve moving to a new place, changing careers, or making other major life adjustments, but more than anything, Bernice emphasizes that getting married is about being proactive, keeping an open mind, and being realistic.

"You can put new windows on the house and paint the shutters," says Bernice, "but at the end of the day, if the bell rings, you have to answer the door!" She warns that some women aren't always thrilled with the men who appear on the other side of the door.

They have their sights set on someone wealthier or taller, and so they keep looking. Sometimes, they find what they want, and other times they just become increasingly disenchanted with the options.

As a rule of thumb in the husband search, Bernice cites an old Chinese saying: "If your life as a wife will be worse than your life as a daughter, don't get married!" Countless mothers, I presume, are bound to disagree, but then again, Bernice isn't there to please them. "I'm just there to read the chart."

The more I learn about Chinese marriages, the more I realize that they're accompanied by a fair amount of lore and superstition. Though now less common, there's also *wang fu lian* (旺夫脸), or what I've come to understand as "feng shui of the face." Essentially, it's a form of physiognomy in which a woman's facial features are evaluated for signs that she might bring her future husband good fortune. Guo Jingjing (郭晶晶), the famous Olympic diving champion from Hong Kong, is considered to be one of the best examples of *wang fu lian*, which is sometimes translated into English as "help husband face." Though interpretations differ, the most common involves an analysis of a woman's mouth, nose, ears, forehead, upper lip (no whiskers!), and hairline. If a woman's nose is high, straight, and with a round and fleshy apex, for instance, she is said to bring luck to her future husband. Her forehead should also be round, as square ones (Angelina Jolie) are indicative of highly opinionated women. Large mouths (Julia Roberts) are considered to mean a woman is a "cash eater," and so wives with smaller, more proportionate puckers are encouraged.

As I later discover, the superstitions surrounding marriage in China even extend to phonetics. On January 4, 2013, for instance, 7,300 couples got married in Shanghai. Why? Because the pronunciation of 13-1-4 (January 4, 2013), "*yi sheng yi shi*," sounds like "love you for a lifetime."

Ultimately, my takeaway from this small foray into Chinese astrology and superstitions is that *ba zi* are a bit like the nutrition facts on a candy bar. They give you an idea of what you're getting yourself into, but at the end of the day, how much you choose to bite off or let melt in your pocket is your own decision. In more practical terms, that means there is no guarantee that June will marry at age thirty-four, as her mother and cousin seem to have interpreted. The results of her *ba zi* reading simply indicate that her spouse star will be optimally positioned in her thirty-fourth year of life. She may get married sooner, later, or not at all—the mix of animals and elements that comprise her *ba zi* chart simply suggest that thirty-four is a propitious age for her to consider marriage.

When I explained this to June, who originally approached *ba zi* with a mix of skepticism and lingering curiosity, I could see her brain begin to percolate. "So I've got seven more years to date around?" she said. "That seems like an eternity, but I got a late start, so I'll take it."

The Classifieds

Christy wasn't quite so optimistic about dating. She's thirty-four, and without any serious suitors in sight, she decided to broaden her potential pool of mates to include foreign men. But where might she find them?

For Beijing women looking to meet Western men online, a common port of call is the personals section of a website called TheBeijinger.com. A bit of a cross between *TimeOut* and Craigslist, it offers an excellent spread of restaurant reviews, a calendar of upcoming cultural and entertainment events, as well as a very lively classifieds section. Using it, one can easily search for an apartment, a job, a secondhand air purifier, or, as the personals section would seem to indicate, a Western boyfriend.

The site is all in English and generally aimed at foreigners in Beijing, with the exception of its personals section, which seems to be heavily dominated by Chinese women.

User goodluckforme writes:

> You cute? You sincerity? You want to fall in love?
> I like the lovely big belly foreign fat man.

sweetygurl writes:

> hello, if you are nature [sic] blonde, please contact me.

wannamarry writes:

> don't be afraid of my username on this website. i come here to find my western Mr. right. but people should be friends first.
> in my free time, i prefer music, reading, dvd's, traveling, talking with friends, going outside and so on. i don't wanna play games so if i am your right one, write to me pls. thanks.

And user goodluckforme posts again, this time targeting a slightly furrier demographic:

> I am a Chinese woman who likes foreign men. I think your chest hair is very sexy and cute.
> what I want is a sincere feeling, hope to have a good start, share life.

I logged on with Christy one afternoon and we perused some

more ads together. We came across one from a woman who only wanted to date Dutch men because the former love of her life was from Antwerp. Then there was another woman who claimed her feet "would make any foreign man suffer" (did they smell of Époisses?), and even a few married women who claimed their husbands—who often traveled—allowed them to be served by foreign boyfriends "who knew how to do things right."

Then there was another category of ads, mostly written by women who had master's degrees from the United States, Canada, Australia, and the UK. Their command of English was always much higher, and they often described themselves as "untraditional." Their ads frequently mentioned that they'd recently returned to China after an extended period abroad, and were struggling to reintegrate. These women sounded much more like Christy, but she seemed reticent to join their ranks. I decided it might be helpful to introduce her to a Chinese friend and former colleague who I knew had a geographically vast rolodex of former boyfriends.

The Mating Game

"I lost my virginia! But I can't get the organism. How to do?"

Those were the first words to come out of Beibei Wong's mouth the morning after she'd been deflowered. It had been no easy task. For years, the young native Beijinger with stilted English had fantasized about losing her virginity, but couldn't quite find the right time, place, or man to lose it with. "China is a crowded place!" she says in retrospect. "There's no space to do these things!"

Fortunately, Beibei's big break came when she left China to become an exchange student in Sweden. Prior to her departure, she had paid a visit to Beijing's Lama Temple, and in front of a large statue of the Buddha, prayed that he might have the benevolence to get her a little action.

Two weeks and one romp with a Stockholm pizza-delivery boy later, her calls to the heavens were answered. That relationship didn't last beyond the evening, but her affinity for foreign men has lasted a lifetime.

"I just cannot date Chinese men," she says. "Eighty-five percent of the ones my age smoke and their fingernails are longer than mine." As much as I'd rather not defame Chinese men, I had to agree with Beibei. Smoking is ubiquitous in China, especially among the men in her age group (thirty-five and up), who also have a curious tendency of growing their pinky fingernails to very unsettling lengths. Having a long pinky finger is said to attract good fortune, but we both agreed, at least visually, all it seems to attract is unsightly black dirt, earwax, nose crust, or worse, depending on where it has last been.

I knew that since Sweden, Beibei had dated a mix of foreign men, including an American. Their relationship ended due to geographic complications, but I could tell she cared deeply for him. Keen to get back onto the singles scene, she decided to try her hand at online dating.

From a research perspective, the idea of online dating in China fascinated me. Numerically, it was impressive—the Chinese online dating industry is the second largest in the world after the United States, and generated US $1.6 billion in sales according to iResearch figures for 2016. Yet beyond the economics of the industry, in a culture where parents and family members still retain such a strong hold on the marital prospects of their offspring but where young people have taken to the Internet so fervently, the advent of online dating seemed like an explosive opportunity for change. To find out just how much it had altered the dating landscape, I scheduled a meeting with Rose Gong, founder and co-CEO of China's most famous dating portal, Jiayuan.com.

Gong is a petite and unassuming woman who created a formidable dating empire, almost by mistake. It was born in her dorm room at the prestigious Fudan University in Shanghai, when she was in full leftover-woman splendor: twenty-seven, single, and studying for a master's degree in journalism. Worried that her bookworm tendencies would prevent her from meeting anyone to date on campus, she turned to the Internet. Upon discovering that the dating sites she had signed up for contained fake profiles and pictures, she taught herself to use Microsoft Office Front-Page, and created her own online dating platform. Gong started small, with only five users, including a timid PhD student who was researching fruit flies. She personally helped him edit his profile, claiming that as it was, it would fail to get the attention of any women.

Now with nearly 90 million cumulative accounts since its launch in 2003, her site is traded on NASDAQ (DATE), and has earned her the much-coveted title of "China's #1 Matchmaker."

Though her *sheng nü* days are behind her (the fruit-fly PhD is now the stay-at-home dad to their young daughter), Gong still has a soft spot for leftover ladies, affirming in an interview, "Most of these so-called leftover women have voluntarily chosen their lifestyle," and stressing, "It's very important to know yourself and what you want before choosing a life partner."

When I sat down with Rose Gong, one of the first things I did was congratulate her: "In a country where the mate search is so often restricted to parents, matchmakers, friends, and colleagues, you've broadened the search parameters. You've allowed millions of young Chinese to—quite literally—search for a mate on their own terms." Gong looked at me, puzzled. "That wasn't my intention at all," she replied. "I just thought that with all of the rural-to-urban migration happening across China, people were losing their traditional networks for finding a partner due to geographic distances. I wanted to fill that void."

And indeed, Gong, as I discovered, was surprisingly no-frills about the mate search. She ascribed heavily to *"men dang hu dui,"* or as mentioned earlier, the concept of "matching doors and matching windows," which has guided matchmakers for centuries. This is apparent on her site, where users can search for mates with parameters like the very popular "salary" function. "It's not there to cater to gold-digging women," she insists. "It just works as a doorstep—the bare minimum a man needs to pass, in order to be considered suitable," she explained. "With hundreds of thousands of users in your city, how else do you begin to narrow things down?"

I asked if it was common for parents to play an active role in the online dating lives of their children and was told by a Jiayuan employee that most of the women signed up on the site are under accounts registered by their mothers. She explained that many singles are even too busy to try to date online—that, or they allowed their parents to create a profile for them as a way of getting them off their backs and alleviating some of the marriage pressure they face. This didn't come as a shock given previous conversations with Christy and June, though I was surprised to learn it was also true for men. Given his salary and general eligibility as a bachelor, my friend Guang had been automatically bumped to diamond status on Jiayuan.com, which means that women had to pay more to message him. (One of the ways that Jiayuan.com monetizes is by offering its more cash-flush users "menus" of the different categories of singles they can pay to access.) Guang had originally filled out his own profile, but then his dad asked to see it. "He made some very aggressive edits," said Guang. "He put an end to my hookups."

During my visit to the Jiayuan.com offices, I was told by Gong's assistant that the website also sponsored many offline events where members could get the chance to meet and mingle. There was one coming up at a huge shopping mall on the west side of the city, and she said I could attend if I wanted to observe how it was organized.

I ran the idea by Beibei, and even though neither of us was in the market for a Chinese boyfriend, we decided to go. When we arrived (about an hour after the event had started), we located the large open space in the middle of the mall where the event was being held. There were bouquets of flowers and a cheerful MC who made announcements through a blaring wireless headset. But where were all of the merry mingling singles? They were at "the wall." On a stretch of sheetrock that was littered with notes, we saw hundreds of profiles of young Chinese singles—men and women—advertising their age, occupation, salary, and QQ number. Much to my amazement, 70 percent of the people at the event just swarmed this area, flipping through different sheets of paper, which, by this point, were so numerous they were overlapping. The wall was divided, with blue sheets on the left from boys, pink sheets on the right from girls. Young Chinese singles (and at least a few parents) were packed in around it, using the zoom functions on their cell phones to see more clearly if they couldn't get close enough to the wall, and taking pictures of the profiles they found most interesting.

Working my way through the pack, I was dumbstruck. Why were the men and women checking out small bits of colored paper instead of talking to one another? Beibei kept her head down and stayed out of the fray. "This is why I can't date Chinese," she said. All eyes were on the wall.

I noticed a man in a newsboy hat nervously looking at the young woman next to him. From what I could tell, he was trying to do the unthinkable and . . . speak with her! The crowd was so tight, it was easy to remain close enough to eavesdrop, so I did. The young man made eye contact with his female target.

"How old are you?" he asked, without even saying hello.

The girl looked flustered, flashed a nervous semi-smile, and turned away into the crowd without responding.

"Next time, you might want to try a less invasive line," I said to him in Chinese, trying to look sympathetic because I got the feeling he was genuinely clueless.

He looked back at me, startled. I was the only foreigner at the event, and clearly the last person he expected to get dating advice from.

"You can even just say, 'Hey, I'm X, what's your name?' " I said.

"I guess I could," he said timidly. "But I usually just ask the age first, because if it's not suitable, there's no need to move forward."

The man honestly didn't seem to understand that his search parameter pickup line wasn't the best way to get a response. Judging by the sprinkling of hairs on his chin, I decided that he was still young and would eventually learn the error of his ways. "Well, next time, just for fun, try something else," I told him, making an escape. Beibei, who had witnessed the entire thing, was howling with laughter in the corner.

As I ventured away from the wall, I discovered a much less concentrated area populated by a handful of cougars, the requisite patches of seedy old men, and a few mother-daughter teams plotting their next move. Mothers seemed universally more excited to be at the event than their daughters. In my conversations with them, I noticed the recurrence of the phrase *zhao gu* (照顾), which means "to look after." Beyond the basics of being able to boast of a son-in-law and eventual grandchild, I could sense that these mothers wanted to find husbands for their daughters so someone would take care of them once their parents passed away. And as unromantic as it sounds, I didn't blame them.

China isn't set up for the single or the childless. For centuries it has been a country where the family unit has unflappably served as the supreme unit of social organization, leaving those who live on its fringes to fend for themselves. A chilling example of the flaws of this paradigm is the devastating 2008 Sichuan earthquake, which killed nearly 70,000 people, with another 18,000 reported missing. Though no exact numbers are available, a large percentage of the deceased were children who perished under the shoddy construction of their school buildings, creating China's earliest example of what would later come to be known as *shidu*, which literally translates as "lose only," or parents who had lost their only child. As Mei Fong writes in her stirring and meticulously reported book *One Child*, "The unmarried and the childless are very low on the societal totem pole." She describes how *shidu* parents found themselves struggling to get into nursing homes and to buy burial plots because their lack of a child to fund and make decisions about care or funeral arrangements were seen as a liability.

Given China's lack of a social safety net, *shidu* parents are also more financially vulnerable than peers who have progeny, and as Fong notes, more prone to depression. The bias against them will have to change in order to protect the elderly (*shidu* support groups suggested using money from violations of the one-child policy to support couples made childless by tragedy, though that idea never got traction), but even broader reforms must be made to accommodate further strains on the traditional configuration of the nuclear family as a result of the country's impending gender imbalance. Beyond the fact that it will soon become numerically impossible for everyone in China to be married and have offspring, it must also be considered that young Chinese—women, especially—are developing a much lower tolerance for marriage for the sake of marriage.

As I spoke with the daughters of the concerned mothers, they confirmed this. They were much more likely to mention things like "common interests" "travel" and "chemistry" in conversations about their search for a partner. They were looking for other halves with whom they could hike or play badminton, backpack around a foreign country, and enjoy as a source of shared laughter and the occasional frisson. The idea of growing old alone troubled them—one told me that she planned to purchase an investment property as a nest egg—but they didn't seem willing to compromise on their partner out of fear. Many spoke good English and were middle-class Beijing natives or current residents (hence the proximity and presence of their mothers), so they had fewer financial concerns and could focus more squarely on their feelings.

On the ride back from our offline dating safari, Beibei told me about the last local she had been introduced to by her family. He was thirty-seven, had never married, and had a good job at a Japanese company in Beijing. "He's really into anime," she said, "which was cool, until I got to know him better." It turns out that Beibei's parents and potential in-laws were so keen to have the young couple married, they conspired to send their children away on an all-expenses paid trip—a preemptive honeymoon, of sorts—to Chengdu, home of China's beloved pandas. Things went OK until their first evening together at the hotel. All along, Beibei had a hunch that her date wasn't the most virile character she'd ever met, but the contents of his suitcase confirmed her suspicions. "He brought a teddy bear to sleep with on our trip," she said. "It's like Mr. Bean, no?" I couldn't help but laugh at the image of minxy Beibei sharing a bed with the Chinese version of Mr. Bean.

Hearing Beibei speak, echoes of conversations I'd had with Christy, June, and Zhang Mei rang through my ears. Like them, she has worked hard to pursue her passions and build a fulfilling life for herself. As an accomplished artist and designer at an international luxury hotel, Beibei has created a nice life for herself. She is keen to share it with someone, but walks a fine line between finding that person on her own terms and her obligation to be respectful of her parents' wishes and society's timelines.

"My parents tried hard to pair me up with this guy because we've known his family for a long time and he owns a house in a very good area," she said. "But I can't imagine that my life would be any happier with him in it or that he'd be any happier with me in his, so I don't see the point. We'd each be better off adopting a panda!"

7

HIGHER CALLINGS

丑妻是个宝

A homely wife is a treasure.

—CHINESE PROVERB

D r. Kaiping Peng, the founding chair of the Department
of Psychology at China's Tsinghua University, has a
theory. Based loosely on Maslow's pyramid of needs, he
argues that when a country reaches a certain level of prosperity,
the focus of people's needs shifts from being primarily material
(food, shelter, clothing) to psychological (spirituality, happiness,
self-fulfillment). While he acknowledges that there are certainly
exceptions, he maintains that the theory adapts itself especially
well to China, where between 2000 and 2016, the size of the middle class grew from 5 million people to 225 million.

"We're going to see an increasingly greater interest in personal
health and well-being, art, innovation, and film," he explains.
"Why do you think China is facing a surge in ethnic conflicts?
Because its people are looking for an identity."

Along with the search for identity, argues Peng, is the drive to be self-actualized. He explains that self-actualization is a complex and coveted cocktail of personal growth, achievement, love, and respect that only about 30 percent of the world's population is able to fully achieve. His bet on who might come the closest in China? Young women.

"The Chinese economic miracle has two secrets," he says. The first are migrant workers, and the second are young, educated women. "You can go to Pudong in Shanghai, you can go to Beijing's Central Business District; of all the international corporations there, I'd say 70 percent of the local employees are young Chinese women. They generally have better English language abilities, they are smart, hardworking, professional, and at ease in global environments. They've been very beneficial to Chinese development; I don't think many Chinese people realize that."

Still, for as much as he defends young Chinese women, Peng spends his days turning them away. In charge of recruitment for Tsinghua's psychology department, he estimates that 80 percent of job applicants are female. Most of them have stellar backgrounds—doctoral degrees from Yale and Harvard, excellent references, and impressive publishing histories. Most of them, Peng also acknowledges, are single.

On paper, these women are pushing toward the upper echelon of the self-actualization pyramid. But as unmarried women, they teeter toward the bottom half of what is socially acceptable in China. What might explain the discrepancy? "These women represent the vanguard of social development in China," says Peng. "They have high standards and they have high expectations," he adds, "and the rest of the country hasn't quite caught up to them."

Indeed, nearly a year into her contract at one of Beijing's mightiest law firms, June realized that she had clocked hundreds of overtime hours and hadn't been paid for a single one. Despite warnings from several colleagues against rocking the boat and receiving negative feedback, she copied all of her emails to a USB drive as evidence of the many late-night work hours she had been putting in, and requested the overtime compensation that was clearly outlined in her contract. In response, her boss threatened to sue her and ask for damages, claiming that by copying her emails to a USB drive, she was in effect stealing intellectual property. Unfazed, June called him out on his "BS legal argument," reminding him that she hadn't leaked any information to any external party. In the ultimate test of her litigation skills, following several heated arguments, June was finally issued the equivalent of six months' salary in overtime payments, and promptly filed her resignation letter.

For perspective on where women like June figure into the grand scheme of China's development, it's helpful to understand the historical place of Chinese women over the past hundred years. Until at least 1906, most Chinese women had their feet bound. Until 1950, they were sold in marriage to the highest bidder. Then there was the Great Famine (1958–1961), which took the lives of over 30 million people and during which it wasn't uncommon for party officials and militia to rape women at will while making their rounds of different communes. Things took a sharp turn in the Cultural Revolution during the '60s and '70s, a time when China had one of the highest female employment rates in the world. Almost overnight, women became "sexless comrades," laboring shoulder to shoulder with men for the greater good of the nation. From a gender viewpoint, this is a special period in Chinese history, the unique conditions of which likely served as the breeding grounds for many of the self-made female billionaires that China has become so famous for, although it came at a huge cost. An estimated 2 million lives were lost during the Revolution, as the result of persecution, torture, violence, and humiliation that began during the bloody summer of 1966, and carried on for a decade.

After Mao's death in 1976, circumstances began to improve. Schools and universities reopened, although the onset of a more sedate period of economic reform and the cultural re-gentrification that accompanied it required that women resume their more traditionally feminine position in society, almost as if nothing had happened. And therein lies the rub: Chinese women have never had their own true feminist revolution—most of the greater opportunities they gained to more actively participate in society were imposed on them, and as a result, could just as easily be taken away.

Until now.

As the world's second largest economy after the United States (in terms of nominal GNP), China has grown at an unprecedented rate, but to avoid losing its position on the global economic leaderboard, it needs to focus on maintaining its size—something it cannot do without the full engagement of its women. This is especially true since one of the country's strongest engines of growth—its power in numbers—is on the wane. Figures from the National Bureau of Statistics of the Chinese Ministry of Human Resources and Social Security show that China's working-age population has been shrinking every year since 2012. Between 2016 and 2030, it is expected to shrink from just over 900 million to 870 million, before dropping to 700 million by 2050. These falling numbers are the logical result of the one-child policy, which has reduced the size of China's overall population, but there's more to it. As China's workforce shrinks, the employment preferences of its workforce are changing. With greater access to higher education, Chinese workers are less likely to want to be employed in the manufacturing sectors that once catapulted their nation's economy to new heights. More want jobs in the service and finance economy, which China is in the process of transitioning to.

Given their educational edge, many of China's young women are especially well positioned to weather their country's transition to a knowledge economy, but as Dr. Peng hinted earlier, what looks good on paper doesn't always translate into practice.

Until it was closed in 2016, the Beijing Zhongze Women's Legal Counseling and Service Center was one of China's most important non-profit organizations for enforcing gender equality. Founded in 1995 around the time of the United Nations Fourth World Conference on Women—which took place in Beijing—it was created during a period when China was trying to remake its image and gain international acceptance following the 1989 military suppression of pro-democracy demonstrations around Tiananmen Square.

I visited the center in 2013 to meet with a lawyer named Lu Xiaoquan, who was working tirelessly to put legal pressure on several universities across China that were requiring female applicants to have a higher *gaokao* score than male students, as a precondition for admission. (The *gaokao* is the closest thing China has to the SAT.) Back during the time when Christy took the exam, parents would flood temples with offerings, but today with a bit more money to throw around, the rules are different. Parents sometimes check their children into special "study suites" at designated hotels, billed as the places where past high-scoring *gaokao* takers are said to have studied their way to success. "Study nannies," charging up to US $50 per hour, have even become an option for moneyed parents who don't trust their children to put in the requisite cram sessions without a bit of stern supervision.

During the exam period, which lasts two days, cities cede themselves to the needs of their students. Internet cafés are closed down, construction stops, traffic is rerouted, and no-honking zones are established. Local newspapers have reported on taxi drivers in Anhui province who give free rides to students on their way to the test, and select McDonald's that have offered free breakfasts for aspiring university students. As chronicled on the popular Chinese web portal, NetEase, in Sichuan province in 2012, local hospitals were flooded with test-takers who studied while hooked up to oxygen machines and intravenous drips of amino acids in order to improve their concentration. At one school in Hebei, the IV drips were offered to students to use in the classroom. Photos show that the IV bags were suspended in the air by a long, dangling rope, which swooped clothesline-style across the classroom, giving students access to a bag from their desks at the discount price of 10 RMB ($1.80).

According to Christy, it has even become common for young girls to take birth control pills during the month before their exam. She cites her younger cousin Emily as an example. At no point during her exam preparation time was there any risk of Emily becoming pregnant. She also wasn't suffering from bad acne, intolerable menstrual cramps, irregular cycles, or any other of the reasons a non–sexually active young woman may be on the pill. She was simply on it because as an aspiring writer with high hopes of attending China's top journalism school, she didn't have a minute of her studying time to waste on maxi pads and monthly blues. As a result, she pumped her 105-pound frame with double doses of estrogen and progesterone.

"It's a very normal thing for young girls in China to do before a big exam," explains Dr. Jin, a gynecologist at the Beijing Sino-American Gynecology hospital. "There are no guarantees, but eight to ten grams of birth control for ten consecutive days before an exam should be enough to keep menstruation at bay for the month."

Yet pill or no pill, Chinese women are outperforming their male peers on the *gaokao* exam. According to data from the China University Alumni Association, female students account for 52.65 percent of the top-scoring students across China's 31 provincial-level regions. Since 2012, they have consistently snatched more and more top slots from male students, even in the sciences, which were formerly the stronghold of the boys. And it's not just in the realm of testing that young Chinese girls are excelling. According to data from the Shanghai Academy of Social Sciences, female students from elementary school to junior high are now outscoring their male counterparts in every subject—math, physics, and chemistry included. While this educational excellence should be something to commend China's young female students for, the stack of correspondence from the Chinese Ministry of Education (MOE) that Lu shows me tells a different story.

Lu explains that discrimination has been happening to a limited degree since 2005, but became notably more severe in 2012, which is when he and his colleagues decided to take action. It mainly affects students who choose *ti qian pi se*, or subjects that are eligible for a type of "early admission." These subjects include foreign languages (with the exception of English), performing arts, international relations, broadcast journalism, cinema studies, and military disciplines, as well as *li ke*, or science-related fields.

For example, in 2012, the admissions requirement for students seeking to study foreign languages at China's prestigious Renmin University was a *gaokao* score of 601 for male students, and 614 for females. At Beijing Foreign Studies University, those same scores for foreign languages were 582 and 590, for males and females, respectively. For science-related fields, the numbers rose to 598 and 639, a discrepancy of 41 points.

Making it clear in his correspondence with the MOE that setting different *gaokao* scores for each sex violated the forty-eighth clause of the Chinese Constitution—among other charters and laws—Lu attempted to find out how and why it was being allowed. He received a series of dispiriting responses, arguing that ratio setting for students in specialized fields was "for the good of the country."

Over the course of various communiqués, the MOE explained that it was necessary to control the gender ratio in certain fields; namely those involving national protection and public safety or in which there's a high element of secrecy or confidentiality and the environment may be deemed "dangerous" for women. They explain that it is necessary to "protect" women by limiting their numbers in fields where they may come to harm, or in fields where educational resources are limited and where society needs a certain level of balance. Without this balance, the MOE argues, the "quality of education and its benefit to society" will be affected. Their responses also hinted that an imbalance might "affect the needs of related ministries," which I was particularly curious to know more about.

"Basically, they're saying that since employers prefer males for certain fields, it's necessary to make sure male enrollment remains high, so employers can be guaranteed a large enough pool of the right gender to choose from," says Lu. "They don't seem to understand that education should meet the needs and expectations of the individual," he adds, arguing that it's not the government's job to try to control who should work in a particular field. "Deciding whether or not someone is suitable for a job is the responsibility of individuals and of HR departments, not the government," said Lu.

Maizi Li, co-founder of the Gender Equality Advocacy and Action Network, a Chinese NGO, agrees. Small and fiery with a pixie cut, Li joined a group of a dozen other women who shaved their heads in protest of the discriminatory *gaokao* scores. A relentless activist, she has raised awareness for everything from China's lack of female toilets—the first time I met her, she gave me a rather slick-looking disposable paper airplane–like device that allows a woman to pee standing up—to domestic violence.

In March of 2015 she rose to international prominence after being detained and eventually imprisoned following a demonstration that she helped organize across several Chinese cities on International Women's Day. Although she and her fellow activists were simply putting stickers on subway cars to draw attention to China's lack of redress for victims of sexual abuse and assault, she and at least nine other women were brought into custody. Five women, including Maizi, were charged with the crime of "picking quarrels and causing trouble"—a common catchall for locking up dissidents—and remained in jail for a total of thirty-eight days. Their case drew an outpouring of support from women around the world, including Hillary Clinton and the former US ambassador to the UN, Samantha Power. The story of "The Feminist Five," as they came to be known, was covered widely by the international press.

Since Maizi's release, she has slightly scaled down her activism. Failing to do so would swiftly get her into trouble with the authorities, who still monitor her actions, though they haven't been able to stop her from having her finger on the pulse of gender inequality in China.

I ask Maizi why the fields chosen for test-score discrimination seem so random, because I can't quite work out the link between more women in broadcast journalism and a threat to national security, for instance. She sighs. "It's impossible to know the true motivations, but I'll tell you what I suspect," she says.

She explains that if it weren't more difficult for girls to enter communications programs than boys, the latter would largely be outnumbered. This is problematic because in China, "one man and one woman means gender equality," she says. If the majority of program hosts on CCTV were female, this wouldn't reflect "equality." If "balance" is so important, what about policies favoring females in fields where women are by far the minority, I ask. She smiles and teaches me a new expression: *qian guize*, which translates literally as "closet rules," but is best interpreted as "unspoken rules."

"The funding of certain schools depends on their being able to show that they've employed a certain number of graduates every year," she explains. "And since males generally have better prospects in the job market, universities want to make sure they have enough of them."

This information throws me for a loop, so I begin to ask around. A source at Renmin University—one of the schools that, as of 2012, had been engaging in the practice of requiring female applicants to have higher *gaokao* scores than males for certain disciplines—tells me that of the students studying to be HR managers in the university's highly reputed program, the majority are women, and yet the only ones who seem to have jobs lined up before graduation are males. Another source, a foreign visiting professor in the literature department at Beijing Normal Capital University, tells me that he is bewildered by his department's choice of a new dean. The department is dominated by female staff, but the newly appointed dean is male—a man not even thirty, who, unlike most of his female colleagues, has not even finished his PhD. "I was very surprised by the choice," said my source, "and by the fact that none of the women seemed to oppose it."

After speaking with a female professor at one of Beijing's top universities, I learned that male students are generally expected to achieve more after graduation. By this logic, most admissions officers reason that the greater the population of male students, the greater the chances that the university will have a star alumnus in the future. The professor is quick to clarify, however, that the university as a whole actually suffers from a shortage of female applicants, given its focus on technology and the fact that fewer women choose to earn degrees in scientific disciplines. Nonetheless, no special effort has been made to recruit more female students. On the contrary, in the Department of Foreign Languages and Literatures where she works, there are generally three to five boys in a class of thirty students. "I once heard a professor at my department meeting say exactly this: 'The severe lack of male students in our department is a big problem. Boys are more likely to become experts in their fields of study in the future, and they have more potential.'"

Before harping for too long about just how terribly unfair things are in China, it might be worth taking a look at the state of college admissions in the United States.

In 2006, a *New York Times* op-ed written by a Kenyon College admissions officer, Jennifer Delahunty Britz, openly admitted that Kenyon often gave preferential treatment to male applicants by making it easier for them to gain admission, despite lower scores. In response to her piece, other admissions officers echoed that such preferences were not uncommon, though many seemed to be surprised at the candor with which she spoke of them. Columbia University law professor Ted Shaw referred to the "help" male students get as an "open secret"—something that everyone in the admissions world was well aware of, but not necessarily something that the outside world needed to know.

In response to the media attention and discussion that Britz's story generated, in September 2009, the US Commission on Civil Rights voted to conduct an investigation of several colleges and universities in the mid-Atlantic states, evaluating for instances of gender discrimination in the admissions process. A study was devised by the late Dr. Robert Lerner, head of the Commission's Office for Civil Rights Evaluation and Research, and over the course of an eighteen-month-long investigation, data was collected from a diverse sample of fifteen colleges and universities.

However, just as the results of the investigation were coming together, three new members of the commission were appointed, two by President Obama and one by Senate Majority Leader Harry Reid. Two of the investigation's original supporters, appointed by President Bush (as well as a member appointed by Reid who had not voted when the investigation was first undertaken) rotated off. In March 2011, a majority of members of the newly reconstituted commission voted to terminate the investigation, though none of the remaining original supporters changed his or her vote. Mostly, those who voted to terminate claimed that shortcomings in data and the limited geographic scope of the project made the study inadequate, but Gail Heriot, a professor of law at the University of San Diego and one of the eight members of the US Civil Rights Commission, suspects there was more to it.

She attributes the shutting down of the investigation possibly being due to political interests, and also brings up a curious point. She cites a column written on the matter, in which the following statistic appears: "For every 100 women who earn a college degree (in the US), only 73 men do." Heriot points out that the author of the column refers to the situation as a "boy crisis," flatly dismissing any possibility of discrimination against female students.

Yet as we've seen in China, these things may be one and the

same. Women can be discriminated against in college admissions and men can be falling behind women in terms of scholastic performance. The former, in fact, seems to be a likely response to the latter. I'll leave the policy ethicists to debate whether or not allowing for this type of "discrimination" is flagrantly unconstitutional, or unfair but somehow justified. Instead, I turn to how those degrees that women need in order to stay afloat professionally appear to be detrimental to their marriage prospects when they get beyond a certain age.

Throughout the twentieth century, white college-educated adults of both sexes in the United States were less likely than their less educated counterparts to be married by age thirty. This was especially true for young college-educated women, who until 1990, got married at much lower rates than their less educated peers. This disparity in marriage rates resulting from education is often referred to by demographers as a "marriage gap," something that, according to a Pew Research Center report, is on the wane. "Among white women under 40, the educational marriage gap has vanished," reads the report, which clearly indicates that as of 2008, 84 percent of college-educated, white thirty-five- to thirty-nine-year-old women had married, matching the rate of white women of the same age without a degree. That same report also predicts that college-educated American women will soon become the majority of married white women.

To compare this information and evaluate its validity in respect to China, it's important to look at a few more numbers. As reported by Barbara Dafoe Whitehead in *Why There Are No Good Men Left*, in 1960, only 185,000, or 1.6 percent, of college-educated American women between age twenty-five and thirty-four in the United States were unmarried. Today, there are 2.5 million of them, or 28 percent of women between the ages of twenty-five and thirty-four. It's also critical to keep in mind that whereas Chinese women have been the dominant gender of college degree earners as of 2011, American women have represented the majority of higher degree earners since 1982. In other words, it has taken over thirty years for well-educated American women to close the marriage gap. Will Chinese women succeed in doing the same?

Smoke and Mirrors

After filing her resignation, June decided it would be a good idea to take some time off to travel and think about whether she'd like to take another job in law or go back to school for a degree in art history. This decision was completely flummoxing to her mother, who didn't fully understand why she left her job in the first place. Nonetheless, to catch up and celebrate her victory over her tyrannical former boss, we meet for dinner and are joined by Ivy, who arrives at the restaurant resplendent as usual.

When the three of us need to communicate, we use Weixin, or WeChat. A cross between Facebook, Twitter, Skype, WhatsApp, and Instagram, WeChat is a convenient way to chat with contacts and follow their lives through a microblog-like feed of "moments" in which users can post pictures, text, links, and other random musings peppered with a magical selection of emojis. I use WeChat daily—it's essentially become my go-to texting app—but I had no idea that it was a key weapon in Ivy's man arsenal.

"You need to post pictures of expensive things," she explains to June. "So the men following you understand that you have exquisite taste."

Ivy opens up the "moments" pages of a few of her protégés, to give examples. She's now beyond this WeChat stage, but reassures June that it was very useful in getting her to where she was now.

"On your birthday, for instance," she says, "post pictures of all the designer gifts you receive."

June looks completely lost. She'd spent her last birthday at a Korean spa with a few of her best gal pals, but hadn't gotten any extravagant gifts to flaunt beyond a few cosmetics. "And if you don't get any expensive gifts, post pictures of other people's gifts, making it seem like they're yours," Ivy continues. "With a few words of gratitude, of course, so it doesn't seem like you're boasting," she adds. "Convincing pictures you can find online are also OK. You just need to make it look like the gifts were given to you."

"The same goes for dinners," she says, as if quoting *The Confucian Analects*. "If you go to a chic restaurant on a date, or even just with friends, post pictures of it. Men need to see you in nice places, so that they know to take you to them. They'll cut corners whenever they can, but if you set the bar very high, their fear of coming up short will ensure they treat you well."

I can see that June is excited to be learning this information, but not yet entirely convincd of the methodology.

"Next, you need attractive photos. Legs and cleavage. Nothing tasteless, but the pictures should be sexy."

Since June doesn't live far from the restaurant where we met for dinner, Ivy offers to help orchestrate a small photo shoot at her apartment that evening.

Once we arrive—Ivy drives over in her Porsche, June and I teeter over on my e-bike—Ivy proceeds to sit on the daybed in June's apartment, which has a magnificent view of the Central Business District of Beijing. "This is the most flattering position for legs," she says, stretching hers out in front of her, with one slightly raised, while arching her back slightly. "You try."

June sits down, lumbering slightly onto the windowsill. Ivy prepares to take a photo. "Stomach!" she says. June inhales. "Stomach!" Ivy repeats, a bit more loudly. June (who is slim to begin with) cinches once again, just before Ivy snaps the picture. "We'll just have to Photoshop," said Ivy as she looks at the picture. Though a few of my Western male friends had fallen all over themselves when they met June, according to Ivy, June's selling point was not physical, but her *qi zhi*, or the air about her. I take this to mean her special mix of charisma and intelligence, though I'm not sure that's what Ivy is referring to.

As Ivy flips through the "Moments" of her other female WeChat contacts to show me more photos, I notice a trend. Many of them had uploaded pictures in the very same position she just suggested to June. Iconic blue Tiffany boxes abound, as do signature black-and-white Chanel ones. Some posts even include photo montages of several different luxury items shown together. Ivy, I was beginning to realize, has disciples.

Following the eye-opening session with coach Ivy, June enacted a more proactive plan of action. Pictures of fine pastries and filet mignon dinners began to pop up on the news feed of her WeChat profile. She even went to a photo studio to have some very sultry glamour shots taken of herself. In one, she was wearing a fitted canary-yellow dress that revealed a stunning hourglass figure.

"The photo shoot was ridiculous. The place was papered in outrageously doctored-up photos of models. One of the male ones was really attractive—he had to be Korean," said June. Noticing her admiration for the man in the photograph, the photographer asked if June wanted to have a romantic photo shoot with one of the male models, as this was a service offered by the studio. "I was tempted," she admitted, "but in the end I decided it would be creepy."

A few weeks after her solo photo shoot, a Korean man popped

up on June's radar. They'd met at a networking event for young professionals, but hadn't really made much of a connection. Her new WeChat images must have caught his eye, however, because he suddenly became more talkative and eventually asked her out.

This was monumental. June loves all things Korean—South Korean soap operas are her guilty pleasure; she is a diehard fan of K-Pop; and in her eyes, South Korean men are the Apollos of Asia. She readily accepted.

8

LOVE, WITH CHINESE CHARACTERISTICS

There are people who would have never fallen in love,
had they never heard of it.

—FRANÇOIS DE LA ROCHEFOUCAULD, MAXIM 136

t was a Sunday morning, just two subway stops after ten a.m. I
approached Beijing's Temple of Heaven Park with high hopes.
As the unofficial playground of the city's vivacious elderly population, you're more likely to be cornered by a Shaolin septuage-
narian than to find a quiet corner to read, lounge, or picnic in, but
none the wiser, I set out to find a few secluded trees.

"Are you looking for a husband?" asked a stout, middle-aged
woman as soon as I made my way through the gate. Standing
about four foot eight, she was plucky, her accent thick with the
heavy twang of a Beijinger. Before I could answer, she took out a
small photo. "This is my son. He's a lawyer. He makes a very good
salary, and just outside this park, we own three *lao fangzi* (traditional Chinese-style row houses). "Would you like to see? One is
already furnished and ready for him to move into with his wife."

I kindly told her that I wasn't on the market, but took a closer
look at the photo.

He had his mother's smile—and her belly. Though seemingly tall, he had a large convex paunch that protruded from his body, giving him the shapeliness of an anvil.

"*Ta shenme dou hui*," she went on, explaining that he was an ace at soccer, basketball, Ping-Pong, badminton, and a few other sports Zhang Mei had not yet taught me the names for in Chinese.

"What do you think?" she asked with a winning grin and a nudge that seemed to say, *Be my daughter-in-law.*

"I have a friend who is a lawyer," I said, in a halfhearted attempt to be polite, and a full-hearted attempt to escape.

"How old?" she asked.

"Twenty-eight," I said, with June in mind.

"He needs a wife, not a dinosaur!" she said. "Anyone younger?"

I bristled, and she could tell. Though I was well aware of how ageist the Chinese can be, especially when it comes to marriage, I wasn't going to encourage it.

She took out a treacly pineapple-coconut hard candy as a peace offering before leaning in a bit closer. "I should probably tell you something," she said, in a hushed whisper. "He's had a girlfriend before. They were even, you know, in love."

"What happened?" I asked, suddenly very curious.

"I didn't approve of her background. I forbade him to see her. He continued for a time, but they eventually split up. It ruined my relationship with him for several years. He wouldn't even speak to me," she said. "Things are better now that I've promised not to meddle in his personal affairs."

"Then, what are you doing here today?" I asked her.

"Helping him find a wife, of course!"

I stopped to take everything in. This woman was one of nearly two hundred parents and grandparents who had attended the "marriage market" that Sunday morning. In addition to the

Xeroxed tomes of information on available mates, there was even a members-only database that one could access for a nominal fee, which is how Christy's grandfather also selects prospective matches for her to consider.

It surprised me that this was still happening in modern China—and smack in the middle of a city as cosmopolitan as Beijing—but I should have known better. What I saw play out that morning were the remnants of a romantic tug-of-war that parents and children in China have been engaged in for the better part of a century.

In 1899, a French novel by Alexandre Dumas, *The Lady of the Camelias*, was translated into Chinese. As one of the first European novels ever translated, it claimed a broad readership upon publication and legend has it that its intrepid translator, Lin Shu, wept so hard while translating its scenes of passion, ill-fated love, and the tragic death of Marguerite Gautier from consumption, that all of his neighbors knew what he was up to.

At this time, the steamy Chinese classic *Dream of the Red Chamber* was past its second printing. Chinese readers had long been exposed to literature laden with ardent emotion, the social paralysis of the aristocracy, and the heroism of renunciation, but as Haiyan Lee, Stanford scholar of Chinese classics, notes in her book *Revolution of the Heart*, Dumas's *The Lady of the Camelias* presented these themes to Chinese readers in a radically new framework: one of romanticism. Through Armand Duval, the son of a tax collector who falls helplessly in love with a Parisian courtesan, and who defies the order imposed by his aristocratic class when he decides to marry her, Chinese readers were given a glimpse of how emotion and the pursuit of romantic love could be a legitimate basis for a new social order—not just a titillating bedtime story.

It's worth keeping in mind that during this period of Chinese history—the Late Qing dynasty and Early Republic periods—there was no phrase to signify "romantic love." The closest linguistic equivalent was the word "*qing*," which translates roughly as "sentiment" and refers primarily to the novels of sentiment, which were popular at the time. More than individual emotions, *qing* was associated with virtue, and people were still expected to keep their identity and accompanying "sentiments" tightly linked to their kinship circles.

Given the all-encompassing nature of social networks, romance—it has been argued—was less necessary and less valued during this time in China, though it certainly wasn't prohibited. Amorous dalliances were allowed in brothels and with concubines to the extent that if a man became so bewitched with his lover, he could bring her into his own home. (Polygamy was widely practiced and legal in China until 1949.) Homosexual relations were also tolerated, and even Confucius—often erroneously portrayed as stalwart and stone-faced—condoned having a good time, as long as it was done in moderation, and with no detriment to the family structure or associated ethical relations. The only real caveat to cavorting was that it needed to be done with great caution.

"Traditional Chinese literature is laden with tales of electrifying love at first sight and erotic bliss," explains Lee. "But most of these tales have a tragic ending—the star-crossed lovers are wrested apart by the will of discordant parents, or one of the lovers (usually the woman) suddenly turns into an evil fox spirit." This is all done on purpose, Lee reassures me, as a way of literalizing the anxieties that people may feel when searching for the appropriate marriage partner, and of reminding them of the perils of deviating from the time-trusted marriage system.

Though often scintillating reads, Lee explains that most of these stories are laced with a similar moral: if you abide by the codes and prescriptions of the process leading to marriage and don't deviate from the structures of your familial network, the system will guarantee that you remain safe. But push the limits of passion a bit too far, and you might find yourself married to a rapturous but cataclysmically evil fox spirit.

By definition, *qing* didn't exclude romantic love or passion, it just required that love and passion be harmonized with other ideals. Among the most important of these were filial piety and patriotic love. Depending on one's family and the political climate, the grand trifecta of unwavering and harmonious devotion to one's family, one's country, and one's beloved could be a rather tall and improbable order.

The May Fourth Movement, which took place in 1919, took the idea of *qing* and kicked it up a few notches. Grown from student demonstrations in Beijing, the driving force behind it was the idea that Confucian values—including arranged marriages—were responsible for the political weaknesses of the country. During the movement, which stretched into the 1940s, activists fervently campaigned for the privileging of the individual over society, and for feeling over formalism. And, as the spirit of the times would have it, one of their largest points of contention was love.

"It was declared (as well as demanded) that love was the sole principle underscoring all social relationships: between parents and children, between husband and wife, and among fellow Chinese," writes Lee. This was so strictly enforced that "any social institution that was not hinged on the existence and continued articulation of love was believed to be impoverished and illegitimate," she adds. Since arranged marriage happened to be one of the biggest obstacles to romantic love, it was dealt with accordingly. In May Fourth literature, parents came under attack and were portrayed as a source of tyranny, their self-interested motives for arranging the marriages of their children ruthlessly exposed.

Ideas of romanticism reached new heights during this period, which—despite being way before Flower Power, Janis Joplin, and the VW Microbus—is generally referred to by scholars as China's "heyday of free love." Incidentally, it was also a period in Chinese history when women writers flourished. They wrote stories of passion highlighting the bravery and resolve of women in love, and with their writings, they challenged the authoritarian family system and the subjugation of women. But perhaps most significantly, it was a time when *qing* morphed into *aiqing*, or the modern translation of "love." Synonymous with freedom, equality, and autonomy, *aiqing* became a trope for the newfound primacy of the individual, and proof that the pursuit of romantic love could be a legitimate raison d'être.

This represented a monumental change for China, a country where identity had traditionally been grounded in kinship or ties to native place. The Confucian system of social relations had previously been so tightly centered on the needs of state and family structures, even friendships outside of these bounds were considered potentially subversive. Though the political ideologues of the time were determined to construct a marriage model that differed radically from the old Confucian model, they feared the heady feelings engendered by romantic love would detract from revolutionary zeal. And they weren't misguided in thinking it might.

Even as far back as 600 BCE, Chinese philosopher Lao Tzu warned, "Love is of all passions the strongest, for it attacks simultaneously the head, the heart, and the senses." These disruptive powers of romance were no secret to the ruling Communist Party. So once they were in power, after a brief but significant stint on the marquee of the Chinese national psyche, love was yet again taken off the billing.

Following the transition to "free-choice" marriages discussed earlier, and by the onset of the Cultural Revolution in the mid-'60s, kissing and hugging—once featured in Chinese films of the 1930s and in classical literature—became strictly forbidden, dismissed as capitalist, degenerate actions. To show their love, Chinese youth were encouraged to lend books to each other or exchange fountain pens or notebooks. When alone together, they were to discuss revolutionary ideals and steer clear of any personal feelings, lest they be accused of *zuofeng wenti*, or "problems of lifestyle"—the type of closeness with a member of the opposite sex that could lead to public disgrace.

Ironically, a term that did emerge amid all of the romantic repression was *tan lian ai*, "fall in love." At the time, it referred more to courtship, or the period a couple should take to get to know each other before getting married. This was condoned because it was seen as a way of phasing out the Confucian system of arranged marriage by allowing couples to *tan*, or "discuss" their relationship before making the decision to wed. Though perhaps a bit more conducive to romance, this "fall in love" approach didn't make finding a marriage partner any easier.

As noted by Elisabeth Croll in *The Politics of Marriage in Contemporary China*, in addition to the socioeconomic requirements that a woman's family still encouraged her to keep in mind, she now had a man's political affiliations to consider. Was he a member of the Communist Youth League? Did she and the young revolutionary share political ideals? These issues were of paramount significance, as reflected in the popular press, where some unaffiliated Chinese youth blamed the Communist Party and the Communist Youth League for their troubles in love. Without being accepted to these organizations, they claimed to be "nonentities," "unable even to get someone to love them."

Marriage, it would seem, returned to being transactional. Romantic love went from being something that young people in the 1920s rallied and fought for—irrespective of class or kin—to being once again overtaken by a stratified, commodified system of family-approved matches that required all involved parties to be in good standing with the party.

Today, things work a bit differently.

It's eight p.m. on a Thursday evening, and a bouquet of roses worth US $10,500 has just arrived at the front door of Maxim's Beijing, an outpost of the famed French brasserie. The bouquet is easily the size of a small elephant. "We're going to have to take the door off," says Corentin Daquin to his staff. "There's no other way," he adds, motioning for someone with the appropriate tools necessary to unhinge the large wooden glass-paned double door. Moments later, four sinewy, flower-bearing Chinese men are cued to come in. Before them looms a steep, two-story staircase. "We can just call the fiancé down," says Daquin with a bit more gesticulating. "Absolutely not," interjects another of his colleagues. "It will ruin the proposal."

According to Daquin, who formerly managed the restaurant, these sorts of floral gymnastics are a regular occurrence at Maxim's, which has been operating in China since 1983. As one of the oldest foreign commercial establishments on the mainland, over the past three decades, it has weathered sudden changes in the Chinese political climate with great finesse. Its first location—just a mile southeast of Tiananmen Square, was wracked by violence on June 3, 1989, as Chinese soldiers shot their way through the capital city in an attempt to quell the legendary pro-democracy demonstrations taking place there. As Beijing's best-known symbol of Western bourgeois elegance, the restaurant was required to close for five months following the Tiananmen massacre, but resumed business as usual that following October.

Today, Maxim's is one of many foreign establishments where Beijing's well heeled convene for fine wining and dining. Pierre Cardin—the now octogenarian couturier whose idea it was to bring the restaurant to China back in the early '80s, is largely credited as a visionary, and enjoys rock-star status in China. When he is in town, streets are closed for his cavalcade and dignitaries convene. At the opening of Maxim's in Hefei—an emerging but otherwise unremarkable city in Eastern China—multiple Chinese heads of state were present for the occasion.

Over time, however, Maxim's has become famed in China for more than its signature French cuisine, meticulously adapted to the Chinese palate. "We have about four to five proposals a week," says Daquin, supervising the small fleet of men who are hoisting the bouquet up the stairs, leaving a trail of shredded rose petals behind them. "We have a special book for keeping track of them all, and every request is more extravagant than the last," he explains, rattling off a list of proposals that includes a man who booked the entire restaurant, requiring that every table be arranged in a heart shape around the area where he and his girlfriend would be seated.

"It's expensive, and it's a lot of work," he says, having a sniff at the oversized bouquet, which has now made its way to the second floor. "These are real roses," he adds approvingly. "Red and fragrant—must have cost a fortune."

As a tall, strapping Frenchman (a quality that, in the eyes of the Chinese, automatically makes him exude romance), Daquin is occasionally asked to bring the ring to the table—sometimes disguised in a cake, looped around a napkin, or poised under a covered platter. "It can be moving," he says. "Especially some-times when the women begin to cry from the surprise or the emo-tion, but most of the proposals are disappointingly superficial."

Two hours later, the man who bought the large bouquet and his soon-to-be wife arrive at the restaurant and are escorted to a table that can accommodate the floral apotheosis planned for the end of their meal. After their five courses are consumed, a vio-linist begins to play, the bouquet is ushered onto the scene, and a ring is presented. The bride-to-be, already covered in sparkles, smiles gently as two glittering carats are slipped onto her finger.

Moments later, the groom-to-be throws the keys to his Ferrari at a busboy and asks him to load up the bouquet. Since getting it into the two-passenger sports car is clearly not possible, the flow-ers are left in the parking lot, where they remain until night staff of the nearby shopping center take notice, and promptly begin to serve themselves.

Long before such extravagant proposals existed or could even be afforded in China, the Cultural Revolution continued to kill any manifestations of romance—real or synthetic—well into the '70s. By the economic reforms of 1979, however, people were ready for some romance. A huge national controversy broke out when *Popular Cinema* magazine published a color photo of a kiss scene from an English film, *The Slipper and the Rose*, on its back cover. As reported by journalist Ginger Huang in *The World of Chinese*, the picture sparked a massive public debate after a pro-paganda officer in Xinjiang called the photo "decadent, capitalist, an act meant to poison our youths." He then clarified: "It's not that we don't want love; the point is what kind of love we want—pure, proletariat love, or corrupted, capitalist love?" In the fol-lowing two months, 11,000 letters flooded the magazine's office, two-thirds of which condemned the attitude of the puritanical propaganda clerk.

Also in 1979, *The Tremor of Life* was screened; a film rumored to have a kissing scene. Before it premiered, people gossiped that the actors had been required to wear plastic wrappings on their lips while filming it. When the kiss scene came, spectators craned their necks and sharpened their eyes in an attempt to spot the plastic. Yet as the actors leaned in for the big moment, Huang reports, "the mother-in-law broke in with a bang and the lovers parted."

As the Mao era came to a close and China began to undergo significant economic and political reforms, love emerged from the rubble as a way of resurrecting a repressed humanity. Perhaps the best proof that it had been missing during the preceding years of turmoil is the fact that it was addressed vigorously and effusively by numerous female writers.

A salient example is Yu Luojin's *Dongtian de Tonghua*, or *A Winter's Tale*—a story drafted in 1974 and published in the fall of 1980. Like so many others in the "wounds literature" genre that was popular in those days, Yu's story details the horrors suffered by her family during the Cultural Revolution. Because of her father's chronic unemployment that resulted from his politics, Yu's mother had to work in a factory (at partial pay, because of her "rightist" label) to support her husband and their three children. Then there was Yu herself, who for some off-color comments on official literary policies made in her (confiscated) diary, was banished to a labor camp. As reported by Ming-Yan Lai, an assistant professor of intercultural studies at the Chinese University of Hong Kong, Yu was then sent to an impoverished village, where she was immediately told by the party secretary of her agricultural brigade to find herself a husband.

Because an unmarried woman in a labor camp was not allowed to remain unwed, Lai writes that Yu was temporarily relegated to a peasant's side room. Eventually, in order to relieve some of her mother's burden of sustaining the family, Yu decided to "sell" herself to a man from a more prosperous region of the country. After describing the dark details of her marriage to a brutal and abusive husband, Yu describes how she realized the hubris in believing that she could repress her inner need for an emotionally and spiritually rich life in her pursuit of a materially comfortable one. She laments falling for what the state vision of national modernity encouraged its citizens to do: devalue their personal feelings and sentiments in favor of financial pursuits.

Yu's recognition of her error generated a tremendous amount of public debate, notes Lai. Adding flames to the fire was the fact that as her story was being published, Yu was going through a second divorce, which she had filed for on the grounds of the absence of love. As per a 1980 amendment to the marriage law stipulating that lack of mutual affection was valid grounds for divorce, Yu's reason for filing was completely legal, though whether it would actually hold up in practice was something many spectators were anxious to see.

But more than anything, the public was fascinated by Yu's very frank revelation of the mercenary nature of her marriages, and what appeared to be her genuine desire to defend a woman's right to satisfy her emotional needs. From informal conversations to popular magazines and newspapers, Lai reports that Yu's admission generated groundbreaking discussions about the meaning of love in marriage and the morality of marriage and divorce. She describes Yu's life as "a public text through which the Chinese people tried to map out changing possibilities for personal lives and the relation between the personal and the public under the new post-Mao regime."

To be fair, when the Maoist era ended in the late '70s, the following regime, anxious to disassociate itself from the extremes imposed by its predecessor, reintroduced the official discourse on marriage and love that was developed in the 1950s. But by the '80s there were yet again official agencies in charge of disseminating the "correct" attitudes toward personal matters, including relationships.

Seen in this light, it would appear that more than a personal struggle for love and self-fulfillment, Yu's writings were about "a public struggle for the general acceptance of women as persons with their own values and rights for happiness." The right to have marital freedom, in other words, is not the quest for a fairy-tale wedding, eternal butterflies, or even daily exchanges of those relatively new words *"wo ai ni"* (I love you). It is, first and foremost, a form of social justice—a form of social justice that, it would seem, has been largely debated and denied in China for the last hundred years.

Small Treasures

My colleague Yanyan had a sheepish giggle and a penchant for round-tipped kitten heels, which she often shuffled around in, reminding me a bit of Minnie Mouse. She smiled often, spoke little, and spent most of her time at the office shopping online or tending to her e-farm. The day I got my first glance of her e-farm—literally, a colorfully animated electronic farm with blossoming crops that required tilling and watering—I couldn't understand how she could possibly find it so engaging. "Everyone has one," she protested, challenging me to take a good look around the office. Sure enough, the office of the media company where we both spent roughly eight hours a day was filled with fields of thriving pumpkin, corn, and red-pepper crops. It all seemed so deliciously ironic. Wasn't China doing everything possible to urbanize? Why, then, were its hardworking rural transplants still tending to virtual cornfields?

While I never fully understood the intrigue of QQ Farm, as the game was called, having a desk right behind Yanyan's was a constant source of entertainment. Piled high with all sorts of electronic appliances, it resembled a miniature space station. One winter morning I arrived to find her desk tricked out with a set of electric mittens chargeable by a USB port so her fingers wouldn't freeze at the keyboard. Below these were heatable slippers that looked like moon boots designed for Baby Spice and a desk humidifier in the shape of a large rubber ducky who artfully released steam from his bottom.

Yanyan had purchased all of her gadgets on Taobao, which has been one of the leading forces behind the commercialization of November 11; what is now popularly known as an unofficial holiday called 光棍节, or Singles' Day. Celebrated across the country, it was allegedly created by a group of bachelor students at Nanjing University in the '90s. Given the four ones in the date (11/11), the students decided it would be a fitting antidote to Valentine's Day—a holiday that would instead celebrate their singlehood and curb some of the negativity commonly associated with it.

Today, Singles' Day has become the largest online shopping day in the world, largely thanks to Alibaba portals like Taobao and Tmall, a B2C platform for official stores featuring a wide range of several foreign brands, from Tom Ford to Target. As a result of clever marketing, heavy commercialization, and improved payment methods, Singles' Day sales on the sites have climbed steadily from $5.8 billion in 2013 to $17.8 billion in 2016. A bit like Cyber Monday, the holiday offers deep discounts to everyone, though there are special products marketed to singles. These include low-calorie instant noodles (for lonely urbanites who can't face cooking for one) and human-sized pillows with arms and legs (for those longing for something to spoon with). In 2016, Ma took the holiday to a new level by prefacing it with a star-studded gala countdown. A-listers such as retired basketball star Kobe Bryant (known in China as Peter Pan for his ability to "fly") as well as David and Victoria Beckham were in attendance. Pop sensation Katy Perry (endearingly referred to by Chinese fans as "Fruit Sister" for her produce-inspired costumes) was supposed to perform, but ended up canceling at the last minute. Some Chinese netizens speculated that Perry was too distressed over the results of the US presidential election to attend.

I knew that many of my female colleagues spent a healthy part of their workday browsing for wares on Taobao, which in Chinese is formally known as 淘宝网, or the "treasure-searching network." I learned this not from leering at their computer screens but from the daily interruptions of *kuaidi* (express delivery). To young working girls in office buildings across China, the arrival of *kuaidi* is a daily yet still much anticipated event. From what I was able to observe, as the *kuaidi* delivery service person arrives at the office door, blips of QQ are momentarily suspended, as are heartbeats. Even the hot-water machine stops humming and gurgling, almost as if in momentary reverence. The women then often flash inquisitive glances at one another—is anyone else expecting a package? Whose might it be? The suspense continues until the deliveryman announces a name. If the woman in question is not in the office at the moment, one of her colleagues will rush up, accept the package for her, and store it safely at her desk, in a bold gesture of e-shopping solidarity.

"You must write about Taobao in your book," Yanyan once told me sternly. "It has changed the lives of so many young Chinese women. It makes us less reliant on boyfriends, because now we can easily and cheaply buy things for ourselves."

What she failed to mention at the time, however, was exactly how much it had changed hers.

"I'm going to give myself a present this year," she confided softly to me one day.

"What's that?" I asked, trying to imagine which kind of electrical heating apparatus she could possibly be lacking.

"A baby," she said.

"Ahhh," I said, wondering if Taobao had a subsection called Tao-baober (*baober* is Chinese slang for "doll" or "baby"). "Well, if you want one of those blond, blue-eyed ones, shipping costs are going to be astronomical!"

But then when she pointed to the middle of her tiny frame, I knew she had other delivery options in mind.

Later that afternoon, I went to lunch with Yanyan and Ryan, an American colleague from Alaska, with whom we were both very close. Over a meal of spicy cabbage, spicy green beans, black-pepper beef, and pickled radishes, she told us all about her pounding ovaries.

Her brother and sister-in-law had just had a baby, and she adored him. (Yanyan's brother was born before the one-child policy was in force, and she was born on the cusp of it.) She had asked Ryan and me to give her nephew an English name—we went with Jack—and she made the trek to the suburbs to see him every weekend. On a regular basis, she showed us pictures of chubby little Jack disguised in elaborate one-pieces—dressed as a dragon, a tiger, a caterpillar, or a donkey. He appeared to spend so much of his life swaddled in layers of fuzzy microfiber that Ryan and I wondered if Jack's parents weren't secretly using him to polish their floors.

But Yanyan was enraptured—she desperately wanted a baby Swiffer of her own!

"Who do you plan to have this baby with?" asked Ryan, noting that there had been no mention of a man.

"Oh, that's not really as important," said Yanyan. "I'm supposed to get married this year anyway, so I'll just find a husband to have one with."

"Do you have any candidates lined up?" asked Ryan. Though we were both more than confident that Yanyan would be able to raise a child on her own, the penalties for having a child out of wedlock—which, as mentioned earlier, prohibit any child born of unwed parents from being legally recognized as a member of society—make it a rather joyless experience.

"No, but I'll find someone. As long as he is *kao pu*"—a phrase that means "reliable" and is pronounced "cow poo"—"doesn't drink too much, and has a steady job to help support our family, it should be OK."

"But don't you at least want to marry someone you love?" said Ryan. I listened quietly, half expecting she was going to tell us that she'd purchased a USB extension on Taobao that would impregnate her on command.

"No, I am too tired for that," she said. "Don't you know work is busy?"

There were a few seconds of awkward silence.

"Well, have you ever been in love?" asked Ryan, who is supremely gifted at breaking silences and asking invasive questions. He was my unfailing sidekick over the course of five years in China, and without him, this book would not exist.

"Mmmm...I don't think so," she said, with a blank expression. Yanyan was twenty-nine when we had this conversation, and Ryan and I had just automatically assumed she had been.

"How about crushes? Little stomach flutters, nervousness, giddiness, like hamsters running on a wheel in your stomach?" asked Ryan, as we both became increasingly baffled.

"Ham-bursters?" asked Yanyan, even more confused. Ryan probably could have chosen a more translation-friendly metaphor, because neither of us could remember how to say "hamster" in Chinese, but in the end, things worked out. Yanyan really liked ham, so much that she called David Beckham (whom she also really liked) "Bacon-Ham." For her purposes, likening love to "ham-bursters" made perfect sense.

"Oh yes, I had them," she said. "But that was in middle school. Those things are not appropriate anymore."

In the early spring, I noticed that the nature of Yanyan's Taobao purchases was beginning to vary. She would no longer open her packages as soon as they arrived, or chat animatedly about her latest knickknacks with the other women in the office. Instead, she seemed to take on a new affinity for eggs. She'd eat a hard-boiled one at her desk every morning, disposing of the shell in the same small plastic bag she ate it out of.

At lunch, we couldn't get her to even taste the spicy vegetable dishes we so regularly enjoyed together. Cold things—like the shaved ice with mung bean or peanut slushies that we'd occasionally indulge in, were also off limits. It wasn't long before she announced to Ryan and me: she was pregnant.

"How did this happen?" I asked, all at once very happy for her, but also concerned, since I had a vague idea what became of mothers who had babies out of wedlock in China.

"I think you probably know how it happened," she said, somewhat abashedly. "It really wasn't planned."

Through the help of a friend, Yanyan had met a man, also from her home province of Anhui. He was four years her junior, and this made her uncomfortable. He also wasn't very well educated and only had a mediocre job, but he was kind to her. As soon as she found out she was pregnant, he immediately suggested they marry.

At first, Yanyan was terrified to be pregnant. Though a baby was something she really wanted, it was coming in the wrong order, and from a father her family was bound to disapprove of. Still, since there was already a bun in the oven, she assumed responsibility and began preparing for motherhood.

Before even informing her family of the wedding, Yanyan and her fiancé spent 5,000 RMB, or nearly US $1,000 to take their wedding photos. Chinese wedding photos are unique in that they are usually taken weeks before the actual wedding, and generally consist of the bride and groom dressed up in a series of funhouse outfits. In the first photo I saw, Yanyan was standing in front of what appeared to be a saloon, wearing an extensively ruffled homage to Scarlett O'Hara. Her soon-to-be husband, dandied-out to the max with a three-piece suit and a fake parted mustache, stood valiantly next to her. In the next picture, they shared a hamburger in what appeared to be a '50s soda-pop shop. Yanyan wore a poodle skirt, and her husband-to-be looked back at her adoringly, his back propped up against a jukebox. For this picture, they had him dressed up in a frilly lime suit trimmed with a lacy white collar, which made him look like a human margarita.

"His face is too fat," she said disapprovingly as she flipped through scenes of them posing playfully in front of a windmill.

Yanyan zoomed in slightly on her computer screen. "His face is kind," I said, because I genuinely thought it appeared to be.

"No matter," she said resolutely. "Next week we will register at the marriage bureau."

The Knot

Curious to know more about what the process was like, I decided to visit the Beijing Chaoyang District Marriage Registration Bureau. Conveniently located down a side alley across from the city's largest soccer stadium (Gongti, home of the mighty green Beijing Guo'an soccer team), it is an unassuming office, which, as I discovered to my great surprise, also doubles as a divorce bureau. In fact, after being directed down a long hallway and ushered toward a room with three long, open desks where I hoped to find at least one resplendent couple forking over the 8 RMB ($1.32) necessary for them to *deng ji* (register as man and wife), I stumbled instead upon a couple in full furor. I quickly deduced from their yelling that they had come to terminate their marriage, but that the husband had forgotten some of the essential paperwork, which meant their separation wouldn't be possible that morning. His almost ex-wife, needless to say, was not pleased.

Sensing they could use some privacy, I returned to the lobby and read through a few of the pamphlets on display. One of them was about adoption, and another listed the requirements necessary to register a marriage. In addition to a birth certificate, health certificate, resident's permit (*hukou*), and a letter of marriageability from one's work unit, I was amused to read that in the cases of a Chinese national wedding a foreigner, a letter from the parents of the Chinese partner giving permission for their child to marry said foreigner—complete with the index fingerprint of both parents below their signatures—was also required.

I meandered back toward the administrative offices and took a seat facing a small open stage with the kind of red curtains you might find at the Great Hall of the People. At its center was a wooden podium decorated with a large bed of red, pink, and white plastic roses in desperate need of dusting. Below them, an electronic sign—the kind one might see at a Yankees game—indicated the date and time. A large red-and-gold mural depicting a dragon and a phoenix meeting in midair loomed in the background, next to an oversize Chinese flag. This was clearly the stage on which newlyweds could take a commemorative photo. Was one included in the 8 RMB fee? I wondered.

From my seat near the door of the marriage office, I could hear the discordance inside growing louder. Eventually, it tapered, and before I had time to camouflage that I'd been eavesdropping, one of the marriage bureau employees walked out into the lobby with the husband.

She sat him down in a chair facing the stage as if he were a small child getting a time-out. "Why do you want to get divorced?" she inquired sternly, standing over him and wagging her finger as he slumped in his chair. He looked back at her, completely depleted, wearing the face of a man who's just been shouted into emotional paralysis by his wife and can no longer process words. He rubbed his head and mumbled something like "We just don't get along." The marriage bureau employee leaned in closer and began to lecture him. After a few more sentences, I realized that she was trying to talk him out of his divorce.

This didn't entirely surprise me. Until 2001, Chinese people had to ask permission from a leader in their work unit before they could get divorced. I had once met a man who had actually been tasked with signing off on divorces in his work unit for twenty years. "I usually denied the requests," he said. "Two years would go by, and then they'd be fine." I also remembered having come across an article on the All China Women's Federation (ACWF) website, where a marriage bureau employee was being honored for having "saved" approximately 240 couples from divorce. She had a trick—she'd say that the office printer wasn't working, so she wouldn't be able to process their divorce papers that day. Many couples, apparently, never bothered to come back.

The marriage bureau employee was being honored in the article—held up as a model worker, citizen, and defender of morality. This in itself was nothing extraordinary. The Chinese government is no stranger to sussing out model citizens and making heroes of them by using the brawn of its various branches and publications (the All China Women's Federation website is one of them). The widely celebrated Lei Feng, a likely fictitious solider who died in service (he was rather un-heroically struck dead by a falling telephone pole) has his own national day of remembrance, and is the subject of poems written by Chinese grammar-school students across the country. Generally, "moral heroes" are developed when it's necessary to raise awareness or shape the public discourse regarding a certain aspect of society. Honoring, I could imagine, might also be on the list of the Aesopian powers that be.

Having increased by 8 percent per year for the past twelve years—or, rather curiously, nearly the same speed at which the Chinese economy had been growing up until 2014—the divorce rate in China is something the government is likely not proud of, especially in urban areas like Beijing, where it is as high as 40 percent.

In an attempt to smooth things over, as one marriage bureau employee worked on the divorced-to-be husband out in the lobby, the other tried to calm his soon-to-be former wife. She appeared to be the more vexed of the two, and though I can't say whether her anger was justified—I didn't know the motivation for their divorce—her treatment of her husband was far from humane. Storming out of the marriage bureau, she demanded that he go to another bureau to get the papers needed in order to divorce that very day. He agreed, saying that he'd be right back. "I will not wait for you!" she said, slapping him on the head with a stack of papers in her hand. I was humiliated for them both.

After they left, I took the chance to speak with the two employees at the bureau who'd been handling their case. "Does this happen often?" was my first question to the younger of the two employees, who seemed a bit more likely to open up.

"Sometimes," she said. "We've had many more divorces recently. In most cases, we try to get them to reconsider." She went on to explain that it's her job to inquire as to why a couple is getting a divorce. In some cases, couples refuse to discuss it and ask to be divorced on the spot. In others, they come back three or four times before they eventually make up their minds to stay together.

Sensing that I was asking questions her colleague shouldn't be answering, the older of the two bureau employees worked her way over.

"The couple you just saw should stay together. They have a common hope," she said, eyes glittering as if she were auditioning to be a marriage fairy. "A seven-year-old son."

She told me that this particular marriage bureau is proud to process five or six marriages a day, though she wouldn't tell me how many divorces. I sensed she was about to launch into a prepared speech, but was saved by a security guard who seemed to need her help with something, and called her away. I tried my luck with the younger employee again, rephrasing my question and instead asking her what the most common reasons for divorce are.

"*Shan hun*," she explained, or "flash weddings"—when people get married after knowing each other for a very short amount of time—are probably the most common reason for divorce. I once heard this term from Zhang Mei, who told me the story of a friend who'd had one. She and her husband had gotten their marriage certificate and were legally man and wife, but before they got around to hosting their actual wedding celebration—the ceremony and the party with all of their extended family and friends—they got divorced because they kept fighting over the plan for their wedding festivities.

Next on the list were *ge ren de wenti*, or what we'd probably refer to as "irreconcilable differences." *Jia ting de wenti*, or "family problems," were the third reason she mentioned. "If a couple can get along, but their respective families cannot, their marriage usually does not last very long."

Luo hun was another type of marriage Zhang Mei had introduced me to. Literally translated as "naked marriage," it refers to a wedding between two (usually very young) people with few assets—no car, house, or other typical prerequisites to marriage. Generally, these marriages are classified as being very romantic, as they're seen to be more about the couple's love for each other, rather than the resources each partner is bringing to the table. They were romanticized on *Luo Hun Shi Dai* [naked marriage generation], a Chinese TV show that premiered in 2011 and scored top ratings, though the general consensus seemed to be that although they sounded nice in theory, few people were willing to put them into practice. "Unless a man spends money on them," said Zhang Mei, "most traditional Chinese girls won't be convinced of his love."

9

CARS, HOUSES, CASH

知足者常乐

Happiness lies in contentment.

—LAO TZU

Chinese New Year was over, and with little hope that their daughter would soon move back to Harbin, where they could usher her transition into wifehood, Zhang Mei's parents came up with another plan.

"If you're not going to come home and get married, we've decided that we'd like you to get married in Beijing," explained her mother. "To help you with that, we've decided to buy you an apartment there. With housing prices the way they are and so many men unable to afford a home, owning property will make you much more of a catch."

Zhang Mei responded to the news like a seasoned marriage ultimatum–averting pro. She dutifully agreed that she'd look into prices and get back to her mother with a detailed report. One week later, her mother called again:

ZMM: Have you looked into any apartments?

ZM: I did, everything is too expensive. It's better to wait for prices to go down.

ZMM: Yes, that's what we've been hearing too. Keep an eye on things though, eh!

In reality, Zhang Mei hadn't made a single inquiry. She was hurt that her parents felt the only way to unload her was to set her up with a dowry that would bait a propertyless man into marrying her. Still, the real reason she was determined not to let her parents buy her a place in Beijing went much deeper than a bruised ego. "The only kind of apartment they can afford for me will be way out of the center of the city," she explained. "It will double my commute to work. Plus, I'll have to share it with a virtual stranger, because once my parents have gone through all the trouble of buying me an apartment, there's no way they'll let me stay unmarried for very long."

I thought about Zhang Mei's current living space. She knew it wasn't ideal—just a modest room—but it was a reasonable distance from her office and she had the freedom of living alone. She could live by her own schedule, and even stay up late to watch movies if she wanted. The rent was inexpensive enough that at the end of the month, she still had money left over for shopping and hotpot dinner outings with friends. She understood it wouldn't be suitable as a long-term arrangement, but she'd worked hard to reach this level of independence and seemed keen to enjoy it at least a bit longer.

Shortly after that first conversation, Chinese media went abuzz with news that the Beijing property market had hit an all-time low. Granted, the low was a very temporary one that lasted only a few weeks, but Zhang Mei's mother still got wind of it. "Go see some agents this weekend!" she urged her daughter during a frantic phone call.

Once again, Zhang Mei expertly handled the situation. "Yes, but that price decrease only applies to Beijing residents; out-of-towners like us still have to pay higher prices," she explained to her mother. This was not entirely true, but China's system of household registration is so convoluted, there was very little risk of Zhang Mei's mother ever becoming any the wiser.

China's *hukou*, or household registration system, was initiated in the 1950s. It was engineered as a way of controlling population movement, which was seen as necessary for the new planned economy. The system was so inhibiting that until the late 1970s, people who wanted to relocate needed the permission of local authorities. These days, Chinese citizens can move more freely, as long as they are willing to leave behind public benefits such as health care and welfare, which are only valid in the jurisdiction of their *hukou*. Transferring a more rural *hukou* (like Zhang Mei's) to an urban address could cost upward of 150,000 RMB or US $22,000 on the black market, and is most difficult in top-tier cities like Beijing and Shanghai.

The quickest route to a *hukou* upgrade is marriage. If a rural woman marries a man with an urban *hukou* (or vice versa), the spouse marrying into the urban *hukou* is entitled to one as well. Like houses, cars, and salaries, the right *hukou* has also become valuable as a marriage bargaining chip. A man with a Beijing *hukou*, for instance, can more easily and cheaply send his kids to school in Beijing, and it's also easier for him to buy property in the city. Though the regulations change often, non-Beijing *hukou* holders have to prove they've lived in the city and paid income taxes for a certain number of years before they're eligible to purchase property, and the financing options available to them are also less favorable. An urban *hukou* makes city life a whole lot easier.

As a result, men with urban *hukou* are in high demand. If a woman without one becomes engaged to a man with an urban *hukou*, it's not uncommon for her to list it as one of his attributes when describing him to her friends. Women with urban *hukou* (June, Christy), however, are considered to have high standards, as their already elevated residential status means they should ideally find a man with the same. The most disadvantaged in this hierarchy are, once again, migrant men. Their lack of a desirable *hukou* or city property (Beijing men are presumed to inherit property from their families) puts them in the bargain basement of prospective mates—just the kind that Zhang Mei's parents thought she could attract. A migrant man with nothing in Beijing would surely be keen to wed a fellow migrant who already owned an apartment in the city.

To put the logic employed by Zhang Mei's parents into perspective, it's helpful to understand that a Chinese man's desirability as a husband is often measured by three things: a house, a car, and cash (房子, 房子, 票子). Known as the holy trinity of *yao qiu*, or "requirements," some Chinese women (but most often their families) use them as the basis for a marriage partner. Finding a man with these three essentials, however, is increasingly harder.

The average yearly salary in a city for a young, male college graduate is roughly 72,000 RMB, or $10,000. The average price of an apartment in Beijing or Shanghai is roughly 25,000 RMB or $3,600 per square meter. The average price of a modest car (not counting the 90,000 RMB registration fee required in Shanghai) is roughly 150,000 RMB, or $20,000. Just to be able to afford a seventy-square-meter apartment and a car, this man would need almost 2 million RMB, or $280,000, approximately twenty-eight times his starting yearly salary. Clearly, the numbers for what he earns and for what he is expected to own before marriage simply don't add up. The struggle average Chinese bachelors face to acquire property prior to marriage has become so prevalent that there's even a word for it: *fangnu*. Literally translated, it means "a slave to the home," and refers not to a woman who is a slave to housework, but to a man who must slave at his job in order to afford a house, and by extension, a wife. In most cases, parents pitch in—and sometimes liquidate their savings—in order to help their sons, but when they can't afford to, marrying into a family like Zhang Mei's may be a convenient alternative.

For Zhang Mei, whether a prospective mate owns a home or not is far down the list of desirable traits in a man. Her ideal would be to jointly purchase property with someone whom she is excited to spend the rest of her life with. In their haste to get her hitched, however, this isn't even a possibility that registers with her parents, or one they'd willingly consider.

Wrecking Homes and Feathering Nests

"Delivery boys and dishwashers can't fall in love in China," said Ivy. "It's simply too expensive." In her teens, she had fallen in love with a man from her hometown of Chengdu, but she ended their relationship because he was of an average upbringing and she wanted a better life for herself and for her family. She left home, went to college, found a lucrative job, and has since maneuvered herself into a comfortable life, with a boost from her male patrons. All along, she has sent generous sums of money home to her parents and has even purchased an apartment in Beijing, though the question of whom she might one day share it with has been increasingly on her mind.

Ivy always knew that she would one day become a wife. Her parents expected it of her, but she also wanted it. Not for love—she was resolutely convinced that she'd passed that phase in her life—but for stability and the chance to become a mother. "There's nothing that would make me happier than to accompany my child to study in the US," she confides to June one evening over dinner. "To give her all of the educational opportunities I couldn't have. I would love to have a daughter like you."

Although it was difficult to imagine Ivy's transition from mistress to mother and wife, it was becoming increasingly probable. A man just a few years her senior had recently proposed to her. He knows that she's involved with other men—or, one married man in particular—but he wants them to be exclusive. As a member of China's *fu er dai*, or "wealthy second generation," he is so rich that he once purposely crashed his $800,000 Mercedes into the back of a pretty girl's Porsche, just because he wanted to get her number. I think it's safe to say that many Chinese women would swoon at the chance to marry into such formidable wealth. Ivy, however, has reservations.

First of all, she knows his family would give her a hard time because she's not from a similarly affluent background. Even the faintest risk of a disapproving mother-in-law does not delight Ivy, whose ideal has always been to marry into a family with more deceased members than living. She had already achieved financial security—for herself and for her parents—although marrying into such wealth would bring her security to a new level, which means a great deal to her. To test the waters, Ivy agreed to accompany the man asking for her hand on a holiday to the Maldives.

The journalist James Palmer once brilliantly referred to mistresses as "the Robin Hoods of the bedroom." By this, he meant that they took from the wealthy to give to the poor—the "poor," in this case, being themselves, but also their families. Likewise, in *Red Lights: The Lives of Sex Workers in Postsocialist China*, Harvard scholar Tiantian Zheng went undercover as a karaoke hostess in the Chinese province of Dalian, conveying to her readers a very unique interpretation of the entertainment and sex trade in China. All of her hostess colleagues at the karaoke bar were women from underprivileged backgrounds who through a combination of sex work and more regular companionship (being a mistress of sorts) had become the economic motors of their families. They'd use the tips and gifts they received from male clients to pay for medicine, clothing, housing, or whatever else their families needed. "A woman's virtue in China comes not from how pure she is, but how filial she is," goes an old Chinese saying. In the case of many mistresses, I was starting to think it might just be true.

The second time I went to Maxim's—the French restaurant that doubles as one of China's premiere destinations for extravagant marriage proposals—was with Ivy. As we sat down, she asked me to take a subtle survey of the people sitting around us. I did, and noticed a pattern: there were many young, attractive Chinese women. Some were sitting in small klatches, others with older women—their mothers, perhaps? There was even a woman in the corner with a teenage girl clearly too old to be her daughter, but perhaps a little sister. Ivy confirmed what I suspected: most of these women were mistresses.

I run this discovery by one of the restaurant's managers, Corentin Daquin, who happens to be a friend. *"Ah oui bien sûr,"* he says. "In addition to being famous for our marriage proposals, we are famous for our mistresses."

My conversation with Daquin also reflects many of the things I'd previously discussed with Dr. X. Namely, that mistresses were not foolhardy faineants but savvy, sultry movers and shakers who have expertly hornswoggled their men into getting exactly what they need from them. "Many of them are supporting their parents—the older women you see with them are their mothers, the younger ones, their little sisters—entire families profit from their relationships," Daquin explained.

He mentioned that many of the women who frequented the restaurant were the mistresses of its shareholders. "They all drive luxury cars and treat the restaurant as if it's theirs," he says. "But they're always extremely polite and on point. I know many of them by name—they make their own reservations and also call on behalf of their gentlemen. I rarely hear from any wives."

Dirty Deeds

Following a reporting trip to India, I had lunch with a Chinese friend named Elliott. As a well-traveled and ambitious adviser at an international private equity firm in Beijing, he was always an excellent source of insight into China's booming e-commerce market. Halfway into our meal, we began chatting about Indra Nooyi, the CEO of Pepsi. I mentioned that I had recently read an interview with her describing the day she found out that she had been made CEO of an American multinational. As she pulled into her garage around ten p.m. after a long day at work, her mother asked her to go back out and buy some milk. Why hadn't her mother asked her son-in-law, who had been home since eight p.m. to get it? He was tired. One of the hired help? She had forgotten to ask. So instead, Indra went out for milk and when she got home, banged the carton down on the counter as she told her mother the big news of her promotion. "You might be president of PepsiCo. You might be on the board of directors," responded her mom. "But when you enter this house, you're the wife, you're the daughter, you're the daughter-in-law, you're the mother. You're all of that. Nobody else can take that place. So leave that damned crown in the garage."

Curious to get a Chinese man's take on this situation, I asked Elliott what he thought. "In China we would not have that problem," he said very matter-of-factly. "Because that woman would already be divorced."

He then rattled off a list of his former female bosses who were all divorced, single moms working deliriously long hours in the highest stratospheres of finance. "They often bring their children into the office," he said. He seemed unfazed and shrugged as if to say that this was the will of the universe.

In 2016, Beijing surpassed New York to become the billionaire capital of the world. This shift happened thanks in no small part to China's rising number of self-made female billionaires, which today account for more than two-thirds or 93 of the 124 self-made female billionaires on the planet. True to Elliott's observations, a fair share—though not all—of China's wealthiest women are divorced, but perhaps more interestingly, their average age hovers around forty-six, which means they were born in the thick of the Cultural Revolution. While it's impossible to say how much the more gender-neutral circumstances of their youth contributed to their eventual success, it's worth noting that more than half of China's self-made women billionaires have made their fortunes in the traditionally male-dominated fields of real estate, finance, and manufacturing.

Beyond what Chinese women have been able to earn on their own, it's equally important to consider that more women in China are inheriting their family's wealth. One of the most prominent cases of a female heir inheriting a huge sum of family wealth is Yang Huiyan, the vice chairwoman and largest share-holder of property developer Country Garden Holdings. When she was twenty-five, her father, Yang Guoqiang—a rice farmer and part-time bricklayer who made his fortune by buying up and developing vacant plots of land in his native southern province of Guangdong—transferred 70 percent of the company to his daughter. This was in 2007, shortly before the company's IPO on the Hong Kong Stock Exchange. Now in her mid-thirties and worth nearly $8 billion, Huiyan is the youngest female billionaire in the world and the richest woman in Asia.

Since middle school, Guoqiang had been grooming Huiyan—the second of his three daughters—to play a key role in the family business. She started participating in board meetings at an early age, and got a degree in marketing and logistics at Ohio State University. When she returned to China, Huiyan worked as the purchasing manager of her father's company before being appointed executive director a year later.

Curiously, Huiyan married at age twenty-four, or just one year before she inherited her father's fortune. Some believe this is because Huiyan's father did not want to risk his daughter marrying a man who would hijack the family's fortune or muscle his daughter out of her role at the helm of it—think Matthew Crawley in *Downton Abbey*. To minimize this risk, Huiyan's husband, Chen Chong, is said to have been carefully chosen. The pair met on a blind date. He held a PhD from China's elite Tsinghua University, and like Huiyan, had also completed his undergraduate degree in the United States. The son of a senior official from a northeastern province, his pedigree was considered to be a good match for Huiyan's money. His more academic proclivities suggested that he would be less likely to interfere with the family business, and the fact that he had been educated at China's top university would bring added prestige to Huiyan, who despite now being well educated and supremely wealthy, was born into a family of farmers.

The logic used to justify the socioeconomic compatibility of Huiyan and her husband is telling of a shifting tide on the Chinese marriage market. Although in order to be considered marriageable, Chinese men are largely still expected to own a car, a home, and have a sizable amount of savings, Chinese women—either through inheritance or their own hustle—are increasingly in possession of these three things too. The result is what economists Xiaobo Zhang and Shang Jin-Wei have referred to as a "tournament effect," or the idea that just as men must strive to attain conspicuous signs of wealth in order to more favorably position themselves in the marriage market, women, by doing the same, can increase their chances of marrying into wealth greater than their own.

Sometimes, however, this system backfires. A friend told me about her cousin Bing—a young woman from a well-to-do family in Beijing, who was planning to marry a man with whom she was very much in love. He was well off and owned property in Beijing, though his apartment paled in size to the one owned by her family. Knowing this might displease him, Bing didn't tell him about her large apartment until just a few days before the wedding. The news of it made him very upset. He wasn't so bothered that she held more impressive assets than he did, but he knew his family would be offended. His parents initially threatened to rescind their blessing on the wedding, but a crafty last-minute solution was devised. After the marriage, the newlyweds moved into Bing's apartment and put her husband's up for rent. All rent collected from the apartment was then directly paid to Bing's parents, in an attempt to reinforce that their son was not living off of his bride.

In yet another property-induced wedding permutation, things didn't end so well. Yue, a research contact, told me about a couple in the second-tier city of Wuhan who had met, fallen in love, and decided to marry. They proceeded to have their wedding pictures taken and began to plan their wedding ceremony before arranging for their parents to meet.

"We don't have 'engagements' in China," Yue explained. "For us, parents from either side meeting to discuss the terms of the marriage symbolizes the official engagement." She stressed the importance of the parents coming to an agreement for the marriage to happen.

In this case, because the boy was from a significantly more affluent class than the girl, negotiations got off to a rocky start. His family was offering to provide the new couple with a home, but insisted, as seems to be common practice in China, that their son's name be the only one to appear on the deed. Were this just a formality meant to reiterate the son's official position as "provider," the parents of the girl likely would have acquiesced. This requirement by the boy's family, however, had much larger implications.

A 2011 amendment states that in the event of a divorce, the marital home belongs exclusively to the person whose name is on the deed. This change was made because the Chinese government decided that too many parents who had sunk their life's savings into a home for their male offspring were losing out when that son later divorced and his former wife received half of the value of the house. While it is reasonable that controls be imposed to prevent the quick acquisition of property through an opportunistic marriage, this amendment heavily disfavors a partner who may have helped with the finances on a marital abode, but whose name isn't on the deed. As is still common in China, a home is most often registered in the man's name, regardless of who is paying for it. That means men end up owning a home that they may have only partially paid for, leaving their ex-wives significantly shortchanged.

In this case, the home already belonged to the boy's family, so the girl wouldn't have had to contribute monetarily to it, but her parents still wanted her name to be on the deed, as a protective measure. They thought it fair that she be considered an equal beneficiary of the marriage, and if the couple were to divorce, they didn't want her to be left high and dry.

The boy's parents responded by saying that the girl's family was "asking for too much," and called off the wedding.

To understand the degree to which property ownership can influence Chinese marriages, it's worth noting that on March 1, 2013, the Chinese State Council announced that local governments should strictly enforce a rule ordering homeowners to pay a new 20 percent tax on the profits from the sales of a secondary home. As housing administration bureaus were swamped by people hoping to put their secondary properties on the market before the new rules took effect, marriage registration centers in Shanghai and other big cities across China saw a spike in divorce filings. In Beijing alone, the divorce rate increased by more than 40 percent in the first three quarters of 2013, as compared to the same time period the year before. Several foreign and local media reports indicated that the sudden uptick in divorces was the result of couples with a secondary home rushing to separate—at least on paper—so that they could claim owning only one home and sell their secondary properties without paying the tax. Most couples interviewed expressed a desire to remarry after the sale of their second home, though others just used the excuse of the legislation as a convenient means of parting ways.

Just how much of an economic impact the lust for property has had on the Chinese economy is impossible to put a precise number on, though it can be safely assumed that it has added some pressure to what has since become a whopping real-estate bubble.

"Whenever you have a system with very rapid expansion in credit and very low interest rates, you get bubbles," explains Mike Pettis, senior fellow at the Carnegie Endowment and professor of finance at Peking University. "And that's exactly what happened in China." Pettis is very careful to point out that the bubble results not so much from the behavior of profit-hungry speculators, but from the nature of the purchases themselves, which has been largely speculative. "People who buy an apartment now because they expect they will need it in five or six years, but won't be able to afford it then, are behaving just like speculators—they are buying early, assuming that prices will go up in the future," he says. "And by buying early, they're pushing prices up; it's self-reinforcing."

But before being able to speculate what the implications of this bubble may be on the marriage market, it's important to understand how things got this way.

In 1998, when its private real-estate market was born, China was still at the top of its economic game. Exports were booming, and the economy was growing enough to sustain and employ the millions of migrants who were making their way from rural areas to big cities. Things remained rosy until roughly 2009, when the growth from China's economy stopped being "real" growth. It was right about this time that the Chinese government injected a massive amount of credit into the economy. Rounding out at near US $5 trillion, this credit was made available through state-backed banks in the form of loans, and siphoned off largely to individuals with government connections, who later used those loans to invest in various projects. Yet since the loans were so easily and cheaply obtained, not all of the projects were very judiciously thought out and have since resulted in feckless investments—infrastructure projects, especially—that have rather misleadingly not added to the growth of the Chinese economy.

Shopping malls are a case in point. They're all over major Chinese cities, and while they may glitter and sparkle and serve as the retail embodiment of the marvels of Chinese buying power, many of them are ghoulishly empty. In some cases, retailers are even offered space, rent-free, in order to draw in customers. While on paper, the act of constructing a shopping mall will be interpreted as a contribution to economic growth, it can only be considered "real" growth if the total economic value generated by the mall's construction exceeds its total building cost. When this doesn't happen, these so-called economy driving "investments" end up as a bank loan that will likely never be repaid.

Who is picking up the tab for these investment flubs? The same people who are paying top dollar for housing: Chinese consumers. Pettis explains that the losses from bad investments are just beginning to be seen, because they were originally hidden in loans. "For a very long time, many companies that should have gone bankrupt, never did," he says. "They had government connections, so they could keep rolling over the loans. Losses grew, but they were hidden in the loans."

Though Chinese banks, as the lenders to the faulty investors, should be the ones shouldering the losses for any loans that their borrowers can't pay back, they compensate for these losses by passing along the debt to Chinese households. The banks pay extremely low interest on the savings accounts of Chinese households and the banks can later reissue these household savings as loans to investors at a very favorable rate—one that absorbs what they can't pay back. Furthermore, by requiring Chinese households to pay very high interest rates on personal loans, banks can use the money from the interest to cover other business losses.

The bottom line: until three years ago when deposit rates were finally liberalized, the savings that Chinese households had in the bank were worth less every year. The less money the households have, the less they're able to consume. The less they're able to consume, the less the economy can depend on consumption for economic growth, and the more it must continue to depend on investments based on government-issued credit, which have a habit of not always creating positive growth.

While there are of signs of change on the horizon and Chinese premier Li Keqiang appears committed to reducing the state's role in funding irresponsible investments, at least for the time being, developers are continuing to build, and real-estate prices are continuing to rise—making it hard on single men. They are still expected to own a home and/or a car before marriage, but are generally not able to afford either. They end up relying on their parents for help, and whenever economically able, their parents seem to aid them.

In exchange, however, parents retain a great deal of decision-making power over their son's bride and are not much concerned about the issue of romance. They put a higher emphasis on the honor and assets that the marriage will bring to the family, especially since China's lack of a social safety net makes Chinese children—many of them only children—the nest eggs of their parents. That works out to two young people supporting four elderly people, which given low salaries and high inflation, is no small order. Yet since parents must save, compete, and make huge economic sacrifices to secure the futures of their children, it is expected that the children will also marry in a way that is conducive to ensuring the social, financial, and emotional well-being of their parents in their golden years.

Only then may the couple begin to live happily ever after.

10

EAST MEETS WEST

兔子不吃窝边草

Rabbits don't eat the grass that surrounds them.

—CHINESE PROVERB

June's Korean crush had trained at a culinary school, and so for their first date, he proposed that she go to his apartment for a cooking lesson one Saturday afternoon. When she arrived, she was dazzled to find a spotless kitchen equipped with a meticulously laid-out arrangement of chopping boards, cooking utensils, and assorted bowls filled with different seasonings. "I forgot the mushrooms!" he said as soon as they began cooking. "I'll have to run down to the store—don't move."

It dawned on June that she knew very little about the man on whose counter loomed a colossal and seemingly very sharp meat cleaver. This, she thought, was her chance to learn more about him. In the spirit of her never-ending quest for information, she decided to do a quick sweep of his apartment. She began in his bedroom. Closet number one revealed a fleet of suits, all starched to perfection. Ties, all suspended on a wooden rack, were arranged methodically, from cool tones to warm ones. Shoes were all lined up neatly and waxed to resplendence—how could this be? Did this guy even have foot odor? She put her nose to a beige leather loafer. It smelled of sandalwood! A tennis shoe might prove more incriminating? She plucked one out from the back of his closet—clearly, this was the place athlete's foot went to die.

While June's foray into a strange man's closet might seem extreme, it's worth keeping in mind that China's dating culture is still in its nascent stages. Whereas in the United States, the invention of the automobile in the 1900s helped prompt the creation of a dating culture—as opposed to a culture of courtship in which a gentleman would come "calling" to a girl's home and meet with her, often in the company of her parents—a similar shift didn't occur in China until the mainstream use of the bicycle in the 1950s. On two wheels, young couples were able to escape the eyes and influence of their elders, although the fully fledged soda-pop shop, movie theater, and dance-hall variety of dating culture that revolutionized the way young men and women socialized in the States has yet to emerge. As a result, singles have few social cues on how to become acquainted with a prospective partner.

Therefore, with little knowledge of how else she might get to know more about the Korean man who had seemingly overtaken her nucleus accumbens—the part of the brain associated with pleasure, addiction, and reward—June pulled open the top drawer of his desk. An identity card—good picture, but was he only twenty-eight? She would have never guessed. A small stack of pages that looked like a medical report was lying just under it in a clear plastic folder. After spending a few moments trying to make out the Korean characters, she realized it was a scalp report. All of the minerals in his hair appeared to be in balance.

In the bathroom, June discovered a bounty of BB creams. Toners, detoxifiers, moisturizers, serums, and sunblock were all stacked neatly on the counter. She was getting concerned that her fastidious Korean friend might be back soon, so she decided to retreat to the kitchen. Wait, what was that on his bed? A cell phone! It couldn't hurt to have a look, just to ensure he didn't have a wife and kids back in Seoul. No password protection, but everything on it was in Korean. Pictures? A quick scan revealed nothing of note.

Back in the kitchen, June popped open the fridge to make it seem like she was trying to be productive while he was away. More creams and serums! These were all in smaller receptacles—some of them even came with eyedroppers. She was beginning to think this man was too metrosexual for her, until he appeared back at the apartment with a heady bag of mushrooms.

"I was so entranced watching him cook," she said, "I forgot all about the frightening order of his shoe collection or the crazy cosmetic rituals his must perform every morning to get himself looking as good as he does."

June was smitten. She reported having "an enchanting afternoon," and was now waiting anxiously by her phone to find out when she might be able to see him again.

Cupid Strikes

After several intense months of work, Christy was also keen to get back onto the dating scene. She'd recently acquired a new celebrity client and had been traveling considerably between Beijing and Nanjing, where this client—a Chinese actress—had been filming a movie. Some of Christy's colleagues had offered to introduce her to bachelors, but none of the dates she'd had with them left her feeling like she wanted a second. The men she met looked good on paper, but for the most part, the dates felt more like business meetings than anything that might turn romantic. "When would you be ready to have a child?" asked one of her blind dates, approximately three minutes after they met in person for the first time. Over the course of their meal, he outlined his desired marriage timeline to her—he planned to wed within six months at the latest. He also described in excruciating detail how he was able to purchase an apartment within the Third Ring Road of Beijing, making sure to emphasize that his address was considered among the city's prime real-estate locations. When they were done eating, he proposed that she accompany him back to his new home. Taken aback by his suggestion, Christy recalls shooting him a look of incredulity. "I'd like to show you the nursery my parents have helped me prepare," he said. "We've even ordered a supply of milk powder from Australia," he added. (Following a toxic baby milk scandal in China in 2009 that killed six babies and caused 330,000 to become seriously ill, imported powders have become the gold standard.) "My parents are looking forward to having a baby to care for and to ensuring that their grandchild will have the very best of everything."

By the time her date said these words, Christy's face had turned as white as the milk powder. She recalls excusing herself from the table, thanking her date for the dinner, and briskly exiting the restaurant. Her experience that evening reminded her of a cautionary tale she'd once heard from a former colleague who had gotten married under pressure to a man she didn't know very well. She became pregnant immediately after their wedding, and upon giving birth, her in-laws seized the spare bedroom. Her mother-in-law made her *zuo yuezi*, or "sit the month," an age-old Chinese tradition. Still widely practiced across China, Taiwan, and Hong Kong, the logic behind *yuezi* is that the female body is fragile after giving birth and requires special care, rest, and nutrition. Traditionally, mothers-in-law are tasked with enforcing the rules of *yuezi*, which in their most draconian form require that postpartum moms refrain from bathing, washing their hair, brushing their teeth, or going outdoors for a period of thirty days. Instead, they must stay in bed, covered from head to toe—socks and a hat, regardless of the season—and eat six traditional meals a day. These meals consist primarily of eggs, soup, pork trotters (pig's feet), chicken, and carp. The dishes must be warm (forget ice cream), cooked (not even raw fruit), and prepared without salt.

It's becoming increasingly common to slightly modernize the rules of *yuezi*—some women, for example, "cheat" and brush their teeth with a special cotton brush or shower after a week instead of thirty days. However, Christy's former colleague explained that her mother-in-law was fierce in enforcing the most traditional formula of *yuezi*. Her mother-in-law also took full responsibility for the newborn baby—a boy—and had him sleep on a hard pillow so that his still malleable head would be flat in the back; something considered aesthetically pleasing by certain elders in China. Although the mother of the child fought repeatedly to allow her baby to develop as nature intended, her efforts were futile. Before long, the back of her son's cranium took on the shape of a cheese grater.

Deciding it might be wise to broaden her search to include Western men, Christy created an account on OkCupid, a popular online dating portal used mainly in the United States, but available internationally. In China, the website features a mix of Chinese and foreign users, including a fair share of expats living in big cities like Beijing or Shanghai. Christy candidly filled out the profile and didn't even lie about her age, which I thought was a nice touch. She uploaded a glamorous picture of herself at a PR event, and another at the beach, with most of her body submerged in the ocean.

Within a few minutes of browsing the site, she spotted a few men she thought might be interesting to meet. She also came across the husband of an acquaintance of hers, who appeared to be using the site to have affairs.

"I just want someone kind, honest, and with a bit of taste," she said. "I feel like most of the Chinese men I meet are lacking in contact with the world. They're just looking to tick boxes and don't realize that a relationship is much more than that."

As Christy continued to try her hand at online dating, Zhang Mei was having a very out-of-character offline experience.

It had been several weeks since I'd last seen her. Once my classes at the school where she worked had ended, I'd taken her on as my private tutor. We'd meet when our schedules allowed us to, but it had been hard to book a lesson in the early spring. It wasn't until we finally met that I fully understood why: my sensible, nose-to-the-grindstone Chinese teacher had been struck by Cupid's arrow.

Naturally, she had to make a lesson out of it.

"There are three stages to falling in love," she explained. "The first is *you hao gan*, or 'to have a good feeling.' The second is *xi huan*, or 'to like,' and the third is *ai*, or 'love.'"

"And where are you on that scale?" I asked her. She scowled back in her playful way, much like she did when I got my tones wrong or forgot a stroke when writing characters. She then took my pen and in my notebook, drew a little tiny line between *xi huan* (like) and *ai* (love).

I probably knew more about Zhang Mei's marriage pressures than anyone around her. For more than two years, I'd heard her tell me about the different ultimatums she'd been receiving from her family to return home and get married. I knew how small her hometown was, and how much she struggled to see herself moving back to it. Although she knew that her parents thought they were acting in her best interest and she didn't want to seem ungrateful, or worse—un-filial—the type of life they envisioned for her was very unlike the one she'd hoped for. "*Wo bu xiang zi ji*," or "I don't think of myself," she would always say. I had long sensed that despite all of her efforts to buy herself a bit more time, she would eventually do exactly what her family expected of her. She didn't seem to have many other options.

After the holiday boyfriend bust, Zhang Mei's mother had offered to come to Beijing and help her look for apartments. If she couldn't find anything suitable, the plan was to have her move back to Harbin by the start of the next teaching semester, when there would be new job openings at a school near her childhood home.

Zhang Mei had agreed with her parents to abide by this plan, until a chance teaching assignment threw everything out of order.

"He's my student," she told me. "He's Japanese."

Zhang Mei explained that she had fallen for him quite organically. Though she'd had many Japanese students before, she never had any particular affinity for them beyond the occasional teen pop star, who was much too young for her anyway. I asked her what made this man so different. "He doesn't smoke. Eighty-five percent of the Asian men my age do; it was so pleasant to meet one who doesn't!" was the first thing she blurted out.

"He's not even good-looking," she said. "But he's kind."

She explained that after class, they'd often go for lunch together. He'd introduced her to spaghetti and lasagna—dishes she'd since grown to love—and to various different Japanese specialties. "When there were certain vegetables in my noodles that

I didn't like" (Zhang Mei despises zucchini), "he'd eat them off my plate," she said.

After lunch, Zhang Mei explained they would sometimes go shopping. "He loves to golf, so I'd go to golf shops with him. He'd make me try on funny hats and shoes, and taught me about different clubs."

As she was sharing these anecdotes, Zhang Mei was trying to deny that she had any special feelings for this Japanese student of hers, but I could practically see the dopamine pulsating through her brain.

"It's hard not to think about him," she eventually admitted. "But I know I shouldn't—we have no future. He's just returned to Japan."

I wanted to get her on the first plane to Tokyo, but a few things needed to be addressed before doing something so irrational. This man's work contract in Beijing was up, and he had no plans to be back in China in the immediate future. He'd tried to have a serious conversation with her about what they were to each other, but Zhang Mei cut him short, as she felt it inappropriate to pursue a relationship with a student. Now she was no longer his teacher— and more important, she was having regrets about not having tried to take things further.

Zhang Mei has never been out of China. She has a passport because she was supposed to go on holiday to South Korea with some of her colleagues, but their plans fell through. Traveling abroad is something that has been on her wish list for years. She had promised herself she would cross a border before getting married, just in case she ended up wed to a man who wasn't much of a globetrotter. She had offers from her job to oversee the opening of new Chinese schools in Thailand and Indonesia, but she'd turned them down because she was scared to go so far on her own. This time, however, she was seriously considering a solo trip to Japan.

Getting visas to travel abroad is often difficult for the Chinese. I know many who have obtained foreign passports (by investing money abroad, for example) in part so that they can travel more freely. Zhang Mei holds only a Chinese passport, however, so as part of the approval process for her visa, she had to show proof of having at least 200,000 RMB ($30,000) in the bank. Zhang Mei didn't have this much money saved.

"I've thought about it, and have decided to ask my parents," she said. "They know that traveling is something I've always wanted to do before getting married, and I think they will support me. This is something I have to do—for myself, and for the chance to be with someone who I think I will be happy with. Even if nothing comes of it, I must know that I at least tried."

Zhang Mei's resolve was admirable. I knew that her courage was being fueled by a rush of emotions, and yet her ability to reason with such a level head and prepare for disappointment was impressive. "If nothing comes of my relationship, I will use the 200,000 RMB from the visa as a down payment on a house in Harbin."

Nearly two years before she had fallen for this Japanese man, Zhang Mei had told me a story about her older sister, Chen. She'd gotten married at twenty-two to her high school sweetheart, but made an agreement with her husband that they wouldn't have children for at least five years. If they got to that point in their lives and she still had no strong desire to be a mother, they agreed that they'd have no children at all. Her husband had no objections, and so Chen accepted to marry him on these terms.

Shortly after their marriage, her husband's grandmother was diagnosed with cancer. The prognosis was grim, and despite being a fighter, she could sense the end was near. As a dying wish, she expressed her desire for a grandson.

Chen didn't know how to handle this request. She had resolutely expressed her desire to remain childless for at least the first five years of her marriage, and not even two had passed. Chen's mother-in-law, who wanted nothing more than to please her dying mother, begged Chen to change her mind. She was relentless. After a few months, she began to insist, and then eventually came up with a plan. "You have the baby, and then just hand it over to me. We'll pay for everything and take care of it—you won't have to do a thing after giving birth." Feeling hopelessly cornered, Chen and her husband conceded. Their child—a baby girl—was born three months after her great-grandmother passed away. Today, that little girl, Pei, is eight years old. She's been raised almost exclusively by her maternal and paternal grandmothers, and her parents, after living in separate cities for several years, are now getting a divorce.

So many of Pei's classmates live with their grandparents—because their parents are away working in bigger cities—that she doesn't feel any different for it. What she does seem to be keenly aware of, however, is that little girls are not valued in the same way as little boys.

It's often said in China that young children can look at the belly of a pregnant woman and accurately predict the sex of the baby inside. There is, of course, no empirical evidence that they can, but that doesn't seem to deter anyone from asking them to try. Pei was once asked to do this when she was four years old, and after having a good long look at her auntie's round tummy, she remained silent for a few moments. Upon further prompting, she said that there was a baby boy inside. Several weeks later when the child was born, it was a girl. When they went to see the baby, Pei quietly confided to her grandmother that she knew the baby would be a girl all along. "Then why did you say boy?" asked her grandmother. "Because I thought Auntie would be upset if she knew she was having a girl."

That there are girls as young as four years old in China who already understand that they're not as desired as boys came as a very disheartening discovery to me. I keep in mind Pei's awareness of gender "differences" at such a young age and the forced circumstances of her birth when trying to understand Zhang Mei's situation. Her future is not something she gets to decide entirely on her own. Marriages are more like stockholder meetings over the course of which many discordant voices lobby for their desired outcomes. I fully supported her determination to go to Japan, but understood everything she had tying her back to Harbin.

Changing Course

As the days went by, Yanyan, my pregnant colleague with the predilection for online shopping, grew rounder. Though she dutifully ate her morning egg and was even adding special proteins to her soy milk, she began to look and feel weary. She was nearly three months pregnant and still hadn't told her family, the majority of her friends, or even our employer. Work was busier than ever before, and these stressors were taking a toll on her.

Then one week, she was absent for three days. She texted to let me know that some complications had required her to spend time in the hospital, but that she was back home and OK. I saw her again at the office for a few weeks, eating her daily egg and starting to dress in baggier clothes to camouflage her burgeoning bump. She seemed to be easing into pregnancy until the beginning of May, when she didn't come to the office at all. I had no news, and couldn't get in touch with her. It was only after the fact that I learned there had been a fatal formation of the baby's heart.

Yanyan was devastated. She had done so much to prepare for the arrival of this little creature, and was so eager to swaddle him (or her) in her arms. Doctors told her that she could try again, but the very fact that'd she'd already lost one baby was making her question her fertility. Another thing she was questioning was her impending marriage. Though her husband-to-be had been by her side throughout the entire pregnancy, he didn't seem very affected by the loss of their baby.

"Seeing him so untouched after losing something that meant so much to me made me question our compatibility," she later told me. "Once the baby was gone, it's like there was nothing holding us together."

She called her wedding off.

After her miscarriage, Yanyan quit her job and went back to her hometown for three months. Returning to Beijing in September, she enrolled in a master's program and began working part-time at a university. She got an edgy new haircut, started wearing more youthful clothing—purchased on Taobao, of course—and when we finally arranged a time to meet up, I was delighted to see her looking so energized. "I am leftover again," she said with a shrug and a smile. "But it was the better choice for me."

11

BAMBOO CEILINGS

Men are looking for women that have ceased to exist and
women are looking for men that have yet to exist.

—ALBERT ESTEVE, DIRECTOR, CENTRE D'ESTUDIS DEMOGRÀFICS

T hough the bulk of these pages have been focused on China, it would be wrong to pretend that the world's most populous nation is the only one with a unique set of cultural, political, and social variables that color the nature of marriage and relationships. More foolhardy yet would be to assume that China is the only place on the planet where women are reorganizing the timetables of their early adult years, choosing instead to get their educations and careers further under way before making legally binding commitments or having babies.

The truth is, a similar shift has been happening across Asia for decades, and in much higher proportions.

In Japan, unmarried women over twenty-five used to be known as "Christmas cakes," in reference to the idea that much like a holiday sweet that loses its appeal after the twenty-fifth of December, a woman loses her appeal after her twenty-fifth birthday. It was replaced in 2003 by the label *make-inu*, which means "defeated dogs," though both expressions have now been substituted in favor of the more popular "New Year's noodles." This term gives women six more years—one for each day after Christmas—before they are categorized as having transgressed their sell-by dates.

If current statistics are any indication, Japan might soon be a nation of noodles. Its proportion of unmarried women has steadily climbed from the 1970s—when fewer than 20 percent of women between the ages of twenty-five and twenty-nine remained single—right up until today, when over 65 percent of Japanese women under thirty have never married. Part of this increase can be explained by a delay in the age of marriage, but for the most part, the numbers represent a shift toward women not getting married at all. At age thirty-five, nearly 35 percent of Japanese women remain unmarried, as opposed to 7 percent in 1970. In a country where fewer than 2 percent of babies are born out of wedlock, these numbers help explain why Japan has one of the lowest fertility rates in the world.

To get a better sense of the economic context under which Japan's marriage rates decreased, it's worth noting that between 1965 and 1980, Japan was considered an "economic miracle." Its nominal GDP soared from $91 billion to a record $1.065 trillion, temporarily turning it into the second largest economy in the world, after the United States. By the mid-'80s, however, Japan became the site of dangerously inflated real-estate prices, over-valued stocks, and unbridled credit expansion, all of which contributed to an asset price bubble that burst in 1992. Since the late '90s, GDP growth has been more or less stuck at under 2 percent and population growth has slowed to the extent that there are now more adult diapers sold in Japan than baby ones. UN data indicate that Japan's current population of 127 million will shrink to 83 million by 2100, and that by then, 35 percent of its population will be over age sixty-five. Its ratio of working-age persons to retirees has already begun to drop—reducing the amount of taxes available to fund the country's social safety net—and there are no signs that the fertility rate will rebound anytime soon. For a country that currently has debt equivalent to two times the size of its economy, this is no small matter.

Stressed by Japan's dwindling population, in a 2007 speech, the former Japanese minister of health, Hakuo Yanagisawa, encouraged his country's "birth-giving machines" to "do their best" to revive the fertility rate. More recently, several male lawmakers in the Tokyo Metropolitan Assembly heckled a Japanese female politician—and there aren't many of those to begin with—as she made a presentation about maternity leave and infertility. "Can't you have babies?" and "Hurry up and get married!" were among the comments directed at her.

Other ill-fated attempts at boosting the fertility rate include the local official in Japan's Aichi prefecture, who proposed that secretly punctured condoms be distributed to young married couples (this is perhaps why more women are needed in government?), and the sudden rise—but limited success of—"konkatsu." Despite sounding confusingly similar to tonkatsu—Japan's signature, panko-covered, deep-fried pork cutlets—konkatsu means "marriage hunting." Coined by Japanese sociologist Masahiro Yamada—who is also responsible for the term "parasite single," which describes singles who live with their parents so they have more disposable income to spend on themselves—konkatsu became a buzzword in 2008. Around this time, konkatsu-related activities were offered everywhere from bars (singles' nights) to temples (special tea services for singles seeking good luck in marriage). As reported in the Wall Street Journal, even The Hokkaido

Nippon-Ham Fighters, a Japanese professional baseball team, got in on the *konkatsu* craze by offering *"konkatsu* seats." Set up in the spirit of speed dating, these seats allowed men and women to rotate between innings so that they could meet several new people throughout the course of a game.

On one level, *konkatsu* helped to fill the void left by employers, which in years of greater economic prosperity were known for funding in-house matchmaking events and trips that would help their unmarried employees partner off with their colleagues. While the idea of a company that encourages its staff members to marry one another may sound like a huge liability—if not a corporate disaster—in Japan, things work a bit differently. Women are largely employed in clerical work, so the "wives" of the newly formed work couples would often quit and become homemakers, thereby leaving space for a fresh crop of nubile secretaries to be hired and married off to the remaining single men at the company.

This culture started to change in the 1990s, when Japan entered its first economic recession. Arguably, the same one it is still facing today. According to Akiko Yoshida, associate professor of sociology at the University of Wisconsin–Whitewater, the recession forced companies to cut back on extracurricular activities for their employees, which meant that opportunities to meet a spouse at work decreased considerably. Office romances could still blossom without company intervention, of course, but given the often segregated nature of employment in Japan—men do the serious work in one place, women do the clerical work in another office or part of the office—there weren't too many chances for cross-pollination. Economic difficulties also meant that companies had hiring freezes, thereby reducing their numbers of eligible male employees. The hiring freezes were especially acute because at that time in Japan, most men were likely to work for the same company throughout their entire careers; once they were in the door, labor laws made it difficult to fire them. As a result, instead of terminating senior, more costly employees— who were more willing to retire later, given the economic uncertainty—firms stopped hiring young ones.

In cases where company-sponsored events failed to end in marriage, Japan's *miai* system—a traditional form of match-making by which singles are introduced through parents, rela-tives, or mediators (much like they are in China)—once served as another way to meet a potential mate. *Miai* has fallen out of popularity as couples now prefer "romantic" marriages to the one-dimensional "good on paper" matches, but even those are hard to come by.

"I hardly see single men [. . .] I wonder whether they really exist," said a forty-six-year-old participant in "No Chance for Romance: Corporate Culture, Gendered Work, and Increased Singlehood in Japan," a study conducted by Yoshida. The results are drawn from in-depth interviews conducted with forty women between the ages of twenty-five and forty-six; twenty-eight of them single, the rest married, but all living in or near Tokyo. The study, which is the basis of a recent book on the same topic, provides insight into how Japan's economy and, by extension, its work culture, have contributed to its bleak marriage and fer-tility rates.

The demands of life as a salaryman in Japan are well doc-umented. They include long, inflexible hours, late nights of drinking with colleagues to encourage office harmony, and a seniority-based system that requires extreme loyalty to one's company in exchange for promotion and lifetime job security. Because none of these professional demands make it easy to raise a family—and because Japan has the added quirk of frowning upon mothers who hire nannies or outsiders to look after their children—it is common for Japanese mothers to exit the workforce after giving birth. This is partially because there are some mothers who simply prefer not to work; the concept of *sanshoku hirune tsuki* ("three meals and a nap") and looking after the home is seen as an appealing alternative lifestyle to the demands of working in an office. "I want to get married because I sometimes feel like quitting my job," said Yuriko Akamatsu, a thirty-five-year-old office worker quoted in the *Wall Street Journal*. "Marriage is like permanent employment."

Although many of the married women in Yoshida's study expressed discontent with their marriages and some single women were turned off by negative stories told by their married friends, the majority of single women she interviewed wished to marry. In fact, popular media suggests that the biggest flight from marriage might not actually come from Japanese women, but from men. Japan seems to have a growing population of "herbivores"—*soshoku kei danshi*, or "grass-eating men" who have no interest in "flesh," or in getting married or finding a girlfriend. The term is also used to refer to men who have lost their "manliness," and according to a poll conducted by Lifenet, 75 percent of single Japanese men in their twenties and thirties label themselves this way.

While some scholars, including Yoshida, believe that the herbivore phenomenon is an overblown, media-induced attempt to create moral panic, there are nonetheless several wild theories that attempt to account for Japan's rise in herbivore men. These include Japanese philosopher Masahiro Morioka's idea that they are the product of Japan's postwar peace. According to Morioka, because Japan has not participated in any wars, men have lost the chance to become manly by being a soldier. Prolonged peace, argues Morioka, has caused Japanese men to become less aggressive, a characteristic that may have tragically spilled over into courtship practices. Another theory is that Japan's manga obsession has made Japanese men prefer fantasy women to real ones.

Manga and masculinity-creating warfare aside, the rise in the popularity of herbivores is most plausibly linked to the decline of the Japanese economy and a growing disillusionment with job opportunities. Young men have witnessed the decline of the salaryman (pronounced sa-ra-ri-man in Japan) and understand the extreme pressure associated with being the dominant (or sole) breadwinner in a society that no longer offers the jobs to make that feasible. According to an informal survey by Kaori Shoji, a journalist with the *Japan Times*, some common reasons that herbivore men don't actively pursue women is because it's "too much of an effort" or "they have no money" or simply, "it's tiring." Perhaps because Japan does not have a culture of *sajiao*—the strategically executed temper tantrum meant to pander to a man's ego that June once tried to master—its men may feel even more vulnerable in the face of their country's growing population of "carnivore" women. These "flesh-seeking" ladies are characterized by their more overt sexuality, their extroversion, and their willingness to make a first move.

Still, there are limits to the types of moves Japanese women can make, especially in the workforce. As reported by Emma Chanlett-Avery and Rebecca Nelson in "'Womenomics' in Japan: In Brief," a paper written for the Congressional Research Service, it's still common for Japanese companies to enforce a two-track hiring system; one for elite, specialized workers known as *sogoshoku*, and another for administrative workers, known as *ippanshoku*. Because worker longevity is highly prized and it is assumed that most women will leave the workforce after having children, few companies are willing to invest in hiring (and training) women for the elite track. This often means that even before having children, women are relegated to the OL or "office lady" career track, which has a huge impact on their career prospects. According to the latest figures available, less than 12 percent of Japan's elite hires are women. As a result of women leaving the workforce for marriage or pregnancy, Japan's female workforce participation resembles an M curve; women are not very present in the workforce between their late twenties and late forties, or during what are usually the most fruitful years of one's career.

Further complicating matters is the Japanese phenomenon of *matahara*, or "maternity harassment," which leads pregnant women to sometimes be bullied by their bosses or colleagues into resigning, as it is assumed they will have to take on extra work while a new mother is on leave. By law, Japan offers new parents up to a year of leave at partial (66 percent) pay, but the frequency of *matahara*—which is experienced by an estimated 1 in 4 Japanese women—suggests that more than a handful of employers are loath to grant it.

Considering the employment difficulties faced by women, it's not surprising that according to the World Economic Forum's *Global Gender Gap Report*, Japan's female employment rate is ranked eightieth out of 144 countries, just above Tajikistan and below Angola. This is already an improvement over past years, thanks to structural reforms mandated by Japan's prime minister, Shinzō Abe.

For perspective, it's worth keeping in mind that the prime minister belongs to his country's conservative Liberal Democratic Party (LDP) and was not always a proponent of reforms and policies that encourage the participation and advancement of women in the Japanese workforce. In fact, back in 2005 when a previous government was taking steps to promote greater equality in Japan, as reported in *The Economist*, Abe and fellow conservatives warned of the damage that could be done to Japan's culture and family values if women were treated more equally. (Imagine the bedlam!) One of the main concerns was that a higher population of working women would be detrimental to the country's already fledgling fertility rate, although it turns out that the exact opposite is true: across the globe, higher levels of female employment are almost always positively correlated with higher fertility.

"It may sound counterintuitive, but it's what the numbers show," said Kathy Matsui, the chief Japan strategist for Goldman Sachs Japan. "In most of the developed world, but also across Japan, higher percentages of employed women positively correlate with a higher birthrate."

Raised on a flower farm in Salinas, California, Matsui first traveled to Japan in 1986 on a Rotary scholarship and has worked in Tokyo ever since. In 1999, keen to stand out in a world dominated by male analysts, she penned what would become a seminal report: *Womenomics*. In it, Matsui argued that the increased workforce participation of women could help counter Japan's economic stagnation. At the time, only 50 percent of working-age Japanese women were employed, which Matsui likened to "running a marathon with one leg."

Matsui has since been credited with coining the term "womenomics"—a system she remains a strong proponent of today. She regularly produces new versions of the report, in which she tracks the country's progress and makes new recommendations for how to continue to enrich female workforce participation, not only by numbers but by the type of work performed. Matsui's work has also earned her the recognition of Prime Minister Abe, who has incorporated elements of it into his similarly titled "Abeonomics"—a set of economic policies based on the "three arrows" of fiscal stimulus, monetary easing, and structural reforms, which were rolled out in 2012.

Following Abe's realization that making it easier for Japanese women to work wouldn't send the country down a dark path of moral destruction, he made some good things happen. Thanks to a push to establish new targets for female workforce participation, the opening of new, desperately needed daycare and after-school care facilities, and a bid to allow more foreign housekeepers— Japan has a notoriously strict immigration policy—female workforce participation in Japan has improved. At 66 percent, it is now just a hair over that of the United States, though as Matsui is quick to add, Japanese women are more likely to be working in part-time, lower-paid positions than their US counterparts. "Still," she said, "for Japan, this is progress."

Matsui explained that the government has also encouraged greater transparency and target setting with regards to female workforce employment by encouraging companies with more than three hundred employees to disclose their numbers of women in positions of leadership. "Companies are not legally required to do this," notes Matsui, "but in a homogenous society like Japan, where there is high pressure to conform, it could work."

An antiquated tax law that discourages married women from fully participating in the workforce by offering a dependent exemption to anyone—usually a man—whose spouse does not earn more than $9,500 per year, has also been revised. Instead of 1.03 million yen, the threshold for claiming the exemption has been raised to 1.5 million yen, or almost $14,000. Although a nice gesture, it's a woefully inadequate move for a country with a very large and highly skilled population of women.

After Japan was defeated in World War II and became occupied by the Allied Forces, there was a shift from a feudal system that largely restricted women to the home, to a more modern system. As the country was demilitarized and democratized, women over the age of twenty were granted suffrage, and regulations preventing women from receiving higher education were removed. Starting in 1949, more than three hundred coeducational universities were established—or upgraded from being single-sex non-degree-granting institutions of higher learning—and two national women's universities were also minted in the cities of Tokyo and Nara. According to statistics from the Japanese Ministry of Education, between 1960 and 1980, the proportion of four-year female university students increased from 2.5 percent to 12.3 percent, and between 1990 and 2000, it more than doubled, from 15 percent to 31 percent. Today, 45.6 percent of Japanese women attend university, as compared with 54 percent of their male peers.

When attempting to make sense of these numbers, it's important to consider that in Japan, higher education for women isn't necessarily meant to lead to a high salary or a lofty career. "It's a bit like the US in the 1950s," explained Akiko Yoshida, the author of the study referenced earlier. "Education is a means to meet future middle-class husbands, or to get an 'Mrs. degree.'" She mentioned anecdotal cases of girls she knew of in the '80s who studied in prestigious two-year colleges, as this increased their chances of getting clerical jobs in Japan's best companies. Although they didn't take these jobs with the exclusive aim of meeting a desirable salaryman to marry—and Japanese parents don't explicitly push their daughters to become educated for the purpose of being considered more "wifely" (that is, capable of managing a home and helping to educate children)—this was considered the ideal trajectory for "smart" girls.

Although this culture is no longer as pronounced, the ideal of a homemaker wife still exists. My good friend Manya Koetse, a Sinologist and editor in chief of *What's on Weibo*—a highly recommended news website that reports the latest trends on the Chinese equivalent of the Twittersphere—went to high school in Japan in the early 2000s. She told me about her best friend, Kumiko—an English teacher who ended up marrying a man who lived in a town five hours away from her family. Kumiko had no friends or job in her husband's town, so she took up a cooking and home economics class that it seems many girls take when they get married. "It's unbelievable," said Manya. "Ten years ago, the girls I went to school with were smoking cigarettes and working as miniskirt-wearing drinking girls in Osaka bars, and now on Facebook and Instagram they're posting pictures of the perfect food they make their husbands." Making bento boxes for her husband (and children) is in fact such an important duty of the Japanese wife, it's also part of how some women communicate with their spouses. There are reports of *Shikaeshi Bento*, or "revenge lunchboxes" in which wives express their displeasure with their husbands through a creative culinary language. Some wives cut messages out of seaweed strips (アホ, the character for "idiot," for example) and delicately place them over a bed of rice, while others choose to punish their mates through less than palatable food combinations, such as a raw egg, a heaping serving of plain yellow corn (have fun eating that with chopsticks!) or an indigestion-inducing bento full of sour pickled plums known as *umeboshi*.

Given the persistence of traditional gender roles, it's no surprise that career-oriented women in Japan are often criticized for being *kawai-kunai* or "unfeminine," and face difficulties when searching for a partner. Many of them want to marry, reiterates

Yoshida, but for lack of exposure to the types of partners they seek—it's worth noting that Japanese men, in part due to their intense work schedules, are consistently ranked at the bottom of global indexes on how much husbands contribute to household chores—they remain single.

I mention Japan because in many ways, it serves as a cautionary tale for China. Like Japan, China passed through a period of being considered an "economic miracle" and is now entering a phase of slower growth, albeit as the result of different circumstances. After years of being the factory of the world, China is attempting to shift its economy away from dependence on heavy industry and cheap exports. This is because labor costs have risen in China, leading corporations to seek out more cost-effective options in countries like Vietnam, Cambodia, Laos, Myanmar, and Thailand, but also because Chinese leaders are keen for their country to make more sophisticated contributions to the global economy.

Accordingly, China has already begun its pivot toward a more knowledge-driven export model. But in order for it to succeed, it needs the support of its entire population. This was true during its boom years—when the push for urbanization moved millions of rural residents into more urban areas, where they took on the manufacturing jobs that became the key drivers of the country's economic growth—and it is even truer now because quality matters more than quantity. Economic growth is no longer strictly a numbers game; it's increasingly about talent, human capital, and productive, income-generating members of society with enough buying power to stimulate domestic consumption.

When evaluating who might be best positioned to help carry China forward, it becomes clear that the country's young, well-educated women are an indispensable part of its future. Channeling their full economic engagement—which includes allowing them to reach their educational and professional potential, without fear that either of these things will jeopardize their chances at marriage or doom them to a sorry life of singlehood—is not only a social imperative; it's an economic necessity.

Many of Japan's current economic and demographic woes can be traced back to its failure to fully engage its women in the formal economy. Even today, only 44 percent of women are employed in the full-time sector, according to numbers published by the Japanese Ministry of International Affairs and Communications. Research from Goldman Sachs indicates that if Japanese women were employed at a rate equal to that of their male peers, Japan's GDP could grow by 13 percent, thereby significantly lessening the pressure imposed by a shrinking population. But the story doesn't end here.

In South Korea, a never-married woman in her thirties or older who has received at least a four-year college education, has her own career, and earns a higher than average yearly income, is known as a "Gold Miss." While this term is softer on the ears than "leftover woman" or "New Year's noodles," it represents an equally significant population of Korean women who have not tied the knot. While many of their reasons for remaining single overlap with those of Chinese and Japanese women—increased access to education, the lack of a desire to forego careers and become homemakers—the consequences of their decision to remain unmarried are also the same.

Like Japan, Korea is on the verge of a demographic crisis. By 2026, 10.7 million Koreans—or more than 20 percent of the population—will be sixty-five or older. As is true in Japan, an increasingly smaller workforce is being squeezed to support a growing elderly population, which, as the result of advances in health care, is also enjoying greater longevity and therefore requiring resources for a longer period of time. Meanwhile, Korea's population has just begun to shrink, and according to a highly futuristic simulation commissioned by the National Assembly in Seoul, Koreans risk becoming extinct by the year 2750. The country's economic boom years—which occurred in the 1970s through the '90s, less than a decade behind Japan's—are over, GDP growth is hovering around a lackluster 2.5 percent, and with few other options for keeping the population ticking, Korea's government is desperate for its people to make some babies.

Less than fifty years ago, Korea was in a very different situation. After the end of the Korean War, South Korea witnessed a baby boom that put further strains on an already desperate economy. The United States encouraged Korea to limit its population growth, which it dutifully did. IUD insertions and sterilizations were carried out in roving clinics that the US Agency for International Development helped to fund, through the donation of reconditioned army vehicles. There were even cases of forced sterilizations and abortions, as reported in Mara Hvistendahl's chilling book, *Unnatural Selection*. As was true in China, they were paid on a per-procedure basis, providing family planners with great incentive to ensure that population controls were being met.

By 1970, the total fertility rate per woman in Korea dropped to 4.71, down from 6.33 in the 1950s. In 1980, the number was further reduced to 2.92; which was around the same time a gender imbalance began to emerge. As it turns out, South Korea was no less immune than China to the Confucian values system that inculcates a cultural preference for sons.

In the 1980s, Korea's new military leader, Chun Doo-hwan,

realized that population control was a pretty good business. It had already been the source of a considerable amount of foreign aid, and he was keen to pursue more of it. "Even Two Is a Lot" appeared as the new slogan on a fleet of mobile clinics funded by a $30 million loan from the World Bank, while millions more in aid came from the International Bank for Reconstruction and Development. As a result of this more restrictive measure—which was not a law, but a stern suggestion—the gender imbalance continued to climb. By 1990, Korea's gender imbalance was the highest in the world—116 boys for every 100 girls born. It held on to this record until 2004, when China—in its most imbalanced year—saw the birth of 121 boys for every 100 girls.

Astonishingly, by the year 2000, Korea's sex ratio at birth made a turnaround, and by 2007, it was back to normal. "South Korea is the only country in modern history to have a highly-abnormal birth ratio and then to reduce that number to fall within normal ratios," writes Hvistendahl. It took a remarkable effort in terms of public-awareness campaigns that promoted the equal value of both male and female offspring, but it also helped that Korean parents could see that it was true. As economic growth helped erode inequalities between the sexes—in terms of their access to education and the labor market—Korean parents became more willing to birth and raise a girl, because it no longer seemed like such a bad deal.

Although the fertility rate is back on track, the imbalances of previous generations are still working their way through society. Between 1980 and 1984, 25 percent more men were born than women of the same age, and for children born in the '90s, that rate is even higher. Unsurprisingly, these imbalances have contributed to a population of leftover men, 1 in 7 of whom is estimated to be unable to find a partner.

Since the imbalance is smaller and more contained—in China, that same figure is 1 in 5 of a much larger population of men—the Koreans have been able to more easily mitigate the effects of the imbalance. Still, the leftover men in both countries share many of the same characteristics. As is true in China, Korean leftover men are overwhelmingly located in the country's most rural areas. In cities, the sex ratio for people between the ages of twenty and thirty-nine is practically normal: about 103 men for 100 women. In rural areas, however, it's as high as 119 men per 100 women of the same age. This is because like their fellow Chinese bare branches, firstborn Korean sons were expected to stay behind and care for their family farms and aging parents, while everyone else who could—young women included—moved to cities to take advantage of Korea's industrialization-fueled boom. The imbalance has created a market for foreign brides, the majority of whom are from rural Vietnam, and for whom Chinese and Korean leftover men now must compete.

Korea's "leftover women," or "Gold Misses," have very different lives. They are concentrated in urban areas and like their Chinese equivalents, they enjoy a good, if not enviable, standard of living. Their "gold" status is less directly correlated with the advantages of being an only daughter, because even in the peak years of family planning efforts, most households still had two kids. However, after centuries of preferring boys, Korean households have started to favor girls.

A component of this counter-trend is certainly economic. Korean men are expected to provide a marital home—a requirement that has become prohibitively expensive in big cities like Seoul and Busan. As in Japan, the country's economic slowdown has atrophied the security and salaries once provided by big corporate jobs, which also require grueling hours and fierce loyalty.

Kwarosa in Korean and *karōshi* in Japanese both mean "death by overwork" and are still serious issues in both countries.

In addition to the effects of an economic slowdown, Korean men have to contend with two years of mandatory military service, which some have complained gives women an unfair advantage in the workforce. This may be true: Korean women are employed at higher rates than Korean men between the ages of twenty-five and twenty-nine—albeit at 52 percent of their pay— but after that, the tables turn.

As is expected of Korean wives, many women leave the workforce in their thirties, spend a decade or so as homemakers and return to the workforce in their forties, often to lower-paying jobs than they had before. They don't face the same work track discriminations as Japanese women, but they are expected to shoulder the majority of the housework, as their husbands—whose long hours and late nights of post-work socializing rival those of Japanese men—do not contribute their fair share of domestic duties. Korea's feverish approach to education adds another element to the responsibilities of raising a child. Because the peninsula has limited land and not many natural resources, there is an extreme emphasis put on human talent in an already fierce job market. To remain competitive, most children are required to attend *hagwon*, or after-school academies, where they study subjects like math, English, science, and history. In PISA (Program for International Student Assessment) test score results, they are consistently ranked among the top-performing students in the world, thanks largely to the extra training, but also the heavy parental supervision they receive.

Given the demands of being a wife and mother in Korea, it's easy to understand how Korea's numbers of Gold Misses have climbed steadily since the '80s, when 15 percent of its women between the ages of twenty-five and twenty-nine were single. Today, 70 percent of women between the ages of twenty-five and twenty-nine are unmarried, and by the time South Korean women hit age thirty-nine, nearly 15 percent remain so. In a country where less than 1 percent of the overall population is unmarried, these numbers represent a significant shift away from coupled life.

"When women's wages rise, more women can choose to stay single than marry traditional husbands," explains economist Jisoo Hwang. Now an assistant professor at Hankuk University of Foreign Studies in Seoul, as part of her PhD research at Harvard, she studied patterns in advanced female education and marriage in South Korea, Japan, Singapore, and the United States. She found that in East Asian "tiger economies," where a burst of rapid economic growth—as seen in Japan in the 1960s–'80s, South Korea in the 1970s–'90s, and Singapore in the 1960s–'90s—led to greater female workforce participation and to an increase in the female-to-male median earnings of full-time employees, the marriage probability for college graduate women sharply decreased.

When considering this information, it's important to note that although women's salaries, relative to those of men, did increase in both South Korea and Japan during the respective boom years of each country, they are still dismal. Japan and Korea rank 111th and 116th, respectively, out of 144 countries on the World Economic Forum's Global Gender Gap Report. Singapore, by comparison, ranks 55th, and China 99th. Nonetheless, writes Hwang, "labor force participation rates of women in the age group 25–34 in Japan, Korea, and Singapore increased by more than 17 percentage points from 1985 to 2006." She notes that in the United States during this same period of time, female workforce participation rates only increased by 5 percentage points, representing a much more gradual increase over the years.

"My generation of women doesn't relate as much with our mothers as previous generations did," says Hwang, who was born in Korea in the mid-'80s. "We can get advanced degrees, pursue professional careers—this is all very different from the options most of our mothers had." She adds that although many women in Korea are at some point forced to choose between focusing on a career or raising a family—because doing both is still very hard to do—there are at least successful Korean female role models who have proven that the professional route is possible.

As far as marriage goes, Hwang believes that because "gender norms don't change as quickly as the markets," Korean and Japanese men are still struggling to process the more modern roles that women have taken up outside of the home, mainly because they conflict drastically with the models that the men were exposed to as children.

To test the validity of her theory, Hwang analyzed the results to the following questions from the Japanese General Social Surveys:

1. If a husband has sufficient income, it is better for his wife not to have a job
2. A husband's job is to earn money; a wife's job is to look after the home and family
3. A pre-school child is likely to suffer if his/her mother works

She found that the probability a man disagrees with the statements increases by about 5 percentage points if his mother worked when he was young, and by more than 10 percentage points if his mother is a college graduate. In other words, her findings support the idea that a mother's work experience and education have an impact on her son's gender attitudes and expectations from marriage, suggesting that men who had working or college-graduate mothers may be more likely to have more egalitarian relationships with their wives. (There was no statistically significant effect based on the father's educational attainment.)

While it's encouraging to see how mothers can help shape their sons' understanding of traditional gender roles, it could also be problematic, argues Hwang. If much of the country's educated, working female population is not married or having kids, they can't contribute to producing a new generation of modern males to help break the cycle of marriage-market mismatch.

Fortunately, women like Youna Lee are finding ways to mainstream alternative ways of thinking. As one of the leaders of the Unni Network, an NGO dedicated to feminist cultural activism in South Korea, she works alongside three hundred other members to serve as a support group for women who live outside the traditional marriage system. These include heterosexual Gold Misses, but also lesbian and transgender women. "Women are individuals. Our existence is not limited to playing the role of wife and mother within a nuclear family," she said. "This is the attitude we're trying to foster in our society, where unmarried women are still seen as abnormal."

To promote its message, the group hosts events, festivals, and also pioneered a "Mouths We Want to Sew Up" mock awards ceremony. Past "winners" include Lee Myung-bak, the former president of South Korea, who once said, "I'm against abortion, except when the child is handicapped" and assemblyman Choi Yeon-hee, who earned a dishonorable mention for harassing a female reporter and later trying to justify it by saying, "I was so drunk that I thought she (the reporter) was the hostess of the restaurant."

In *Plan B*, a publication published by the Unni Network that was partially funded by the Seoul Metropolitan government, readers are invited to take a quiz measuring their fortitude to survive life outside the traditional confines of marriage. Based on the results, they can either be classified as soft tofu (in need of some stir frying to toughen up their skin); a watermelon (more resilient, but still a work in progress); or a walnut (ready to triumphantly face the world!).

For women who aspire to have a family but have been discouraged by the cost—professional, monetary, or otherwise—it should also be acknowledged that Korea's government has made earnest attempts to improve work-life balance. It has increased paternity leave—although only a very small percentage of new fathers have taken it—and contributions to public and private childcare. Subsidies per child and tax breaks have also been introduced, although there is room for more.

"The government needs to be more aggressive and focused with policies regarding childcare and work-life balance," said Hwang. "If they can help ensure that children are taken care of while their parents work, changes in traditional gender roles can follow."

Although it's uncertain how long a transition of that magnitude might take, Hwang is hopeful. "My grandmother still can't believe that parents these days like girls as much as boys," she said. "But when people saw that girls were doing just as well in school and in the labor market, their thinking changed," she added. "It can change again."

It's National Night

Although governments all over the world have done crazy things to either restrict or boost population growth, Singapore—

a tiny island nation of 5.4 million people—has by far been the most creative.

Since 1984 (a very Orwellian year), Singapore's Social Development Unit (a very Orwellian name for a government institution) has been hard at work trying to get the country's most well-educated women married and pregnant by similarly well-educated men. This push stems from the notion advanced by Singapore's former prime minister, Lee Kuan Yew: "If you have two white horses, the chances are, you breed white horses." In a nation as ethnically diverse as Singapore, which is home to a vibrant Chinese, Indian, and Malay population, "white" was a poor word choice, which the prime minister only made worse by adding that, occasionally, two gray horses breed a white one, but that they were "very few."

At first, the Social Development Unit (SDU) operated under what is now known as the Ministry of Social and Family Development. It was created "to promote marriages and nurture a culture where singles view marriage as one of their top life goals," in reaction to a 1980 census which revealed that a large number of highly educated Singaporean women above the age of forty were still unmarried. The census also showed that the more educated a woman was, the fewer children she had, which the Singaporean government seems to have interpreted as a plea for help. Prime Minister Yew expressed concerns that a decrease in the number of children born to educated women would lead to a social and economic downturn, and promised that the government would take strong measures to reverse this alarming trend.

In addition to the unfortunate coincidence of having an acronym that could stand for "single, desperate, ugly," the SDU didn't get off to a roaring start. The graduate women it targeted were offended that their personal lives had suddenly become the target of public discourse, while non-graduate women—and their parents, in particular—were upset that the government was dissuading graduate men from marrying them. They were especially angry that their tax dollars were being used to fund activities like SDU-sponsored cruises, barbecues, dance lessons, and other matchmaking events, which graduate civil servants sometimes even got extra work leave to attend. A year after the SDU was formed, a sister organization called Social Development Services (SDS) was set up to foster marriages among "gray" or non-graduate singles. Interestingly, this was all happening while Singapore's neighbors, China and South Korea, were in full-blown population-control mode.

In its first year of operation, the SDU spent nearly US $300,000, and its efforts resulted in only two weddings. Despite this low conversion rate, as time went by, the numbers of couples introduced through SDU activities began to climb. By the early 2000s, the organization reported that it had facilitated over 30,000 marriages. It's hard to say how many of these marriages wouldn't have happened without the SDU, though the numbers helped make the existence of the organization easier to justify.

Realizing the value of shedding its institutional origins, in 2006, the SDU was opened up to the private sector, and instead of organizing dating events, it has since become more of an agency that accredits individual operators. These include "Lunch Actually," a platform that relies on a team of dating consultants to partner professional singles over a midday meal, and the more explicitly titled, but now defunct, "Get Them Dates." In a sign that its elitist graduate-only system was eroding, in 2009, the SDU merged with the SDS to become the Social Development Network, or SDN. According to the SDN website, this was done to "reap economies of scale, enlarge the outreach, and provide more opportunities for singles to meet." Its mission is "to be a credible, leading agency and one-stop resource centre on relationship skills, social interaction opportunities and information." The SDN website features a seemingly endless list of activities such as leather-crafting lessons, terrarium-making workshops, and whiskey and chocolate pairings. For the more active, it also holds events like "Why Walk When You Can Salsa?" and "Be My Bait"—an outing in which singles go prawning. Most of these activities are subsidized by the SDN, which funds up to 80 percent of approved dating projects through "The Partner Connection Fund." In addition to being abundant, the SDN's offerings are inexpensive. A weekend getaway to the charming colonial Malaysian town of Malacca that includes transportation, two meals, and a night of shared accommodation—in one of many private villas built on stilts over the water and arrangd in the shape of a giant Hibiscus—costs US $130.

Still, these government-backed efforts to boost marriage and fertility rates haven't been sufficient to stymie the "silver tsunami," or the fact that by 2030, one in five Singaporean residents will be over age sixty. The country's current rate of 1.29 births per woman puts it at just a hair under South Korea and a tenth of a point under Japan. This number is far off track from the government's desired population of 6.9 million people by 2030, but for a place as geographically small as Singapore, more modest population growth might not necessarily be a bad thing. Already one of the most expensive cities in Asia—especially in terms of housing costs—Singapore would not be able to accommodate another 1 million people without severe overcrowding, and its infrastructure would struggle under the weight of a million more bodies to support and transport. While these concerns are unsettling to the thousands of citizens who expressed their discontent with a government white paper that detailed the country's plans for

growing its population by a million people over the next decade—
four thousand Singaporeans even went to Speaker's Corner, the
only place on the island where people can apply for a license to
make a speech and "protest"—from an official standpoint, they
are secondary to the threat of slowing economic growth. Despite
being an important financial center, Singapore is half the size of
Greater London. A shrinking workforce and a growing population of dependent citizens—who happen to have among the highest life expectancies in the world—could jeopardize its economic
momentum; an outcome that the government is trying to avoid
at all costs.

To get a sense of just how fervently the population agenda is
being pushed, it's worth noting that every Singaporean prime
minister since Lee Kuan Yew has been a proponent of it. In
August 2001, the *Straits Times* (which has been called a government mouthpiece) published a twelve-page special section on
how Singaporeans should "rise to the occasion" and procreate on
National Day, a holiday celebrating the country's independence
from Malaysia in 1965. It even included tips on how couples could
use newspaper to tape up the windows of their cars for greater
privacy while partaking in their national duty. (A more permanent solution would have been to make housing more affordable/
abundant so that young couples didn't have to live with their parents.) This, in a country where chewing gum has been banned
since 2004 because officials want to maintain cleanliness and
order in public spaces, comes as quite a shock.

Taking things a step further, in 2012, National Day in Singapore was marked by the release of a rap song produced in part-
nership with Mentos (yes, the mints) that urged married couples
to "let their patriotism explode."

"I'm a patriotic husband, you're my patriotic wife, so let me
book into your camp and manufacture life," goes one of the more

memorable lines of the song, which is reminiscent of something Usher might sing.

Other highlights of the song include "Singapore's population needs increasing, so forget waving flags, August ninth we be freakin.'" After a male voice sings about the appeal of a "baby bonus," a female voice responds, "I can't wait to buy a $900 stroller" in a sultry contralto.*

While the entire population of Singapore is often called upon to participate in its "national duty," women—as the ovens that can bake future buns—are given a bit of extra attention. As part of an SDN sponsored activity, four final-year university students were awarded money to create "The Singaporean Fairy Tale," or a retelling of fairy-tale classics with slightly more agenda-serving morals.

The retelling of Snow White reads as follows:

> *Mirror, mirror, on the wall*
> *Who in this land is the richest of all?*
> *Snow-White, beyond the mountains with her seven children*
> *Who learn, play and give her kisses every day.*
> *Snow-White is the richest of all.*

The fairy tale is accompanied by an image of a resplendent Snow White surrounded by her dwarfs (who seem to have magically morphed into charming, non-grumpy, sneezy, sleepy, or dopey little blond boys in matching pink short-sets) and the following caption:

* It should be noted that faced with a similar population problem, Vladimir Putin invited Boys II Men to perform in Russia ahead of Valentine's Day in 2013. This was an addition to previously held "Day of Conception" festivities, which gave couples time off from work to procreate. Couples that gave birth to baby patriots exactly nine months from Russia's national day became eligible to win refrigerators, cars, cash, and other prizes.

"Sperm cells can live in your reproductive tract for 3–4 days, so having sex two to three times a week would mean that when an egg is released there will be sperm waiting!"

The retelling of "The Golden Goose" is also worth a mention:

The Golden Goose was prized for her eggs
That shone light in brilliant gold
But there soon came a time she could make them no more
Because her egg-making device was rusty and old.

These tales, along with Cinderella, the Three Little Pigs, and Rapunzel, were distributed as leaflets to university students in the hope that they would become educated on "what it takes to start, live, and be a family in Singapore," as Chan Luo Er, the project manager of the series, told the *Guardian*.

Instead of assailing its population with directives on how to live, Singapore might be better served by making it easier to live there. Government records indicate that in 2012, over half of the abortions performed in Singapore—where abortion is legal—were on married women. The majority were college-educated women who didn't want a child because they were still climbing career ladders and were concerned that taking time away to care for a child would derail their professional ambitions. There were also women who already had a child, but decided to terminate their pregnancies because they didn't feel they could afford another one.

It's also worth noting that more than 80 percent of Singaporeans live in public housing, which is more abundant, but still not plentiful enough to go around. In addition to being controlled by race—if an Indian family moves out of their housing unit, for example, they will likely be replaced by another Indian family, to ensure a certain degree of balance and avoid racial ghettos—

public housing is granted based on marital status. Unmarried citizens under the age of thirty-five are not eligible for public housing subsidies; they must purchase in the private sector, where housing costs are at least double. For this reason, many Singaporean couples joke that being able to apply for public housing is one of the biggest perks of getting engaged.

To further discourage those tempted to live on their own, the Singaporean government offers a segment of build-to-order (BTO) flats. BTOs are priced much more cheaply than public flats on the market—up to $100,000 cheaper—but singles are restricted to buying only the smallest two-room model of them. Likewise, the Urban Redevelopment Authority recently required property developers to limit the number of "shoebox" apartments they build. At less than 500 square feet, these apartments are popular and sell quickly, but as reported by the BBC, new guidelines have been released that require developers to build a greater proportion of larger, family-friendly apartments, in the hopes that a shortage of other options will inspire people to require them.

"You can't just badger people into having children—they need support," said Jolene Tan, head of advocacy and research at Singapore's Association of Women for Action and Research (Aware). She explains that although there is growing recognition among local politicians that costs and care are going to be huge factors in people's reproductive decisions going forward, there is still a very embryonic understanding of gender equality in Singapore. "It is a value that needs to be actively and explicitly promoted from a young age," she said. "Instituting compulsory paternity leave is a step in the right direction, but it isn't enough to change entrenched traditional norms and attitudes."

Mandy Li, a professional matchmaker from China who is based in Singapore, agrees. "Men in Singapore struggle to find

Singaporean women who correspond to the type of wife they're looking for," she explains, a problem she has managed to turn into a lucrative business. Specialized in pairing Southern Chinese women with Singaporean men, Li explained that since street food and takeaway in Singapore is very cheap, clean, and accessible, barely anyone cooks at home. Unlike in China, where moneyed men must always eat in private VIP rooms in upscale establishments, men of all socioeconomic classes in Singapore can eat at the same curbside stalls. "They don't need homemaker wives who will cook for them," she said. "They want partners—women who will help out with their businesses and support whatever industry they happen to be in." But many Singaporean women don't want this—"they have businesses or careers of their own that they prefer to pursue," added Li, which is where Chinese women come in.

Generally speaking, Chinese women are more willing copilots to their husbands' careers, and when the added bonus of immigration to Singapore is factored in (along with the prospect of cleaner air, safer food, and better social benefits), according to Li, many a happy match can be made. "They're just more compatible," she said. As a native of China's Fujian province, she herself is a testament to the success of the Chinese female/Singaporean male marriage model, and has been in the business of matchmaking from her home office in a well-manicured suburb of Singapore for over twenty years. "The men are happy because they have a wife more willing to follow their lead, and the women are happy because they have a husband who is more likely to treat them as an equal," she said, seated on a salmon-colored couch in her living room, surrounded by photos of beaming couples. "Everyone wins."

12

THE WAY FORWARD

当风向改变时，有的人筑墙，有的人造风车

When the winds of change blow, some people build walls
and others build windmills.

—CHINESE PROVERB

On January 1, 2016, China ended its one-child policy. After thirty-six years of what is widely considered the most radical human experiment of the last century, parents in China are now allowed the slightly greater reproductive freedom of having two children.

When the one-child policy was conceived in the 1970s, few people could foresee the full magnitude of its human consequences. This includes one of the policy's lead architects, a rocket scientist named Song Jian, who at the time was one of China's top cyber-ballistics and missiles specialists. Although he may sound like a peculiar choice to help engineer the nation's most aggressive population-control effort, it turns out that at least from a military perspective, missiles and mating patterns have more in common than meets the eye.

Song Jian studied mathematics and systems analysis in the

Soviet Union. He earned a PhD from Moscow University and published seven papers (in Russian) on the theory of optimal control, a mathematical optimization often used to predict and calculate the path to a desired outcome, in very simple terms.

Following the Sino-Soviet split in 1960, Song returned to China and quickly rose in the ranks of the Ministry of National Defense to become the country's foremost authority on missile guidance and control systems. Although the Red Guards ransacked his home during the Cultural Revolution—a common story for all members of the Chinese academic elite at the time—he was promptly put on a select list of scientists who enjoyed special state protection. Because Mao feared attacks from the United States and the Soviet Union, he treated military scientists—especially strategic-weapons scientists like Song, who could build atomic bombs—as a privileged coterie. They worked in modern facilities and had rare access to foreign materials, data, and powerful computers, according to Susan Greenhalgh, a professor of anthropology at Harvard and the author of *Just One Child: Science and Policy in Deng's China*.

Perhaps most important (and dangerous), they had a direct line of communication with the highest levels of government and were involved in important national political decisions, the most significant of which would eventually become the one-child policy.

I must stress that Chinese social scientists and even some politicians had considered the need for population control long before Song's time. As far back as the 1930s, they had identified China's population as a burden, but since China's wartime Guomindang government cherished military might and high population numbers, there wasn't much they could do. Once the Chinese Communist Party took power, they followed the lead of the Soviet

Union, where Stalin had reinstated pre-revolutionary family norms. In contrast to the birth-control initiatives of imperialist, capitalist states, these norms included the promotion of child-bearing, which was also enforced in Communist-controlled areas of China. This was true to the extent that between 1931 and 1948, abortion was penalized, and only allowed in the case of danger to a mother's life, writes German demographer Thomas Scharping, in his seminal book, *Birth Control in China, 1949–2000: Population Policy and Demographic Development*. By September 1949, on the eve of the founding of the People's Republic, Mao declared: "It's a very good thing that China has a big population. Even if China's population multiplies many times, she is fully capable of finding a solution; the solution is production."

By the 1950s, Mao's hard stance against population control began to erode. China was facing food shortages and difficulty providing education for a growing number of children, as well as employment and health care challenges. Still, his revolutionary zeal led him to execute the Great Leap Forward—a campaign to quickly transform China from an agrarian economy to a Socialist one, through industrialization and collectivization. The strains of the transition contributed to the Great Chinese Famine, which, through the tens of millions of lives it tragically claimed as a result of malnutrition, underscored the need for population control and helped put it back on the political agenda.

Zhou Enlai, who served under Mao as first premier, became the government's main promoter of population control policies. "A large population is a good thing, but as we are already the most populous country in the world, we already have plenty of this good thing, and if we still let the population grow rapidly in an unplanned manner, it won't be a good thing anymore," he said in a 1963 speech cited by Scharping.

By 1970, the Chinese politburo, including Mao, agreed that

population control needed to be revisited in the context of economic development and food security. However, by this point, the social scientists who had originally lobbied for population control had already been banished to reeducation in remote areas of the country. As the only remaining scientists in China who were allowed to work in their chosen field, Greenhalgh notes in *Just One Child*, military scientists like Song—who had spent most of the Cultural Revolution in the Gobi Desert, where he studied nuclear physics, astronomy, and other areas of science that he would later channel into his defense work upon returning to Beijing—took on new importance.

During this time in China, but also globally, there was a general nervousness about the size of the global population, which had grown at the fastest rate in human history during the second half of the twentieth century, as reported by Chinese demographers Wang Feng, Yong Cai, and Baochang Gu in their paper, "Population, Policy, and Politics: How Will History Judge China's One-Child Policy?" Organizations around the world were just starting to see a more crowded planet as a threat to economic prosperity, and in some cases, political stability. This uncertainty was further fueled by *The Limits to Growth*, a report commissioned by the Club of Rome, a global think tank that counts David Rockefeller among its founders. Published in 1972, it sold 30 million copies and was translated into thirty languages, making it the best-selling environmental book in world history.

Even today the book's message is a valid one. Based on the work of an international team of researchers at MIT in the 1970s, it is essentially a study of the implications of continued worldwide population growth. It examines how agricultural production, nonrenewable resource depletion, industrial output, and pollution relate to population increases and concludes that "man can create a society in which he can live indefinitely on earth if he imposes limits on himself and his production of material goods to achieve a state of global equilibrium with population and production in carefully selected balance."

In the spirit of the times, Song emphatically made the case that China needed to implement drastic measures to limit its population growth in order to thrive as a nation. "He gave the idea scientific credibility and urgency," explains Susan Greenhalgh. "He made the case that without a radical, scientific plan, China would collapse under the weight of overpopulation."

Communist Party leaders responded to Song's calls for alarm because they aligned well with their new objectives. As part of his plan to modernize China very quickly, Deng Xiaoping, who was on his way to becoming paramount leader of the Communist Party, believed that the country needed to rely on science instead of Marxist and Leninist ideologies, as Mao had. Greenhalgh explains that because Song's branch of science was very complex and highly quantitative in nature—and few people actually understood it or could do it themselves—it had a certain prestige attached to it, which Song deftly parlayed into power.

It should be noted that by the 1970s, Chinese social scientists were allowed to practice in their respective fields again and were also working to find a solution to China's population problem. The difference was Song had access to a cutting-edge computer, which had been developed for military applications. The most sophisticated instruments the social scientists had were calculators. In addition to this material disadvantage, Greenhalgh argues in her book that China's social scientists were still shell-shocked from their recent persecution. The military scientists, in contrast, "possessed the self-assurance to enter an entirely new field, borrow a set of foreign techniques they had encountered only briefly, modify them in significant ways, and then employ those techniques to quickly develop and press for a radically new solution to social problems."

And so they did. On a visit to the Netherlands in 1975, Song visited a Dutch mathematician named Geert Jan Olsder. A professor at the University of Twente, Olsder was co-writing a paper called "Population Planning: A Distributed Time-Optimal Control Problem," in which he attempted to calculate the optimal birthrate for an imaginary island with no emigration or immigration; just births and deaths. This paper is believed to have inspired Song to use his knowledge of missile-control techniques to develop an optimization problem for the best fertility trajectory that would produce a future ideal population target for China. Although different parameters were involved (missile velocity, position, and thrust were swapped out for population density, death rate, and migration), Greenhalgh reports that the mathematics of partial differential equations used in the two cases was virtually identical.

Outside of academic circles, what often gets overlooked in the sequence of events leading up to the one-child policy is that it may not have been necessary. The Chinese government has been in the business of seriously trying to curtail its population growth since as early as 1964, or nearly fifteen years before the one-child policy was put into force.

Starting in 1973, the government experimented with the *wan, xi, shao*, or "later, longer, fewer" policy. Considered a more benign precursor to the one-child policy, it encouraged couples to marry later; to leave a three-to-four-year gap between children so as to ensure that each child received proper health care, education, and parental attention; and to have fewer children altogether, so that each of their offspring could enjoy a more comfortable life. It was followed by a slightly more explicit "One Is Best, Two at

Most" campaign in 1978, which was easy to enforce because at the time in China, most people belonged to work units, which also provided them with food and housing. Officials or work unit leaders could easily revoke the food rations or housing privileges of couples who didn't obey the rules, explains Greenhalgh. And overall, the modest population policy proved very effective. Between 1970 and 1980, China's total fertility rate per woman fell from 5.8 to 2.7. In other words, it more than halved itself before the one-child policy even began.

Still, the Chinese government pressed on with more severe measures because demographic data indicated that a population increase was to be expected in the '80s, as the result of the baby boom that had taken place in the '60s. Adding to the urgency for control was the fact that Deng Xiaoping had just replaced Mao as the leader of the Communist Party. Deng inherited a difficult job; the country had just been devastated by the Cultural Revolution and the mandate of the Chinese Communist Party was in peril. In an attempt to set the nation on a healthier path to the future, Deng made economic development the cornerstone of his tenure. Because GDP growth was considered the best way to measure a country's economic success, he favored strategies and policies that would help increase it.

Song's ideas on population control were well aligned with Deng's objectives. In addition to creating optimal conditions for economic growth—reducing the population would make it easier to increase per-capita GDP—Song reinforced the need for population control with a mix of coveted foreign science and the Malthusian fear that was rising in the West, where it was believed that the population was going to devour the environment, leading to famine and disaster. On the heels of the devastating food shortages that China had just been through, Song's ideas had almost automatic appeal, and so along with China's remaining scientists—again, mainly weaponeers—he was tasked with finding a strategy to ensure China's healthy transition into a new era.

As a result of their work and of the Chinese government's continued desire to limit population growth, on September 25, 1980, the universal one-child policy was put into force and positioned as a solution that would help ensure that the Chinese population would remain under 1.2 billion by the year 2000, the number that was deemed optimal for China to quadruple its GDP to $1,000 per capita between 1980 and 2000.

As early as 1982, the Chinese authorities started adding exemption clauses to the one-child policy in an attempt to alleviate some of its restrictions. I mention this not to make excuses for them, but to illustrate that contrary to popular belief, the one-child policy has not been strictly universal. In fact, by the year 2000, as reported by Chinese demographers Gu Baochang, Wang Feng, Guo Zhiguang, and Zhang Erli in the *Population and Development Review*, there were seventeen exemption clauses and only 35 percent of the population (namely, urban residents) were still required to respect the policy in its original form. Fifty-four percent of Chinese people (primarily non-urban residents) were required to respect a 1.5-child policy, which meant that if a couple's first child was a girl, they'd be allowed a second child, while 10 percent of the population—residents of remote areas— could have two children, even if the first was a boy. It should also be noted that 1 percent of the population—mainly ethnic minorities—was even allowed to have up to three children.

In line with these exemptions, a friend whose grandmother was in charge of enforcing the one-child policy in the city of Wuhan told me that the team of nurses that her grandmother oversaw would toss aborted but not-yet-dead babies born to urban parents in a designated place, where rural families would pick through the babies and could then take the live ones home with them. This should not have been allowed, but according to my friend's grandmother, as long as it was done discreetly—the babies were carried away in trash bags—she and many of the nurses turned a blind eye.

Beyond the countless and often heartrending stories associated with population control in China, the reality is that today, 150 million households there have only one child. Like its fellow East Asian tiger economies, the country faces the threat of a rapidly aging population, with the added complication of a severe gender imbalance. As a result of the policy and the draconian methods used to enforce it, China has earned a top billing on the list of the world's most egregious human rights offenders, and even still, by the year 2000, the population had grown by 60 million more people than desired. Despite this growth—and perhaps even because of it—the GDP goal of $1,000 per capita was reached within half the time, putting China on track to becoming an economic powerhouse.

Regardless of the economic gains, the human and emotional sacrifices caused by the one-child policy must not be underestimated. As was true during the Cultural Revolution, individual rights and welfare were sacrificed in the name of short-term gains, with little regard for long-term consequences. Although the policy has contributed to an increase (completely unintentional) in the status of urban girls born in China since the 1980s, it's important to understand how it has also made things worse for other women, especially the ones who had to endure forced abortions or sterilizations, or the ones who will be trafficked from places like Vietnam, Cambodia, and North Korea, in order to serve as wives for China's rural bachelors. China will continue to pay the consequences of the one-child policy for decades, both in demographic terms, but also social terms. The inhumanity of being treated as reproductive units, rather than as people, will not easily be forgotten. Now that the policy has been amended, the government is also discovering that getting every fertile woman in China to give birth to two children is much more difficult in practice than in theory.

On the same day that the policy was lifted, Chinese authorities strategically repealed a "marriage leave" that gave twenty days of paid holiday to any couple marrying after the age of twenty-five. The original idea behind this leave was to discourage couples from getting married and having children in their early twenties, and to instead entice them to wait until they were older before starting families. In a country where the average annual leave rarely exceeds five days of paid personal leave, it was a very generous incentive that was met with considerable backlash as soon as it was repealed.

In another sign that the Chinese government is (quite literally) pulling out all the stops in order to increase the birthrate, it has also started offering free removal of the intrauterine contraceptive devices—IUDs—with which it had forcibly outfitted women after giving birth to one child. According to official statistics, over 320 million Chinese women were fitted with IUDs between 1980 and 2014. As reported in the *New York Times*, unlike the devices used in most parts of the developed world—which often have strings attached to them and are made to be rather painlessly taken out by a gynecologist after a period of five to ten years—the Chinese *shang huan*, or "loop installation" process is more invasive. Until the mid-'90s, a low-cost stainless-steel IUD ring was installed by state gynecologists. It was meant to be worn indefinitely and was designed to be so hard to extract, surgery would be required to take it out. Now, the Chinese government is offering free surgery to remove the devices, but so far, there have been few takers. The ones in line for operations are often women who have suffered complications resulting from their IUDs, which can embed in the uterine wall and require a hysterectomy.

In an unprecedented legal maneuver and in the hope that older couples might also want to have a second child, the Chinese government also reversed a draft law banning surrogacy that had already been widely publicized and was about to take effect. Despite now being legal in China, it is still common for Chinese to seek out surrogate moms in the United States, as a baby born there comes with the added advantage of US citizenship. The government is also expanding sperm banks and has begun to publish "guidelines" for potential donors, in which it is rather comically stipulated that men "know how to masturbate." Absurdly, unmarried women are still not legally eligible to freeze their eggs, although those who can afford to simply travel to the States for the procedure—a move that was popularized by the Chinese actress Xu Jinglei. Like double-eyelid surgery (a procedure that many Asian women have done in their late teens or before entering the workforce in order to make their eyes look bigger), egg freezing is becoming part of the package of goods and services that young Chinese women seek out. I've read accounts of Chinese women still completing university degrees in the United States who are freezing their eggs for peace of mind. Friends will sometimes go through the process together, as if getting a manicure.

Because the Chinese government has relieved its ballistics specialists of population-control duty and is being informed on how to best reverse the one-child policy by social scientists, it also has a better grasp on the numbers and age structure of its population. Currently, 16 percent of the population is over age sixty, and that percentage is set to double by 2050. The majority of the country's residents now live in urban areas—793 million, versus 590 million in rural areas—and there is a gender imbalance of 30 million more men than women of marriage age. To help recalibrate the country from both age and gender perspectives, the government has set a population target of 1.42 billion by 2020, which means that the population would need to grow by roughly 70 million over the next two years. If recent fertility rates are any indication, this goal is highly ambitious. In the first year since the one-child policy was replaced by a two-child policy, there was only an increase of 1.31 million childbirths over the previous year, which clearly indicates that Chinese families aren't as keen to have as many children as their government would like them to.

The low fertility rate is the result of many factors, starting with the simple reality that it is very expensive to raise a child in China in accord with middle- to upper-class expectations. Parents with means have lavished their only children with private tutors and foreign educations; such expenses add up and are considered too high to double without significantly compromising on quality. China remains highly competitive and in order to maximize their children's chances for success, many parents now believe they must not dilute the opportunities they are able to give to one child by having another.

"My mom became pregnant with a second child when I was three," explained Cara, a Chinese friend of mine now living in New York City. Born in Shanghai in 1988, she was raised primarily by her grandparents, as her mother and father worked long hours and didn't have time to care for a child. Her mother ended up aborting the second baby—a boy—because her family couldn't afford to raise both children. "China was growing considerably at the time, and my parents wanted to use every opportunity they could to improve our living conditions." Their hard work paid off, and Cara's parents were able to fund a college degree for their daughter in the United States and now live comfortably among China's upper middle class. "They are *baofa hu*," she explains, part of the wave of Chinese "upstarts" who rose from humble origins to a position of wealth.

"My life would have been so different with a brother," said Cara. "To have a sibling to play with as a child would have been nice, though it would have definitely impacted my lifestyle as an adult." As uncomfortable as it may be to think about, she's probably right. Cara's parents paid for her to go to college in New York, where they bought her an apartment, and a luxury sports car to drive to and from Flushing, a predominantly Chinese neighborhood in Queens, where she likes to buy groceries, dine out, and get manicures.

While Cara works nine to five in New York, her now retired parents spend their days traveling. Their social media "moments" on WeChat show that they've visited Sweden, the Maldives, Hawaii, and the Egyptian pyramids in the span of less than ten months. They spend lavishly wherever they travel and once gifted Cara a souvenir pink diamond from Nepal that is certain to intimidate any man hoping to ask for her hand. (When a former suitor was taking too long to pop the question because he was still in grad school and couldn't afford a ring, Cara's mom—who is very eager to be a mother-in-law—cheerfully suggested that she just seal the deal with the pink diamond.)

At home in Shanghai, Cara's mother busies herself with singing karaoke (she's on a social media platform that allows others to rate her singing, and is apparently quite the sensation) while her dad busies himself with traditional ink-and-brush paintings. Although they enjoy their life as jet-setters—they often travel in gaggles with other jolly Chinese retirees—they are both very keen for their daughter to return to Shanghai, where they expect her to get married and give them not one, but two grandchildren.

"Since they were robbed of the chance to take care of me as a baby, they are especially eager to be grandparents," explains Cara. "But because they know that the parents of my future husband will be equally keen to take care of a baby, they want one for themselves," she explains. Sensing my confusion, she clarifies. "One baby should take my husband's last name, and the other should have mine."

Cara herself isn't crazy about the idea of having any children, much less a designated grandchild for both her parents and her in-laws. She reassures me, however, that this is becoming a trend among more well-to-do families who have invested heavily in their daughters, and that it's adding to the pressure on her to settle down.

"They want me to get started as soon as possible so that they can care for their grandchildren while they're still healthy," she said. "They have it all planned out—all I'm expected to do is give birth."

Another one of my Chinese female friends in New York is facing similar, although slightly more intense, pressure to procreate. She's already had one child (a boy), and while her in-laws are already encouraging her to have another, her dad has even more ambitious plans. "Anyone in China these days can have two," he told her. "You live in the US now, you should have three!"

Double Trouble

From an employment perspective, the two-child policy has also made things more complicated for Chinese women. "Before, employers would discriminate against women who were not married or who did not have a child," explains Lily, who works at a foreign firm with offices in Beijing. "Now," she explains, "the discrimination has escalated."

Lily got her current job in her twenties, and at the time she was applying, she didn't realize that age and marital status would play so heavily into her future career prospects. "I thought a greater amount of work experience would give me better opportunities in the future, but I didn't realize that my age and gender would eventually work against me."

Now in her mid-thirties, Lily has been struggling to get a new job and believes she has been unsuccessful because she is not married. "I had no idea that this was a real concern for HR managers, but they take no pains to hide it," she explains. "I recently applied for a position with a multinational company and was interviewed by a Taiwanese manager who very bluntly told me that if I were in my early twenties, she wouldn't have bothered asking about my plans for marriage and motherhood, but now that I was in my early thirties, she was required to," said Lily.

"This has happened to me on several occasions, and the craziest thing is that it's usually women discriminating against other women," she added.

Because most employers in China require that prospective employees list their age and marital status on their CV, HR managers know that Lily is single. She believes this contributes to "invisible discrimination" and once tried to leave this information off of her CV, but prospective employers called and asked her to include it before considering her for an interview.

In addition to fielding personal questions about her future plans, Lily is often offered employment under constricting circumstances. "Even after I openly stated that I had no plans to have children, one employer asked if I would be OK with signing a contract promising that I wouldn't get pregnant for up to two years," she said, mentioning that this was a common occurrence in her friends circle, among both single and married women.

As tempting as it may be to assume that this sort of discrimination only happens at local Chinese companies, Lily reassures me that these anecdotes are from her experiences applying to work for multinationals operating in China. "When it comes to their HR departments, most of the employees are Chinese, and so they follow more local rules," she said. She adds that since the two-child policy, things have become slightly more complicated. Employers now fear that they might eventually have to pay for up to two rounds of maternity leave (amounting to about ninety-eight days) for currently childless women, and so they are ever more fearful of employing women who have no kids but are at an age where they might.

At this rate, it's difficult to imagine that the number of babies born in China will soar anytime soon. Chinese government figures rather optimistically predict that with the two-child policy, the total fertility rate will rise to 2.1 (22 million births per year) in 2018, then gradually decline to 1.72 in 2050. If this were to happen, China's population would peak at 1.45 billion in 2029, then decline to 1.38 billion in 2050. However, Chinese demographer Yi Fuxian, a scientist at the University of Wisconsin–Madison, projects a very different trajectory. Because the mere existence of a two-child policy doesn't mean that Chinese women are suddenly all going to be having two babies—fertility cannot be switched on and off, contrary to what the Chinese government might like to believe—Fuxian predicts that the total fertility rate will temporarily rebound from 1.05 in 2015 to 1.3 in 2017, then decline even further. Ultimately, he estimates that China's population will drop to 1.1 billion in 2050, and that by 2100, there will be 500 million Chinese people left in China—most of them elderly.

For China's population to halve in the next sixty years is a very big deal. Much of what the country has achieved—socially and economically—has hinged on its power in numbers, and its youth. In 1980, the average age in China was twenty-two, explains Fuxian. That number rose to thirty-eight in 2015 and is predicted to increase to fifty-six by 2050, putting it among the oldest populations in the world. (By 2050, the average age in the United States will be forty-two and in India it will be a spry thirty-seven. The world average is expected to be around thirty-six.) And while China had 7.6 people of working age supporting every person over sixty-four in 2010, by 2050, Fuxian estimates that the number will decrease to a harrowing 1.7 supporting every senior. This is nearly the equivalent of each person taking care of their parents as they age—a heavy responsibility for a married couple with one or two children besides.

These estimates are based on current fertility rates, which don't fully account for the rising percentage of Chinese women who are choosing to get married and have children later in life, or not at all. In the context of Eastern Asia, China's numbers of unmarried women are still comparatively low, but it's important to remember that China's socioeconomic level is an average of twenty years behind that of its neighbors. In the 1980s, when China still had a near universal marriage rate for women by age thirty (there were few alternatives to marriage at the time), in Japan, Singapore, and South Korea, approximately 20 percent of women remained unmarried at age thirty. Today, the average percentage of unmarried women under thirty in Japan, South Korea, and Singapore has soared to 70 percent, and even by age thirty-nine, over 20 percent of women in those countries still remain unmarried. For added perspective, Hong Kong and Taiwan follow a similar pattern: an average of 68 percent of women under thirty are unmarried, and 19 percent remain so by age thirty-nine. In China, the percentage of unmarried women at age thirty-nine is still a modest 5 percent, though given everything Chinese women have achieved over the past thirty years, there is strong reason to believe that these numbers will increase.

In the United States, by contrast, the opposite has happened. As mentioned earlier, college-educated women are now more likely to marry than their lesser-educated counterparts, and in addition, American women as a whole have taken on a greater share of breadwinning responsibilities. According to the US Center for American Progress, 42 percent of mothers are the sole or primary earners in US households.[*] Biological anthropologist Helen Fisher believes this represents an exciting return to our "hunting-and-gathering past," in which women would forage and usually came home with 60 to 80 percent of what their families ate. Their ability to consistently provide for their families— it wasn't every day that their husbands would manage to hunt down and slaughter a boar—made them as economically and sexually powerful as men. They could leave bad relationships if they wanted to because they weren't financially dependent on their partners—until the tractor was invented and put them out of commission.

Jisoo Hwang, the Korean researcher mentioned earlier, posits that because GDP growth has been more gradual in the United States, and because women have entered the workforce and seen an increase in their wages over a longer period of time, they've avoided the "shock" that results when economies grow quickly

---

* It should be noted that this figure also includes single-parent, often less affluent, households in which mothers are the only breadwinners.

and female workforce participation rates and salaries increase suddenly. Hwang argues that this "shock" often results in high rates of single women as men struggle to adapt to a new role for women so different from the one they grew up with. There is a risk that the same might happen in China, where the same economic growth pattern readily applies—but I don't think it will.

Making an educated guess, I'd venture that the biggest challenge Chinese men and women will face in terms of partnering off will be an increasingly larger supply of college-graduate women and a shrinking pool of college-graduate men. This situation is nothing new—it's true in virtually all developed countries in the world, including in the United States, where Jon Birger explains in *Date-onomics* (a fascinating read) that young American millennial women are entering a dating pool of 134 college-educated women for every 100 college-educated men. For perspective, he notes that today's forty-year-old college-educated woman started out with a dating pool of 117 college-educated women for every 100 men, which wasn't ideal either, but certainly preferable to the current situation. Although the gender imbalance on US college campuses shows signs of becoming even more acute, it has existed for at least three decades, and marriage patterns have started to adjust accordingly. It is not uncommon for women in the United States (or in most of the developed world, as mentioned earlier) to marry men with less education than themselves. In China, that's still a hard pill to swallow; men remain more hesitant to marry up, and women less likely to marry down, with parents usually reinforcing this reluctance. Mathematically, if this does not change, it will add to a decrease in marriage rates over time and could bring China up to the numbers seen in the East Asian countries examined earlier.

While this may make it even more tempting to draw parallels between China and its neighbors—at this point, China is probably just a rap song away from begging its population to reproduce—it's important to underscore certain differences that have the potential to send China down an alternate path.

After years of economic growth driven by higher manufacturing and rural-to-urban migration, China is at an important crossroads. In order to sustain its economy, it must increase consumer spending and shift its focus away from heavy industry and exports, in favor of services and consumer products. On many levels, it is well placed to make this transition. Just ten years ago, 1 in 20 college-age people in China pursued higher education; now it's 1 in 3. While we in the United States still swipe credit cards, fiddle with coins, and sign receipts, China has become a cashless, paperless society. Almost anything can be purchased with the scan of a barcode, from street-side dumplings to sports cars. You can book a car, a massage, or a vacation all from the same app, and pay for it with funds that may earn more interest from being in a Web bank account than they would in an actual bank. WeChat is the world's most versatile social media platform and Alibaba is the world's largest e-commerce platform; both are Chinese and neither show any signs of disappearing anytime soon.

In addition to this futuristic digital edge, China—unlike its East Asian tiger economy counterparts—has a huge, growing class of professional women who are engaged in the formal workforce. Already, they contribute to 41 percent of Chinese GDP, which is one of the highest rates in the world. Forcing them to conform to an antiquated timeline for marriage and motherhood or failing to acknowledge the critical role they play in Chinese society—aside from ensuring it doesn't go extinct—would risk undoing all of the progress that China has made over the last thirty years.

Yet beyond its domestic potential to blaze a brighter path for itself, China is also favorably placed to set the tone for many other countries across the world, namely because no other country straddles the developed and the developing world as China does at this precise moment in time. Home to one-quarter of the world's female population, it is the pitch-perfect composition of a prodigious change that has already worked its way around most parts of the developed world. How China makes room for women whose careers, educations, and lifestyles may make them more likely to marry and have children later in life, or not at all, will have an effect on legions of women to come.

When you add India to the equation, the scope for change nearly doubles. India's female population is almost as large as China's. It is a country that also suffers from a severe gender imbalance, and although from a socioeconomic perspective, it is light-years behind China, there are areas where the two countries intersect. According to research from the McKinsey Global Institute (MGI), there is a wide variation in gender equality among India's thirty-two states, largely because of disparities in work opportunities. The top five states closest to gender parity are on par with China, Argentina, and Indonesia; India's bottom five states on gender parity are more in line with Chad and Yemen. In other words, there is a strong correlation between a woman's perceived value in the workforce and her value in society; without both those things being valued, neither one is possible.

If 68 million Indian women could be brought into the non-farm labor force over the next decade, MGI estimates indicate that the country could boost its GDP by $0.7 trillion by 2025. The process for bringing them into the workforce involves doing things that China has already done well: closing gender gaps in secondary and tertiary education, expanding the reach of financial and digital services to enable women entrepreneurs, and challenging entrenched attitudes regarding the role of women in work and society. At present, women in India contribute the lowest share of GDP among all regions in the world, putting it on par with the Middle East and North Africa, where in many places, female employment is restricted by law. The economic growth potential from advancing gender equality and improving female workforce participation in India is the highest in the world.

Behind India is a host of other heavily populated South Asian, Middle Eastern, and African countries, where women are just starting to get a bit more autonomy over their lives and bodies. Women in Bangladesh are being sent to school in higher numbers because they've become an important source of talent in the country's factories, which require skilled labor. Women in Pakistan are racing motorbikes to promote gender equality. Women in Afghanistan are riding skateboards to do the same, because they're still not allowed to ride bikes. Women in Iran are training in karate and martial arts to protect themselves against gender-based violence. Women in Egypt are taking to the streets in wedding gowns to protest marriage by a certain age. Women in Malawi are helping one another escape child marriage. Women in Saudi Arabia just gained the right to drive. However small, these are all signs that women around the world are standing up against the people or traditions that prohibit them from being fully participating members of society. Although these are not the same women who are rallying in marches around the world—none of the aforementioned countries, with the exception of India, Malawi, and Saudi Arabia, even had a Women's

March—their small victories must be nourished, because they need them most.

I wrote much of this last chapter on a trip through Africa, which ended in Mozambique. While there, I met a young Mozambican entrepreneur of Portuguese descent who has developed a line of inexpensive, reusable feminine napkins, which are of significant value in a country where most women still rely on leaves, sticks, or shreds of *capulanas*—rags, essentially—to absorb blood during their periods. The initial idea was to employ Mozambican women to promote and sell this product at local markets, although it quickly became clear that this was unwise. Women in Mozambique have such little purchasing power, that despite being the end users of the product, they were not the ones making the decision on whether or not to buy it. Husbands (or fathers) were the ones who needed to first be convinced of the sanitary benefits of reusable pads; a sales pitch that most women in Mozambique— where menstruation remains highly stigmatized—were loath to make. The founder of the company decided that she needed to recenter her marketing efforts on universities—where female students might have a bit of disposable income—and on mosques, where, if convinced of the cost-saving benefits of these pads, an imam might buy a bundle for his wives.

On many levels, Mozambique provided me with a fresh lens through which to see China, which has invested heavily across Africa, but in Mozambique, in particular. The country's main airport was built by the Chinese, as was the city's largest hotel. The skeleton of the longest suspension bridge in Africa—which will connect Maputo, the capital, with the town of Catembe—is already visible from the shoreline. Funded by the Export-Import Bank of China, built with China's Angang Steel, and developed by China Roads and Bridges Corporation, it is expected to replace the poor network of roads currently used to transport goods and tourists between Mozambique, South Africa, and Swaziland.

Beyond investments, however, it was fascinating to learn that Mozambique has the twelfth highest fertility rate in the world— 5.26 per woman. It is located in a part of the globe where in stark contrast to most of Asia, the population is expected to double by 2050. Infant and maternal mortality rates are high and female education rates are low. The average life expectancy is forty-nine, which often means that when parents die, their eldest children have to drop out of school and find a job to support their siblings, thereby limiting their opportunities to become educated and build better lives for themselves. Although women in sub-Saharan Africa already contribute to 39 percent of GDP, they are also responsible for an overwhelmingly large share of domestic work, and child marriage and young motherhood complicate their efforts to find more lucrative jobs. They are at the tail end of the development spectrum that China currently straddles, but over time, as they gain greater access to education and more autonomy over their marital and reproductive choices, that should change.

Already, signs of that change are emerging. In China, one of the most telling indicators of the progress that women have made over the last thirty-odd years is the fact that the lives of women in their twenties and thirties are very different from those of their mothers and grandmothers. While that isn't yet true in Mozambique, it's starting to be. While there, I visited my friend Sigrid, who was formerly working in China, and had just taken up a new posting as a diplomat in Maputo. The daughter of diplomats, she had grown up in Mozambique, with a housekeeper who had worked for her parents for over a decade. When the housekeeper—whom Sigrid was very fond of—passed away, her eldest daughter, Cresencia, had to help provide for her younger sister. She's now employed by Sigrid as a housekeeper, tending to the exact same chores as her mother did when she worked for Sigrid's family—in the same high-rise apartment building overlooking the ocean that Sigrid grew up in, and chose to move back into as an adult.

Like her mother, Cresencia is a single mother, with the additional responsibility of a sibling to look after. History could easily repeat itself and she could work as a housekeeper until her final days, except that she's resumed classes at the local university and is studying to be an accountant. Her little sister is studying international relations. They are able to fund their studies thanks to Sigrid's parents, who are footing some of the bills—a luxury that not all people have in Mozambique, of course—but to see the sisters both so enthusiastic about going to school leaves hope that they'll achieve a different life for themselves, if that's what they desire.

Although the access that women in Mozambique gain to higher education will not be as comprehensive or of the quality that it has been for Chinese women, it's important that a transition has begun.

While China is an extreme example of how quickly things can change, the speed of its transition has not come without a cost. The country's oppressive pollution is not to be taken lightly and is already beginning to cause severe health issues. It continues to have a dubious human-rights record; freedom of the press (or of speech) is a slippery slope; socioeconomic inequality is growing, despite an overall reduction in poverty; territorial disputes and tensions between Han Chinese and ethnic minorities often lead to violent conflict; and government corruption remains rampant, even after serious crackdowns under President Xi Jinping. In addition to the inequalities mentioned earlier, women earn less than their male counterparts, spend more time on unpaid work, are frightfully underrepresented in roles of political leadership— something that regrettably shows little signs of changing—and are just starting to get a bit of legal recourse when it comes to domestic and sexual violence.

Still, I am rooting for China. I believe in its women, I have faith in its men, and most of the time—when I feel like I can get a reasonably accurate reading of the tea leaves—I am not distrusting of the government's stated goals. But more than anything, I believe that China desperately wants to reach the next level of development. It wants to build better cities, generate cleaner air, and improve its public service. It knows that it has to ensure more inclusive growth, especially with regards to its "leftover men," who have traditionally found employment in heavy industry and manufacturing, much like their disillusioned US counterparts who overwhelmingly helped elect a populist president. It longs to become internationally recognized for the quality of its education, the power of its technology, and the value of its advances in health care. It wants to play on a more sophisticated field and show the world that it is a creator, not an imitator. And it can.

Yet, as is true for almost all countries, if China continues to cling to its established gender roles and allows tradition to trump the professional and economic potential of its young women, it will stagnate. High-achieving Chinese women will seek out more open-minded foreign husbands. Instead of returning to China after studying abroad (which many female Chinese students do to be closer to their parents), they will more doggedly pursue work opportunities away from home and become part of the Chinese diaspora. Contributing to a significant drain on the domestic talent pool, they will cause China to lose the valuable ground it has gained on the path to becoming a more civil and truly developed society.

Ultimately, the stories of China's leftovers are a mosaic depicting the lives of women from around the globe, a flagrant reminder that even in the world's most developed nations, there still exists a pathological scrutiny of women who are not wed by a certain age. Domestically, these women are the single most powerful force ushering China into a new future, but in larger terms, they are the protagonists of a global narrative starring ambitious young women with revised timetables and expectations for their early adult years and relationships. They hold the keys to balancing economies and reducing poverty, infant mortality, domestic violence, and hunger—all proven to decrease when women have greater control over their careers, finances, and fertility. Neglecting the very generous returns on these three foundational freedoms and failing to recognize the promise and the transformative value of women seeking out more fulfilling lives, careers, and partnerships puts any country at perilous risk of being not only leftover, but left behind.

NEW BEGINNINGS
TO HAPPY ENDINGS

Something was in the air. I caught up with Yanyan one afternoon at 798, Beijing's trendy art district. She'd gotten new hair extensions and bumped up her kitten heels to a full three inches. "I am meeting an old classmate this evening," she told me. "I haven't seen him in sixteen years!"

Fast-forward three months, and I'm sitting in the living room of their apartment. As they welcome me, Yanyan's soon-to-be husband, Li Ming, whom I've just met for the first time, offers me a glass of orange juice and some sweets. It's not yet four p.m. on a brisk November afternoon, and shortly after I arrive, he changes into a fleecy pair of navy-blue pajamas with bright yellow moons and stars all over them. I start to wonder if everyone in Yanyan's family has a thing for microfleece, as these look suspiciously like the pajamas Baby Swiffer would always be dressed in. Li Ming looks inquisitively at Yanyan, and asks, "You won't change?" She giggles, and tells him that she'll change later.

Over a meal prepared by Yanyan that includes my absolute favorite dish, *gan bian doujiao*—spicy fried green beans—the pair tells me all about how they reconnected. In high school, Li Ming had a crush on Yanyan's best friend. He asked Yanyan to give her friend a note he'd written for her—a small declaration of his feelings—and Yanyan dutifully complied. The friend wasn't very impressed, but Yanyan always had a soft spot for Li Ming, especially after having witnessed this kind gesture.

Three weeks after their first date, he proposed to her on a small piece of paper. "Finally, I wrote to the right girl!" he says, laughing.

After dinner, they take me on a tour of their apartment, which they've purchased from a relative and have since been working hard to renovate. It's filled with ready-to-hang wedding photos featuring the classically outlandish repertoire of Chinese wedding backdrops, and all sorts of decorative stickers and gadgets, which Yanyan proudly confirms she's purchased on Taobao. Before the tour is over, Yanyan pulls me aside into a spare bedroom. Under a big sunny window I spot a wire cage, inside which can be seen two hilariously plump critters chowing down on Chinese cabbage. "Our ham-bursters!" she said. "As soon as Li Ming gets a pay bump, we'll start a litter of our own."

It's now September, and June has just finished a series of summer courses at the prestigious Yonsei University in Seoul. Her infatuation with the South Korean chef in Beijing didn't work out, but the weeks she spent wondering why led to a new academic interest—philosophy—and the moxie to one day pursue a master's degree in it. Contrary to the warnings from her former colleagues (who are still clocking overtime hours without being paid for them), her legal career has not been destroyed, and she's landed a plum position at a top-ranked law firm in Hong Kong. Recently settled into a spectacular apartment overlooking Kowloon, she is dating vigorously and putting all of the tactics she learned from Ivy to good use.

Christy has landed an account doing PR for one of China's biggest female celebrities. Quickly picking up on Christy's discerning style, her client started asking Christy to shop for her as well—serving as a personal shopper, of sorts—which involves several trips a year to New York, where virtually every designer brand is cheaper than it is in China. Meeting her one evening for dinner in Midtown, she arrives with $75,000 worth of clothes for her client in a bag from Bergdorf Goodman. She has disregarded her mother's mandate against higher education, and is pursuing an MBA at the Cheung Kong Graduate School of Business, considered the Wharton of China.

She has also suspended her OkCupid account and is "going steady" with an American pilot who is a few years her senior and wants to put some roots down. "On our first date he told me that he was looking for a wife, and that he owned three houses in Colorado," said Christy. "And all I could think was: Why is he being so Chinese?!" But then they feasted on burgers, went dancing, and drank until the wee hours as he told her all about his adventures piloting private planes for the Saudi royal family.

Zhang Mei is proud to have the first stamp on her passport, though she's already back in Harbin after her much-anticipated trip to Tokyo. "The feelings just weren't the same when I got there," she explained upon her return. "I knew deep in my heart that a life in Japan with that man wasn't for me, so I've decided to just cherish it for what it was. We had *yuan* [affinity] but no *fen* [destiny]." As she spoke, she sounded serene and from what I could tell, at peace with her decision. I think it also helps that on her flight back to China, she met a friendly Chinese graduate student returning home after completing a degree in Japan. His hometown is not very far from hers, and they've been doing a good job of staying in touch. "I really need to take planes more often!" she said, hinting that a trip to Thailand was next on her wish list. Harbin, after all, would always be there.

The last time I saw Ivy, her status update came in the form of a visual cue—a sparkly new diamond on her left hand resting over an almost imperceptible baby bump. Following an underwhelming trip to the Maldives with the obscenely wealthy man who had been trying to marry her, she met a recently divorced surgeon who was keen to make her his new lady. He was by far the least wealthy of her conquests, but he was kind and had a very special way of igniting a twinkle in her almond eyes. "I'm in a good place," she said, patting her stomach gently before adding, "it's time for someone else to be the third wheel."

ACKNOWLEDGMENTS

Thanks are owed to my Beijing 朋友们, who made life in China such an adventure: Beibei Wong, Sigrid Ekman, Gianvito D'Onghia, Marina Martin, Manya Koetse, Alessandra Marino, Jeanie Wang, Iris Wang, Daisy Sun, Elkin Bello, Angela Köckritz, Alexia Pestre, Marjorie Quach, Katia Loridon, Ana Fernanda Hierro Barba, Fergus Ryan, Guillermo Bravo, Valentina Salmoiraghi, Anne Li, Daphné Richet-Cooper, Paloma Sánchez, Mu Gao, Ma Shanshan, Cong Niu, Xin En Li, Annie Wang, Jordi Fakiani Axelsen, Weiwei Zuo, Liu Fang, James Flanagan, the inimitable Yolanda Wang and the entire cast of *The Leftover Monologues*. To Maya Reid for capturing me at my best. To Aziz Hoque for asking me to dance. To Leo Lee for turning everything to Technicolor. To Ryan Myers for being the "kittastrophe" to my "apopcolypse," and with fondest of thanks to Celine Lange. Ça y est, j'ai fini de couver!

I am equally grateful to those who selflessly offered their expertise, advice, and research, and who helped me remain connected to China after moving away: Mingjie Wang, Jessie Shi, Queenie Lin, Nina Huang, Janice Leng, and especially Wanda Wang, Carol Liu, Li Maizi, Yue Qian, Albert Esteve, Xiaobo Zhang, Yong Cai, and John Xenakis. To Xinran for being an inspiration, and with heartfelt thanks to Trena Keating and Amy Cherry for believing in this book.

BIBLIOGRAPHY

Bailey, Beth L. *From Front Porch to Back Seat: Courtship in Twentieth-Century America*. Baltimore: Johns Hopkins University Press, 1989.

Beibei, Ji. "Female Astronauts: Single Women Need Not Apply." *Global Times*, March 17, 2011.

Birger, Jon. *Date-onomics: How Dating Became a Lopsided Numbers Game*. New York: Workman, 2015.

Coontz, Stephanie. *Marriage, a History: How Love Conquered Marriage*. New York: Penguin, 2005.

Croll, Elisabeth. *The Politics of Marriage in Contemporary China*. Cambridge, MA: Cambridge University Press, 2010.

Economist, The. "Japanese Women and Work: Holding Back the Nation." March 28, 2014, http://www.economist.com/news/briefing/21599763-womens-lowly-status-japanese-workplace-has-barely-improved-decades-and-country.

Esteve, Albert, Joan Garcia-Roman, and Iñaki Permanyer. "The Gender-Gap Reversal in Education and Its Effect on Union Formation: The End of Hypergamy?" *Population and Development Review* 38 (2012): 535–46. doi:10.1111/j.1728-4457.

Feng, Wang, Yong Cai, and Baochang Gu. "Population, Policy, and Politics: How Will History Judge China's One-Child Policy?" *Population and Development Review* 38 (2012): 115–29.

Fong, Mei. *One Child: The Story of China's Most Radical Experiment.* Boston: Houghton Mifflin Harcourt, 2015. Kindle Edition.

Fry, Richard. "The Reversal of the College Marriage Gap." *Pew Research Center Social and Demographics Change,* October 7, 2010, http://www.pewsocial trends.org/2010/10/07/the-reversal-of-the-college-marriage-gap/.

Greenhalgh, Susan. *Just One Child: Science and Policy in Deng's China.* Berkeley: California University Press, 2008.

Huang, Ginger. "30 Years of Kissing." *The World of Chinese,* June 6, 2012, http://www.theworldofchinese.com/2012/06/30-years-of-kissing/

Hvistendahl, Mara. *Unnatural Selection: Choosing Boys over Girls, and the Consequences of a World Full of Men.* New York: Public Affairs, 2011.

Kristof, Nicholas D. *Half the Sky: Turning Oppression into Opportunity for Women Worldwide.* New York: Vintage Books, 2010.

Lai, Ming-yan. "Telling Love: The Feminist Import of a Woman's Negotiation of the Personal and the Public in Socialist China." *NWSA Journal* 12, no. 2 (2000): 24–25, https://muse.jhu.edu/article/25220.

Lee, Haiyan. *Revolution of the Heart: A Genealogy of Love in China, 1900–1950.* Palo Alto: Stanford University Press, 2010.

Osburg, John L. *Engendering Wealth: China's New Rich and the Rise of an Elite Masculinity.* Ann Arbor: ProQuest, Umi Dissertation Publishing, 2011.

Parry, Simon. "The Queen of Mistresses: Meet the Unlikely Heroine Whose Lovers Made Her a Billionaire—and Who She Repaid by Landing Them in Jail." *Daily Mail,* March 20, 2011, http://www.dailymail.co.uk/femail/article-1367968/Li-Wei-Meet-Chinas-unlikely-heroine-lovers-billionaire.html#ixzz4jBRWQVhq.

Qian, Yue, and Zhenchao Qian. "Gender Divide in Urban China: Singlehood and Assortative Mating by Age and Education." *Demographic Research* 31 (2014): 1337–364, http://www.demographic-research.org/Volumes/Vol31/45/ DOI: 10.4054/DemRes.2014.31.45.

Scharping, Thomas. *Birth Control in China 1949–2000: Population Policy and Demographic Development.* London: Routledge, 2002.

Stockard, Janice E. *Daughters of the Canton Delta: Marriage Patterns and Economic Strategies in South China, 1860–1930.* Palo Alto: Stanford University Press, 1989.

Wee, Sui-Lee. "After One-Child Policy, Outrage at China's Offer to Remove IUDs." *New York Times*, January 7, 2017.

Wei, Shang-Jin, Xiaobo Zhang, and Yin Liu. "Home Ownership as Status Competition: Some Theory and Evidence." *Journal of Development Economics* 127 (2017): 169–86, https://doi.org/10.1016/j.jdeveco.2016.12.001.

Whitehead, Barbara Dafoe. *Why There Are No Good Men Left*. New York: Penguin, 2003.

Woetzel, Jonathan, Anu Madgavkar, Kweilin Ellingrud, Eric Labaye, Sandrine Devillard, Eric Kutcher, James Manyika, Richard Dobbs, and Mekala Krishnan. "How Advancing Women's Equality Can Add $12 Trillion to Global Growth." McKinsey Global Institute, September 2015.

Yoshida, Akiko. "No Chance for Romance: Corporate Culture, Gendered Work, and Increased Singlehood in Japan." *Contemporary Japan* 23, no. 2 (2016): 213–34, http://dx.doi.org/10.1515/cj.2011.011.

———. *Unmarried Women in Japan: The Drift into Singlehood*. United Kingdom: Taylor & Francis, 2016.

Zheng, Tiantian. *Red Lights: The Lives of Sex Workers in Postsocialist China*. Minneapolis: Minnesota University Press, 2009.